BLACKOUT WARS

STATE INITIATIVES
TO ACHIEVE PREPAREDNESS
AGAINST AN
ELECTROMAGNETIC PULSE (EMP)
CATASTROPHE

Dr. Peter Vincent Pry

contributors

Dr. William R. Graham
Ambassador R. James Woolsey
Ambassador Henry F. Cooper
Rep. Andrea Boland
Senator David Farnsworth
Senator Bryce Reeves
Senator Ralph Shortey
Rep. Michelle Rehwinkel Vasilinda
Dr. George H. Baker III
Dr. William Radasky
John Kappenman
William R. Harris
Thomas Popik
Michael Hoehn
Lori Frantzve & Larry Guinta

Congress of the United States
Washington, DC 20515

17 November 2011

CONGRESSIONAL EMP CAUCUS:
Task Force on National and Homeland Security

We strongly endorse and approve the Task Force on National and Homeland Security as it pertains to Electromagnetic Pulse (EMP) applications. This newly established task force is under the leadership of Dr. Peter Vincent Pry, its Executive Director. Dr. Pry played a key role in establishing and serving on the Congressional Commission To Assess The Threat To The United States From Electromagnetic Pulse Attack.

We, as Co-Chairs of the Congressional EMP Caucus, support policies and legislation that will protect against nuclear, non-nuclear, and natural EMP threats to the critical infrastructures of the United States that sustain the U.S. economy and the lives of the American people.

Unfortunately, no credible official body, like the Congressional EMP Commission, now exists to inform and support the Congress on issues of national and homeland security related to EMP.

Accordingly, a Task Force on National and Homeland Security may serve, to the extent possible, as a surrogate for the Congressional EMP Commission, by providing expert views and advice on any and all technical, operational, and policy matters of relevance to EMP. Protection of the critical infrastructures--including electric power, communications, transportation, energy, banking and finance, food and water--is a very broad challenge. Issues for the Task Force on National and Homeland Security include: EMP, proliferation, energy security, financial issues, missile defense, intelligence and any other issues of relevance.

It is understood that, as there are no congressional monies available for the support of the Task Force on National and Homeland Security, the Task Force must be self-sustaining by means of private contributions of funding, labor, and other support.

Sincerely,

Trent Franks
Member of Congress

Roscoe Bartlett
Member of Congress

Yvette Clarke
Member of Congress

DEDICATION

This book is dedicated to

Andrea Boland

who led the way
with courage and grace
and to

Bronius Cikotas
and
David Schriner

who gave their lives
in our cause.

BLACKOUT WARS
IS AVAILABLE IN B&W OR WITH FULL COLOR
PHOTOS AND FIGURES
FROM CREATESPACE.COM, AMAZON.COM,
AND OTHER RETAIL OUTLETS,
AS ARE OTHER BOOKS BY THE
EMP TASK FORCE:
APOCALYPSE UNKNOWN
AND
ELECTRIC ARMAGEDDON

ACKNOWLEDGEMENTS

My deepest admiration, gratitude, and thanks are extended to all the contributors to this book--especially to Representative Andrea Boland, Representative Michelle Rehwinkel Vasilinda, Senator David Farnsworth, Senator Bryce Reeves, and Senator Ralph Shortey-- who have the courage of their convictions. They are among the first to try, against formidable obstacles, to protect their States and peoples from the existential threat that is EMP.

Dr. William Radasky, John Kappenman, Bronius Cikotas, Dr. George Baker, William Harris and Kevin Briggs have long been the scientific and intellectual shock troops for national EMP preparedness--and have often come to my rescue.

Dr. William R. Graham, Ambassador R. James Woolsey, and Ambassador Henry F. Cooper are the generals of our cause, and are always in the forefront when their troops need them. Heartfelt thanks to these mentors and friends for always answering the call, for being our Winston Churchill, and by their example inspiring us to, "Never, never, never give up."

Special thanks to Nadia Schadlow of the Smith Richardson Foundation whose help made possible not only this book, but the truly heroic efforts described here.

Thanks to Brent Thomas for designing the covers for this book and for the other two books by the EMP Task Force: *Electric Armageddon* and *Apocalypse Unknown*.

Any errors in these pages are mine alone.

Dr. Peter Vincent Pry
Executive Director
EMP Task Force on National and Homeland Security
September 23, 2015

CONTENTS

FOREWORD

Blackout Wars is about the historically unprecedented threat to our electronic civilization from its dependence on the electric power grid. Most Americans have experienced temporary blackouts, and regard them as merely an inconvenience. Some Americans have experienced more protracted local and regional blackouts, as in the aftermaths of Hurricanes Sandy and Katrina, and may be better able to imagine the consequences of a nationwide blackout lasting months or years, that plunges the entire United States into the dark.

In such a nightmare blackout, the entire population of the United States could be at risk. There would be no food. No water. Communications, transportation, industry, business and finance--all of the critical infrastructures that support modern civilization and the lives of the American people would be paralyzed by collapse of the electric power grid.

Millions could die.

How could a catastrophic blackout happen? Threats to the electric power grid are posed by cyber attack, sabotage, a geomagnetic super-storm, and electromagnetic pulse (EMP) from the high-altitude detonation of a nuclear weapon.

Blackout Wars warns that terrorists and rogue states are developing a revolutionary new military strategy that could exploit all of these threats in combination, including exploiting the opportunity of severe weather or a geo-storm, to collapse the national electric grid and all the critical infrastructures. It would be the fall of American civilization.

For the first time in history, the most dysfunctional societies, like North Korea that cannot even feed its own people, or even non-state actors like terrorists, could destroy the most successful societies on Earth--by means of a Blackout War. Attacking the electric grid enables an adversary to strike at the technological and societal Achilles Heel of U.S. military and economic power.

Blackout Wars likens this new Revolution in Military Affairs to Nazi Germany's Blitzkrieg strategy, secretly developed and tested in low-profile experiments during the 1930s, sprung upon the Allies in 1939-1941 in a series of surprise attacks that nearly enabled the Third Reich to win World War II. Just as the West was asleep to the threat from the Blitzkrieg, so today U.S. and Western elites are blind to the looming threat from a Blackout War.

Yet the threat of a catastrophic blackout is not merely theoretical, but real:

--On April 16, 2013, North Korea flew its KSM-3 satellite on the optimum trajectory and altitude to evade U.S. radars and missile defenses and apparently practiced a surprise nuclear EMP attack on the United States.
--On the same day, parties unknown used AK-47s, the favorite assault rifle of rogue states and terrorists, to attack the Metcalf transformer substation that services San Francisco and the Silicon Valley. Jon Wellinghoff, the former chairman of the U.S. agency responsible for grid security, and the U.S. Navy SEALS warn that Metcalf is probably a dry run for a future large-scale attack on the national electric grid.
--In July 2013, a North Korean freighter that had transited the Gulf of Mexico was discovered, while undergoing inspection in the Panama Canal for smuggling illegal drugs, to have two nuclear capable SA-2 missiles, mounted on their launchers, hidden in the hold under bags of sugar. Although the missiles were not nuclear armed, the incident

demonstrates North Korea's capability to use a freighter in U.S. coastal waters to launch a nuclear EMP attack anonymously, in order to escape U.S. retaliation.

--On October 27, 2013, the Knights Templars, a criminal drug cartel, blacked-out Mexico's Michoacan state and its population of 420,000, so they could terrorize the people and paralyze the police. The Knights, cloaked by the blackout, entered towns and villages and publicly executed leaders opposed to the drug trade.

--On June 9, 2014, Al Qaeda in the Arabian Peninsula used mortars and rockets to destroy transmission towers, plunging into darkness all of Yemen, a country of 16 cities and 24 million people. It is the first time in history that terrorists have put an entire nation into blackout.

--In July 2014, according to press reports, a Russian cyber-bug called Dragonfly infected 1,000 electric powerplants in Western Europe and the United States for purposes unknown, possibly to plant logic bombs in powerplant computers to disrupt operations in the future.

--On January 25, 2015, terrorists attacked transmission towers and blacked-out 80 percent of Pakistan, a nuclear weapons state.

--On March 31, 2015, a mysterious nationwide blackout temporarily plunged into chaos Turkey, a NATO member and important U.S. ally, reportedly from a cyber attack by Iran.

--In 2015 the White House issued a draft executive order acknowledging that natural EMP from a geomagnetic super-storm is a potentially catastrophic threat to the nation. A NASA report (July 23, 2014) warns that on July 23, 2012, Earth narrowly missed experiencing a geomagnetic super-storm that could have collapsed electric grids worldwide, and put at risk the lives of billions. NASA estimates that the likelihood of a catastrophic geo-storm happening over the next decade is 12 percent.

Blackout Wars is also about, is primarily about, failure of the U.S. Government to protect the electric grid, and the heroic struggle of a small number of experts, political leaders, and State governments to meet this challenge.

Terrible and unprecedented as is the danger from any of the threats above singly or in combination as a Blackout War--solutions that are technologically sound, and not only cost-effective but inexpensive relative to the threat, are readily at hand. Protecting the electric grid against nuclear EMP attack is key.

Nuclear EMP is the worst threat, even worse than natural EMP from a geo-storm, because it can damage small electronic systems and inflict deeper damage on the grid and other critical infrastructures. If the grid is protected against the worst threat--nuclear EMP--this would significantly mitigate all the other threats.

However, the biggest obstacle to protecting the American people from a catastrophic blackout is not technological or financial, but political.

The Federal government is failing spectacularly to protect the electric grid and the American people from nuclear EMP, or from any of the other catastrophic threats, because of a self-interested and wholly improper relationship between the electric power industry, represented by the North American Electric Reliability Corporation (NERC), and the U.S. Federal Energy Regulatory Commission (FERC). Attorney William R. Harris, an eyewitness to NERC-FERC chicanery and a former legal advisor to the Reagan Administration, writes, "The NERC-FERC relationship has elements of a suicide pact." Harris:

The NERC-FERC relationship has elements of a suicide pact. NERC and FERC are engaged in a mutually beneficial parasitic relationship. Each needs the other, and thrives on magnification of the monopolistic powers of the other. Only NERC can propose reliability standards. Only FERC can ratify standards, however defective and however damaging to the society at large....NERC works hard to prevent the Congress from authorizing FERC to modify or otherwise improve NERC-proposed reliability standards. FERC discourages the Congress from providing authority for more adaptive and protective FERC powers...FERC has sufficient authority to mandate new standard development that the member utilities of NERC need to make generous political contributions to Members of Congress. And most Members of Congress are content with a regulatory system that provides liability protection to the utilities, and keeps the Members in elective office.

Fortunately, where the Federal government is failing to protect the national electric grid, State governments have legal authority and the technical capability to protect their electric grids within their State boundaries, and so spare their citizens from the worst consequences of a protracted blackout.

Maine, Virginia, Arizona, Florida, Oklahoma Texas, Colorado and other States have initiatives underway to protect their grids and their peoples from the existential threat that is nuclear EMP attack, and from other hazards that could cause a catastrophic blackout. Ominously, this necessary trend toward decentralization of a vital national security responsibility from the Federal government to State governments is eerily reminiscent of the late Roman Empire. When Rome could no longer defend its cities from the barbarians, the cities built walls to defend themselves.

Now that Washington cannot or will not defend the United States from nuclear EMP attack, some States are "building walls" to protect their electric grids and peoples from the new barbarians.

Blackout Wars is the story of these heroic efforts by individual legislators and citizens to be "Horatio on the Bridge" defending their States and peoples against perhaps the greatest threat that has ever challenged civilization. Most of all, **Blackout Wars** is a handbook on why and how the States must meet this challenge, and a clarion call to the States to defend themselves. We agree with the author that it is, "Time for the States to succeed where Washington has failed....Time to prevent, figuratively and literally, a blackout of civilization, that could cancel Mankind's monumental progress in science, industry, and human rights made since the Age of Enlightenment--by the advent of a New Dark Age."

Dr. William R. Graham was Science Advisor to President Ronald Reagan, Administrator of NASA, and Chairman of the Congressional EMP Commission. Ambassador R. James Woolsey, former Director of Central Intelligence, is Chancellor of the Institute of World Politics and Chairman of the Leadership Council of the Foundation for Defense of Democracies.

KEY JUDGMENTS

Political gridlock in Washington has prevented the Federal Government from protecting the electric grid and other critical infrastructures from a protracted blackout lasting months or years, that would have catastrophic consequences for national survival. Such a blackout is a clear and present danger. It could be caused by a geomagnetic super-storm, physical sabotage, cyber attack, or electromagnetic pulse (EMP) attack. The grid is not even adequately protected from blackouts induced by severe weather, like Hurricanes Katrina and Sandy. Protecting electric grids from nuclear EMP attack--the worst threat--would also protect against and mitigate all lesser threats, including severe weather, sabotage, cyber attack, and geomagnetic storms. (Chapter I)

A protracted blackout catastrophic to our electronic civilization could be caused by all of the above used in combination by terrorists or rogue states who have developed a revolutionary new military strategy based on blacking out the national electric grid and collapsing the other civilian critical infrastructures--waging in effect a combined arms Blackout War. The key to defeating this new strategy is protecting the grid and other critical infrastructures from the worst threat--nuclear EMP attack. (Chapter II)

State governments have the opportunity and duty to act, where the Federal Government has failed, by protecting the electric grids within their States. State governors, legislatures, and public utility commissions have legal authority to order utilities to protect the electric grid within their State from EMP attack and all hazards that could cause protracted blackout. (Chapter III)

Technically, even though most States are part of a larger regional electric grid, a State can harden its portion of the grid to survive an EMP attack using proven technologies such as blocking devices, surge arrestors, faraday cages and other technologies. Protecting the State grid will "keep the lights on" and save the people within the State and facilitate rescuing and more rapidly recovering neighboring States from a protracted blackout. Grid protection against nuclear EMP attack and all hazards is cost-effective. (Chapter III)

Maine, Virginia, Arizona, Florida and Oklahoma have introduced initiatives to protect their State electric grids and peoples from an EMP catastrophe. Lessons learned from these initiatives include the following (Chapters III-VIII):

State initiatives to protect electric grids from EMP and other threats are already working, in sharp contrast to the lack of progress in Washington. Inspired by Maine's EMP legislative initiative, Virginia passed its own initiative and is the first state in the nation to commence protection of its grid from EMP. Maine, Florida, and Arizona are not far behind.

Governors have broad authority to provide for the homeland security of their State and can invoke their emergency powers to protect the electric grid within their State. This may be the fastest way to achieve EMP and all hazards preparedness for a State electric grid.

State legislatures can pass a bill to protect the electric grid within their State. Education of the State legislature and governor on the EMP threat and the necessity of grid security should be thorough preceding the introduction of any bill. Hearings featuring independent experts and providing scientific and technical reports on the EMP threat and solutions should be provided to policy makers. A media campaign to educate the public is highly desirable. Personal one-on-one meetings between the legislator introducing the bill and his colleagues to explain the importance of the bill is highly desirable. The bill should be simple and easily understandable to a legislator without requiring technical explanation.

State legislatures can amend the charter of the State emergency management agency or agencies to require them to be prepared to protect and recover the State from an EMP catastrophe. Legislatively, this may be less challenging and easier to accomplish than a bill aimed directly at the utilities requiring them to protect the electric grid. It could also be a stepping stone toward a more ambitious bill to protect the State electric grid.

State legislatures can pass a popular referendum giving the people an opportunity to vote directly on the question of protecting the electric grid within their State. Legislatively, this may be less challenging and easier to accomplish than a bill requiring the utilities to protect the grid. Enlisting support of the people for grid protection will make easier subsequent passage of more ambitious bills requiring the utilities to act.

Public Utilities Commissions work closely with the utilities, often have a "rotating door" between the PUC and the industry they are supposed to regulate, and intuitively look to the utilities and the electric power industry for advice and expertise on grid security. Yet most PUCs and utilities know little or nothing about EMP. State legislatures, especially the energy committees that are supposed to oversee the PUCs, should be aggressive in soliciting and requiring the PUCs to work with objective independent experts who have real expertise on the EMP threat and protecting electric grids.

Expect opposition from the utilities, and especially from the North American Electric Reliability Corporation (NERC). NERC and its allies in the utilities will aggressively lobby against any bill requiring the State electric grid to be protected from EMP:

-- Be prepared to rebut NERC claims that protecting the grid from nuclear EMP attack is the responsibility of the Department of Defense. (Chapter X)

--Be prepared to answer NERC that their proposed federal standard to protect the grid from geomagnetic storms is based on "junk science" and has been proven by independent experts to be grossly inadequate against a geomagnetic super-storm. (Chapter X)

--Be prepared to rebut NERC's admonition that the States should take no action, but should wait for Washington to solve all problems related to electric grid security. (Chapters X)

Congress is trying to pass the Critical Infrastructure Protection Act and re-establish the Congressional EMP Commission, which would greatly advance progress toward EMP preparedness nationally and among the States (Chapter XI).

Dr. George Baker proposes a plan to protect nuclear power reactors from natural and manmade EMP and other threats, which would eliminate the grave danger from widespread radioactive contamination, and make nuclear reactors one of the most important resources for quickly recovering the national electric grid and society. (Chapter XII)

Ambassador Henry Cooper, former Director of the Strategic Defense Initiative, proposes a plan to quickly strengthen and plug holes in the National Missile Defense against nuclear EMP attack, in order to buy time to EMP harden the national electric grid. (Chapter XIII)

"The history of the failure of war can almost be summed up in two words:
too late.
Too late in comprehending the deadly purpose of a potential enemy.
Too late in realizing the mortal danger.
Too late in preparedness.
Too late in uniting all possible forces for resistance.
Too late in standing with one's friends."

--General Douglas MacArthur

I

A CLEAR AND PRESENT DANGER

Introduction

Natural EMP from a geomagnetic super-storm, like the 1859 Carrington Event or 1921 Railroad Storm, or nuclear EMP attack from terrorists or rogue states, as apparently practiced by North Korea during the nuclear crisis of 2013, are both existential threats that could kill up to 9 of 10 Americans through starvation, disease, and societal collapse. A natural EMP catastrophe or nuclear EMP attack could blackout the national electric grid for months or years and collapse all the other critical infrastructures--communications, transportation, banking and finance, food and water--necessary to sustain modern society and the lives of 320 million Americans.

The objective of this book is to advance national preparedness against an EMP catastrophe and other threats to the electric power grid by educating State governments and the public about the EMP threat and how to achieve preparedness.

Most State governments are unaware of the EMP threat and that:

- **Political gridlock in Washington has prevented the Federal government from implementing any of the several cost-effective plans for protecting the national electric grid;**
- **Most State governments are unaware that they can protect that portion of the grid within their State and so protect their citizens from the catastrophic consequences of a national blackout;**
- **The electric grid is the keystone critical infrastructure necessary to recover all other critical infrastructures;**
- **Protection of the grid from EMP, which is the worst threat, will also enhance overall grid security against all other threats, including cyber attack, sabotage, and severe weather.**

All Hazards Strategy--EMP Protection Key

The Congressional EMP Commission warned that an "all hazards" strategy should be pursued to protect the electric grid and other critical infrastructures. An "all hazards" strategy means trying to find common solutions that protect against more than one threat--ideally against all threats.

The "all hazards" strategy is the most practical and most cost-effective solution to protecting the electric grid and other critical infrastructures. Electric grid operation and vulnerability is critically dependent upon two key technologies--Extra-High Voltage (EHV) transformers and Supervisory Control and Data Acquisition Systems (SCADAS).

Extra-High Voltage (EHV) Transformers

EHV transformers are the technological foundation of our modern electronic civilization as they make it possible to transmit electric power over great distances. An EHV transformer typically is as large as a house, weighs hundreds of tons, costs millions of dollars, and cannot be mass produced but must be custom-made by hand. Making a single EHV transformer takes about 18 months. Annual worldwide production of EHV transformers is about 200 per year.

Unfortunately, although Nikolai Tesla invented the EHV transformer and the electric grid in the U.S., EHV transformers are no longer manufactured in the United States. Because of their great size and cost, U.S. electric utilities have very few spare EHV transformers. The U.S. must import EHV transformers made in Germany or South Korea, the only two nations in the world that make them for export.

Mitsubishi and some other companies based in the U.S. have announced that they plan to begin manufacturing EHV transformers--which would again create a domestic source for EHV transformers located in the United States. Whether these companies will actually be able to deliver on their promises remains to be seen. Each EHV transformer is unique, custom designed for a particular role in the electric grid. Moreover, crucial parts of EHV transformers, like the coil windings, must be done by hand--requiring a craftsmanship not easily duplicated.

The design and construction of EHV transformers is such a significant technological challenge that it typically takes years before a manufacturer knows whether or not they have succeeded. Brazil, for example, attempted to build its own EHV transformers. They discovered something was going wrong with Brazilian EHV transformers, causing them to fail after 5 years, when they should have a lifetime of 30 years. Brazil gave up and went back to importing EHV transformers.

An event that damages hundreds, dozens--or even as few as 9--of the 2,000 EHV transformers in the United States could plunge the nation into a protracted blackout lasting months or even years.

Supervisory Control And Data Acquisition Systems (SCADAS)
SCADAS are basically small computers that run the electric grid and all the critical infrastructures. For example, SCADAS regulate the flow of electric current through EHV transformers, the flow of natural gas or of water through pipelines, the flow of data through communications and financial systems, and operate everything from traffic control lights to the refrigerators in regional food warehouses.

SCADAS are ubiquitous in the civilian critical infrastructures, number in the millions, and are as indispensable as EHV transformers to running our modern electronic civilization.

An event that damages large numbers of SCADAS would put that civilization at risk. SCADAS are typically highly vulnerable to nuclear EMP and non-nuclear EMP from radiofrequency weapons.

Nuclear EMP--The Worst Threat
High-altitude nuclear EMP attack is the greatest single threat that could be posed to EHV transformers, SCADAS and other components of the national electric grid and other critical infrastructures. Nuclear EMP includes a high-frequency electromagnetic shockwave called E1 EMP that can potentially damage or destroy virtually any electronic system having a dimension of 18 inches or greater.

E1 EMP is unique to nuclear weapons, although non-nuclear radiofrequency weapons can produce a similar phenomenon, typically less energetic and less damaging, over much shorter distances.

Consequently, a high-altitude nuclear EMP event could cause broad damage of electronics and critical infrastructures across continental North America, while also causing deep damage to industrial and personal property, including to automobiles and personal computers.

Nuclear EMP can also produce E2 EMP, comparable to lightning.

In contrast, natural EMP from a geomagnetic super-storm generates no E1 EMP, only E3 EMP (technically called Magneto-Hydro-Dynamic EMP, MHD EMP, or E3 for short). E3 EMP has such long wavelengths that it requires a large "antennae" of about 1 kilometer or more in length, such as power lines, telephone lines, pipelines, and railroad tracks. E3 EMP cannot enter directly relatively small targets such as automobiles or personal computers.

However, while a geomagnetic super-storm would not directly damage relatively small electronic systems, a protracted nationwide blackout resulting from such a storm would within days stop everything. Personal computers cannot run for long on batteries, nor can automobiles run without gasoline.

Nuclear EMP can also produce E3 EMP comparable to or greater than a geomagnetic super-storm. Even a relatively low-yield nuclear weapon, like the 10-kiloton Hiroshima bomb, can generate an E3 EMP field powerful enough to damage EHV transformers.

The Congressional EMP Commission recommended protecting the electric grid and other critical infrastructures against nuclear EMP as the best basis for an "all hazards" strategy. Nuclear EMP may not be as likely as other threats, but it is by far the worst, the most severe, threat.

The EMP Commission found that if the electric grid can be protected and quickly recovered from nuclear EMP, the other critical infrastructures can also be recovered, with good planning, quickly enough to prevent mass starvation and restore society to normalcy. If EHV transformers, SCADAS and other critical components are protected from the worst threat--nuclear EMP--then they will survive, or damage will be greatly mitigated, from all lesser threats, including natural EMP from geomagnetic storms, severe weather, sabotage, and cyber attack.

The New "Lightning War" or "Blackout War"
The "all hazards" strategy recommended by the EMP Commission is not only the most cost-effective strategy--it is a necessary strategy. U.S. emergency planners tend to think of EMP, cyber, sabotage, severe weather, and geo-storms in isolation, as unrelated threats

However, potential foreign adversaries in their military doctrines and actual military operations appear to be planning an offensive "all hazards" strategy that would throw at the U.S. electric grid and civilian critical infrastructures--every possible threat simultaneously

Russia, China, North Korea and Iran appear to be perfecting what Moscow calls a "Revolution in Military Affairs" that is potentially more decisive than Nazi Germany's Blitzkrieg ("Lightning War") strategy that nearly conquered the western democracies during World War II. The New Lightning War would attack the electric grid and other critical infrastructures--the technological and societal Achilles Heel of electronic civilization--with coordinated employment of cyber, sabotage, and EMP attacks, possibly timed to leverage severe space or terrestrial weather.

While gridlock in Washington has prevented the Federal Government from protecting the national electric power infrastructure, threats to the grid--and to the survival of the American people--from EMP and other hazards are looming ever larger. Grid vulnerability to EMP and other threats is now a clear and present danger.

Geomagnetic Storms

Natural EMP from geomagnetic storms, caused when a coronal mass ejection from the Sun collides with the Earth's magnetosphere, poses a significant threat to the electric grid and the critical infrastructures, that all depend directly or indirectly upon electricity. Normal geomagnetic storms occur every year causing problems with communications and electric grids for nations located at high northern latitudes, such as Norway, Sweden, Finland and Canada.

For example, the 1989 Hydro-Quebec Storm blacked-out the eastern half of Canada in 92 seconds, melted an EHV transformer at the Salem, New Jersey nuclear power plant, and caused billions of dollars in economic losses.

In 1921 a geomagnetic storm ten times more powerful, the Railroad Storm, afflicted the whole of North America. It did not have catastrophic consequences because electrification of the U.S. and Canada was still in its infancy. The National Academy of Sciences estimates that if the 1921 Railroad Storm recurs today, it would cause a catastrophic nationwide blackout lasting 4-10 years and costing trillions of dollars.

The Carrington Event

The most powerful geomagnetic storm ever recorded is the 1859 Carrington Event, estimated to be ten times more powerful than the 1921 Railroad Storm and classed as a geomagnetic super-storm.

Natural EMP from the Carrington Event penetrated miles deep into the Atlantic Ocean and destroyed the just laid intercontinental telegraph cable. The Carrington Event was a worldwide phenomenon, causing fires in telegraph stations and forest fires from telegraph lines bursting into flames on several continents. Fortunately, in the horse and buggy days of 1859, civilization did not depend upon electrical systems.

Recurrence of a Carrington Event today would collapse electric grids and critical infrastructures all over the planet, putting at risk the lives of billions. Scientists estimate that geomagnetic super-storms occur about every 100-150 years. The Earth is probably overdue to encounter another Carrington Event.

NASA in a July 23, 2014 report warns that, two years earlier, on July 23, 2012, a powerful solar flare (technically a coronal mass ejection) narrowly missed the Earth. According to NASA, it would have generated a geomagnetic super-storm, like the 1859 Carrington Event, and collapsed electric grids and life sustaining critical infrastructures worldwide.

The National Intelligence Council (NIC), that speaks for the entire U.S. Intelligence Community, published a major unclassified report in December 2012 *Global Trends 2030* that warns a geomagnetic super-storm, like recurrence of the 1859 Carrington Event, is one of only eight "Black Swans" that could by or before 2030 change the course of global civilization. The NIC concurs with the consensus view that another Carrington Event could recur at any time, possibly before 2030. If it did, electric grids and critical infrastructures that support modern civilization could collapse worldwide.

NASA estimates in its July 2014 report that the likelihood of a geomagnetic super-storm is 12 percent per decade. This virtually guarantees that Earth will experience a natural EMP catastrophe in our lifetimes or that of our children.

NERC "Operational Procedures" Non-Solution

The North American Electric Reliability Corporation (NERC), the lobby for the electric power industry that is also supposed to set industry standards for grid security, claims it can protect the grid from geomagnetic super-storms by "operational procedures." Operational procedures would rely on satellite early warning of an impending Carrington Event to allow grid operators to shift around electric loads, perhaps deliberately brownout or blackout part or all of the grid in order to save it. NERC estimates operational procedures would cost the electric utilities almost nothing, about $200,000 dollars annually.

Critics rightly argue that NERC's proposed operational procedures is a non-solution designed as an excuse to avoid the expense of the only real solution--physically hardening the electric grid to withstand EMP.

NERC's operational procedures for coping with geo-storms depend upon the obsolete ACE satellite.

The ACE satellite is aged and sometimes gives false warnings that are not a reliable basis for implementing operational procedures. While coronal mass ejections can be seen approaching Earth typically about three days before impact, the Carrington Event reached Earth in only 11 hours. Moreover, the Ace satellite cannot warn whether an incoming coronal mass ejection is positively or negatively charged (negative is bad news), and so will likely generate a geo-storm on Earth until merely 20-30 minutes before impact.

Most recently, on September 19-20, 2014, the National Oceanic and Atmospheric Administration and NERC demonstrated again that they are unable to ascertain until shortly before impact whether a coronal mass ejection will cause a threatening geomagnetic storm on Earth.

The ACE satellite will be replaced eventually with another satellite that has been in storage for years, originally called Discovery, and originally designed to collect data on global warming. Critics rightly warn that Discovery may be inadequate to replace ACE because it too is aged, and is not purpose built to monitor and provide warning of coronal mass ejections that generate geo-storms.

There is no command and control system for coordinating operational procedures among the 3,000 independent electric utilities in the United States. Operational procedures routinely fail to prevent blackouts from normal terrestrial weather, like snowstorms and hurricanes. There is no credible basis for thinking that operational procedures alone would be able to cope with a geomagnetic super-storm--a threat unprecedented in the experience of NERC and the electric power industry.

NERC has not helped its case by being caught red handed peddling "junk science" that grossly underestimates the threat from another Carrington Event, as detailed in the book *Apocalypse Unknown.*

States Should EMP Harden Their Grids

NERC rejects the recommendation of the Congressional EMP Commission to physically protect the national electric grid from nuclear EMP attack by installing blocking devices, surge arrestors, faraday cages and other proven technologies. These measures would also protect the grid from the worst natural EMP from a geomagnetic super-storm like another Carrington Event. The estimated one time cost--$2 billion dollars--is what the United States gives away every year in foreign aid to Pakistan.

Yet Washington remains gridlocked between lobbying by NERC and the wealthy electric power industry on the one hand, and the recommendations of the Congressional EMP Commission and other independent scientific and strategic experts on the other hand. The States should not wait for Washington to act, but should act now to protect themselves.

Catastrophe from a geomagnetic super-storm may well happen sooner rather than later--and perhaps in combination with a nuclear EMP attack.

Paul Stockton, President Obama's former Assistant Secretary of Defense for Homeland Defense, on June 30, 2014, at the Electric Infrastructure Security Summit in London, warned an international audience that an adversary might coordinate nuclear EMP attack with an impending or ongoing geomagnetic storm to confuse the victim and maximize damage. Stockton notes that, historically, generals have often coordinated their military operations with the weather. For example, during World War II, General Dwight Eisenhower deliberately launched the D-Day invasion following a storm in the English Channel, correctly calculating that this daring act would surprise Nazi Germany.

Future military planners of a Blackout War may well coordinate a nuclear EMP attack and other operations aimed at the electric grid and critical infrastructures with the ultimate space weather threat--a geomagnetic storm.

Severe Weather

Hurricanes, snow storms, heat waves and other severe weather poses an increasing threat to the increasingly overtaxed, aged and fragile national electric grid. So far, the largest and most protracted blackouts in the United States have been caused by severe weather.

For example, Hurricane Katrina (August 29, 2005), the worst natural disaster in U.S. history, blacked out New Orleans and much of Louisiana, the blackout seriously impeding rescue and recovery efforts. Lawlessness swept the city. Electric power was not restored to parts of New Orleans for months, making some neighborhoods a criminal no man's land too dangerous to live in. New Orleans has still not fully recovered its pre-Katrina population. Economic losses to the Gulf States region totaled $108 billion dollars.

Hurricane Sandy on October 29, 2012, caused blackouts in parts of New York and New Jersey that in some places lasted weeks. Again, as in Katrina, the blackout gave rise to lawlessness and seriously impeded rescue and recovery. Thousands were rendered homeless in whole or in part because of the protracted blackout in some neighborhoods. Partial and temporary blackouts were experienced in 24 States. Total economic losses were $68 billion dollars.

A heat-wave on August 14, 2003, caused a power line to sag into a tree branch, which seemingly minor incident began a series of cascading failures that resulted in the Great Northeast Blackout of 2003. Some 40-50 million Americans were without electric power--

including New York City. Although the grid largely recovered after a day, disruption of the nation's financial capital was costly, resulting in estimated economic losses of about $6 billion dollars.

On September 18, 2014, a heat wave caused rolling brownouts and blackouts in northern California so severe that some radio commentators speculated that a terrorist attack on the grid might be underway.

NERC and Electric Utilities Underperform

Ironically, about one week before the California blackouts of September 18, 2014, on September 8-10, there was a security conference on threats to the national electric grid meeting in San Francisco. There executives from the electric power industry credited themselves with building robust resilience into the electric power grid. They even congratulated themselves and their industry with exemplary performance coping with and recovering from blackouts caused by hurricanes and other natural disasters.

The thousands of Americans left homeless due to Hurricanes Katrina and Sandy, the hundreds of businesses lost or impoverished in New Orleans and New York City, and the residents of California, would no doubt disagree.

The U.S. Government Accountability Office (GAO), if it had jurisdiction to grade electric grid reliability during hurricanes, would almost certainly give the utilities a failing grade. Ever since Hurricane Andrew in 1992, the U.S. GAO has found serious fault with efforts by the Federal Emergency Management Agency, the Department of Homeland Security, and the Department of Defense to rescue and recover the American people from every major hurricane (as detailed in the book *Electric Armageddon*). Blackout of the electric grid, of course, seriously impedes the capability of FEMA, DHS, and DOD to do anything.

Since the utilities regulate themselves through the North American Electric Reliability Corporation, their uncritical view of their own performance reinforces a "do nothing" attitude in the electric power industry.

For example, after the Great Northeast Blackout of 2003, it took NERC a decade to propose a new "vegetation management plan" to protect the national grid from tree branches. NERC has been even more resistant and slow to respond to other much more serious threats, including cyber attack, sabotage, and natural EMP from geomagnetic storms.

NERC flatly rejects responsibility to protect the grid from nuclear EMP attack.

New York and Massachusetts Protect Their Grids

New York Governor Andrew Cuomo and Massachusetts Governor Deval Patrick would not agree that NERC's performance during Hurricane Sandy was exemplary. Under the leadership of Governor Patrick, Massachusetts is spending $500 million to upgrade the security of its electric grid from severe weather. New York is spending one billion dollars to protect its grid from severe weather.

Unfortunately, both States are probably spending a lot more than they have to by focusing on severe weather, instead of an "all hazards" strategy to protect their electric grids.

The biggest impediment to recovering an electric grid from hurricanes is not fallen electric poles and downed power lines. When part of the grid physically collapses, an overvoltage can result that can damage all kinds of transformers, including EHV transformers, SCADAS and other vital grid components. Video footage shown on national television during Hurricane Sandy showed spectacular explosions and fires erupting from transformers and other grid vital components caused by overvoltage.

If the grid is hardened to survive a nuclear EMP attack by installation of surge arrestors, it would easily survive overvoltage induced by hurricanes and other severe weather. This would cost a lot less than burying power lines underground and other measures being undertaken by New York and Massachusetts to fortify their grids against hurricanes--all of which will be futile if transformers and SCADAS are not protected against overvoltage.

According to a senior executive of New York's Consolidated Edison, briefing at the Electric Infrastructure Security Summit in London on July 1, 2014--Con Ed is taking some modest steps to protect part of the New York electric grid from nuclear EMP attack. This good news has not been reported anywhere in the press.

I asked the Con Ed executive why New York is silent about beginning to protect its grid from nuclear EMP? Loudly advertising this prudent step could have a deterrent effect on potential adversaries planning an EMP attack.

The Con Ed executive could offer no explanation.

New York City because of its symbolism as the financial and cultural capitol of the Free World, and perhaps because of its large Jewish population, has been the repeated target of terrorist attacks with weapons of mass destruction. A nuclear EMP attack centered over New York City, the warhead detonated at an altitude of 30 kilometers, would cover all the northeastern United States with an EMP field, including New York State and Massachusetts.

Hopefully, New York and Massachusetts will not have reason to regret that their governors failed to implement the Congressional EMP Commission's recommended "all hazards" strategy for electric grid protection.

A practitioner of a Blackout War may be more likely to exploit a hurricane, blizzard, or heat wave than a geomagnetic storm, when launching a coordinated cyber, sabotage, and EMP attack. Terrestrial bad weather is more commonplace than bad space weather.

New York and Massachusetts have both been frontline States in the war on terrorism. Nuclear EMP attack could potentially put in the frontlines--and in the crosshairs of a Blackout War--all the States.

All the States should prepare themselves for all hazards in this age of the Electronic Blitzkrieg.

Sabotage--Kinetic Attacks

Kinetic attacks are a serious threat to the electric grid and are clearly part of the game plan for terrorists and rogue states. Sabotage of the electric grid is perhaps the easiest operation for a terrorist group to execute and would be perhaps the most cost-effective means, requiring only high-powered rifles, for a very small number of bad actors to wage asymmetric warfare--perhaps against all 320 million Americans.

Terrorists have figured out that the electric grid is a major societal vulnerability.

Terror Blackout in Mexico

On the morning of October 27, 2013, the Knights Templars, a terrorist drug cartel in Mexico, attacked a big part of the Mexican grid, using small arms and bombs to blast electric substations. They blacked-out the entire Mexican state of Mihoacan, plunging 420,000 people into the dark, isolating them from help from the Federales. The Knights went into towns and villages and publicly executed local leaders opposed to the drug trade.

Ironically, that evening in the United States, the National Geographic aired a television docudrama "American Blackout" that accurately portrayed the catastrophic consequences of a cyber attack that blacks-out the U.S. grid for ten days. The North American Electric Reliability Corporation (NERC) and some utilities criticized "American Blackout" for being alarmist and unrealistic, apparently unaware that life had already anticipated art just across the largely unprotected U.S. border with Mexico.

Life had already anticipated art months earlier than "American Blackout" and not in Mexico, but in the United States. A fact suppressed by the utilities and their national spokesman, the NERC.

The Metcalf Attack

Six months before "American Blackout" aired on television, on April 16, 2013, apparently terrorists or professional saboteurs practiced making an attack on the Metcalf transformer substation outside San Jose, California. Metcalf services a 450 megawatt power plant providing electricity to the Silicon Valley and the San Francisco area.

The North American Electric Reliability Corporation (NERC) and the utility Pacific Gas and Electric (PG&E), that owns Metcalf, claimed that the incident was merely an act of vandalism. They discouraged press interest.

Consequently, the national press paid nearly no attention to the Metcalf affair for nine months.

Jon Wellinghoff, Chairman of the U.S. Federal Energy Regulatory Commission, conducted an independent investigation of Metcalf. He brought in the best of the best of U.S. special forces--the instructors who train the U.S. Navy SEALS. They concluded that the attack on Metcalf was a highly professional military operation, comparable to what the SEALS themselves would do when attacking a power grid.

Footprints suggested that a team of perhaps as many as six men executed the Metcalf operation. They knew about an underground communications tunnel at Metcalf and knew how to access it by removing a manhole cover (which required at least two men). They cut communications cables and the 911 cable to isolate the site. They had pre-surveyed firing positions. They used AK-47s, the favorite assault rifle of terrorists and rogue states. They knew precisely where to shoot to maximize damage to the 17 transformers at Metcalf. They escaped into the night just as the police arrived and have not been apprehended or even identified. They left no fingerprints anywhere, not even on the expended shell casings.

The Metcalf assailants only damaged but did not destroy the transformers--apparently deliberately. The Navy SEALS and U.S. FERC Chairman Wellinghoff concluded that the Metcalf operation was a "dry run" like a military exercise, practice for a larger and more ambitious attack on the grid to be executed in the future.

Military exercises never try to destroy the enemy. Most exercises try to keep a low profile so that the potential victim is not moved to reinforce his defenses. For example, Russian strategic bomber exercises only send a few aircraft to probe U.S. air defenses in Alaska, and never actually launch nuclear-armed cruise missiles. They want to probe and test our air defenses--not scare us into strengthening those defenses.

Chairman Wellinghoff was aware of an internal study by U.S. FERC that concluded saboteurs could blackout the national electric grid for eighteen (18) months by destroying just nine (9) crucial transformer substations.

Much to his credit, Jon Wellinghoff became so alarmed by his knowledge of U.S. grid vulnerability, and the apparent NERC cover-up of the Metcalf affair, that he resigned his chairmanship to warn the American people in reports published by the Wall Street Journal (February 5, March 12, August 28, November 20, 2014). The Metcalf story sparked a firestorm of interest in the press and investigations by Congress.

Consequently, NERC passed, on an emergency basis, a new standard for immediately upgrading physical security for the national electric grid. PG&E promised to spend over $100 million over the next three years to upgrade physical security.

Terror Blackout of Yemen
On June 9, 2014, while world media attention was focused on the terror group Islamic State in Iraq and Syria (ISIS) overrunning northern Iraq, Al Qaeda in the Arabian Peninsula (AQAP) used mortars and rockets to destroy electric transmission towers to blackout all of Yemen, a nation of 16 cities and 24 million people.

AQAP's operation against the Yemen electric grid is the first time in history that terrorists have sunk an entire nation into blackout. The blackout went virtually unreported by the world press.

Metcalf Again--NERC and Utilities Negligent
Two months later, amid growing fears that ISIS terrorists may somehow act on their threats to attack America, on August 27, 2014, parties unknown again broke into the Metcalf transformer substation, stole cameras and other equipment for detecting intruders, and again escaped PG&E security guards and the police. PG&E claims that the second Metcalf affair is, again, merely vandalism.

Yet after NERC's emergency new physical security standards and PG&E's alleged massive investment in improved security--Metcalf should have been the Rock of Gibraltar of the North American electric grid. If terrorists or someone is planning an attack on the U.S. electric grid, Metcalf would be the perfect place to test the supposedly strengthened security of the national grid.

Does stolen equipment prove that Metcalf-2 was a burglary? In the world of spies and saboteurs, mock burglary is a commonplace device for covering-up an intelligence operation, and hopefully quelling fears and keeping the victim unprepared. Theft of cameras and other equipment for detecting intruders would obviously be of great interest to terrorists planning to sabotage the grid.

If PG&E is telling the truth, and the second successful operation against Metcalf is merely by vandals--this is an engraved invitation to ISIS or Al Qaeda or rogue states to attack the U.S. electric grid. It means that all of PG&E and NERC's vaunted security improvements cannot protect Metcalf from unsophisticated vandals, let alone from terrorists. The "vandals" must have been extremely daring, or perhaps illiterate, to burglarize Metcalf after all the national publicity about its improved security.

About one month later, on September 23, 2014, another investigation of PG&E security at transformer substations, including Metcalf, reported that the transformer substations are still not secure. Indeed, at one site a gate was left wide open. Former CIA Director R. James Woolsey, after reviewing the investigation results, concluded, "Overall, it looks like there is essentially no security."

Terror Blackout of Pakistan
On January 25, 2015, terrorists in Pakistan sabotaged key transmission towers causing a nearly nationwide blackout across 80 percent of Pakistan's national electric grid. Temporarily, the blackout caused widespread disruption of business and social life.

Pakistan repaired the transmission towers and fully recovered from blackout after a few days. Fortunately, no EHV transformers were destroyed, which would have put Pakistan in the dark for weeks or months.

Pakistan's terror blackout of January 25, 2015, might be a dry run for a more ambitious future attack aimed at overthrowing the government--or stealing one of Pakistan's nuclear weapons.

Terror Blackout of Turkey
On March 31, 2015, virtually all of Turkey was plunged temporarily into a chaotic blackout that disrupted businesses, transportation, and had fire departments rescuing people from stalled elevators in nearly every major city. The blackout of Turkey, a nation of 75 million people, a member of NATO, and a crucial U.S. ally in the Middle East, reportedly resulted from a cyber attack from Iran.

Iran, the world's leading sponsor of international terrorism, is also allied with Syrian dictator Bashar al-Assad, whose regime is threatened by Turkish aid to anti-Assad rebels.

Connecting the dots--Metcalf, Mexico, Yemen, Pakistan, and Turkey--terrorists and rogue states clearly are learning and experimenting with ever more ambitious versions of Blackout War. America and Western Civilization are probably their ultimate intended victims.

States Should EMP Harden Their Grids
State governments and their Public Utility Commissions should exercise aggressive oversight to ensure that the transformer substations and electric grids in their States are safe and secure. The record of NERC and the electric utilities indicates they cannot be trusted to provide for the security of the grid.

State governments can protect their grid from sabotage by the "all hazards" strategy that protects against the worst threat--nuclear EMP attack.

For example, faraday cages to protect EHV transformers and SCADAS colonies from EMP would also screen from view these vital assets so they could not be accurately targeted by high-powered rifles, as is necessary in order to destroy them by small arms fire. The faraday cages could be made of heavy metal or otherwise fortified for more robust protection against more powerful weapons, like rocket propelled grenades.

Surge arrestors to protect EHV transformers and SCADAS from nuclear EMP would also protect the national grid from collapse due to sabotage. The U.S. FERC scenario where terrorists succeed in collapsing the whole national grid by destroying merely nine transformer substations works only because of cascading overvoltage. When the nine key substations are destroyed, megawatts of electric power gets suddenly dumped onto other transformers, which in their turn get overloaded and fail, dumping yet more megawatts onto the grid. Cascading failures of more and more transformers ultimately causes a protracted national blackout.

This worst case scenario for sabotage could not happen if the transformers and SCADAS are protected against nuclear EMP--which is a more severe threat than any possible system-generated overvoltage.

Cyber Attack

Cyber attacks, the use of computer viruses and hacking to invade and manipulate information systems and SCADAS, is almost universally described by U.S. political and military leaders as the greatest threat facing the United States. Every day, literally thousands of cyber attacks are made on U.S. civilian and military systems, most of them designed to steal information.

Joint Chiefs Chairman, General Martin Dempsey, warned on June 27, 2013, that the United States must be prepared for the revolutionary threat represented by cyber warfare (Claudette Roulo, *DoD News*, Armed Force Press Service): "One thing is clear. Cyber has escalated from an issue of moderate concern to one of the most serious threats to our national security," cautioned Chairman Dempsey, "We now live in a world of weaponized bits and bytes, where an entire country can be disrupted by the click of a mouse."

Cyber Hype?

Skeptics claim that the catastrophic scenarios envisioned for cyber warfare are grossly exaggerated, in part to justify costly cyber programs wanted by both the Pentagon and industry at a time of scarce defense dollars. Many of the skeptical arguments about the limitations of hacking and computer viruses are technically correct.

However, it is not widely understood that foreign military doctrines define "information warfare" and "cyber warfare" as encompassing kinetic attacks and EMP attack--which is an existential threat to the United States.

Thomas Rid's book *Cyber War Will Not Take Place* (Oxford University Press, 2013) exemplifies the viewpoint of a growing minority of highly talented cyber security experts and scholars who think there is a conspiracy of governments and industry to hype the cyber threat. Rid's bottom line is that hackers and computer bugs are capable of causing inconvenience--not apocalypse. Cyber attacks can deny services, damage computers selectively but probably not wholesale, and steal information, according to Rid. He does not rule out that future hackers and viruses could collapse the electric grid, concluding such a feat would be, not impossible, but nearly so.

In a 2012 BBC interview, Rid chastised then Secretary of Defense Leon Panetta for claiming that Iran's Shamoon Virus, used against the U.S. banking system and Saudi Arabia's ARAMCO, could foreshadow a "Cyber Pearl Harbor" and for threatening military retaliation against Iran. Rid told the BBC that the world has, "Never seen a cyber attack kill a single human being or destroy a building."

Cyber security expert Bruce Schneier claims, "The threat of cyberwar has been hugely hyped" to keep growing cyber security programs at the Pentagon's Cyber Command, the Department of Homeland Security, and new funding streams to Lockheed Martin, Raytheon, Century Link, and AT&T, who are all part of the new cyber defense industry. The Brookings Institute's Peter Singer wrote in November 2012, "Zero. That is the number of people who have been hurt or killed by cyber terrorism." Ronald J. Delbert, author of *Black Code: Inside the Battle for Cyberspace*, a lab director and professor at the University of Toronto, accuses RAND and the U.S. Air Force of exaggerating the threat from cyber warfare.

Peter Sommer of the London School of Economics and Ian Brown of Oxford University, in *Reducing Systemic Cybersecurity Risk*, a study for Europe's Organization for Economic Cooperation and Development, are far more worried about natural EMP from the Sun than computer viruses: "a catastrophic cyber incident, such as a solar flare that could knock out satellites, base stations and net hardware" makes computer viruses and hacking "trivial in comparison."

Aurora Experiment
The now declassified Aurora experiment is the empirical basis for the claim that a computer virus might be able to collapse the national electric grid. In Aurora, a virus was inserted into the SCADAS running a generator, causing the generator to malfunction and eventually destroy itself.

However, using a computer virus to destroy a single generator does not prove it is possible or likely that an adversary could destroy all or most of the generators in the United States. Aurora took a protracted time to burn out a generator--and no intervention by technicians attempting to save the generator was allowed, as would happen in a nationwide attack, if one could be engineered.

Nor is there a single documented case of a even a local blackout being caused in the United States by a computer virus or hacking--which it seems should have happened by now, if vandals, terrorists, or rogue states could attack U.S. critical infrastructures easily by hacking.

Stuxnet Worm and Gaza Cyber War
Even the Stuxnet Worm, the most successful computer virus so far, reportedly according to White House sources jointly engineered by the U.S. and Israel to attack Iran's nuclear weapons program, proved a disappointment. Stuxnet succeeded in damaging only 10 percent of Iran's centrifuges for enriching uranium, and did not stop or even significantly delay Tehran's march towards the bomb.

During the recently concluded Gaza War between Israel and Hamas, a major cyber campaign using computer bugs and hacking was launched against Israel by Hamas, the Syrian Electronic Army, Iran, and by sympathetic hackers worldwide. The Gaza War was a Cyber World War against Israel.

The Institute for National Security Studies, at Tel Aviv University, in "The Iranian Cyber Offensive during Operation Protective Edge" (August 26, 2014) reports that the cyber attacks caused inconvenience and in the worst case some alarm, over a false report that the Dimona nuclear reactor was leaking radiation: "...the focus of the cyber offensive...was the civilian internet. Iranian elements participated in what the C4I officer described as an attack unprecedented in its proportions and the quality of its targets....The attackers had some success when they managed to spread a false message via the IDF's official Twitter account saying that the Dimona reactor had been hit by rocket fire and that there was a risk of a radioactive leak."

However, the combined hacking efforts of Hamas, the Syrian Electronic Army, Iran and hackers worldwide did not blackout Israel or significantly impede Israel's war effort.

Dragonfly
But tomorrow is always another day. Cyber warriors are right to worry that perhaps someday someone will develop the cyber bug version of an atomic bomb. Perhaps such a computer virus already exists in a foreign laboratory, awaiting use in a future surprise attack.

On July 6, 2014, reports surfaced that Russian intelligence services allegedly infected 1,000 power plants in Western Europe and the United States with a new computer virus called Dragonfly. No one knows what Dragonfly is supposed to do. Some analysts think it was just probing the defenses of western electric grids. Others think Dragonfly may have inserted logic bombs into SCADAS that can disrupt the operation of electric power plants in a future crisis.

Cyber Command Warning, China-Russia Cyber Aggression, Blackout of Turkey
Tomorrow's cyber super-threat, that with computer viruses and hacking alone can blackout the national electric grid for a year or more, and so destroy the United States, may already be upon us today. Admiral Michael Rogers on November 20, 2014, warned the House Permanent Select Committee on Intelligence that sophisticated great powers like China and Russia have the capability to blackout the entire U.S. national electric grid for months or years by means of cyber attack, according to press reports.

Admiral Rogers, as Chief of U.S. Cyber Command and Director of the National Security Agency, is officially the foremost U.S. authority on the cyber threat. "It is only a matter of the when, not the if, that we are going to see something traumatic," Admiral Rogers testified to Congress, as reported on CNN (November 21, 2014).

However, Jonathan Pollett, a cyber-security expert, in an article challenged Admiral Rogers' warning as wrong, or misunderstood and exaggerated by the press: "No, hackers can't take down the entire, or even a widespread portion of the US electric grid. From a logistical standpoint, this would be far too difficult to realistically pull off," writes Pollett in "What Hackers Can Do To Our Power Grid," *Business Insider* (November 23, 2014).

In June 2015, congressional hearings revealed the discovery, about a year earlier, that China, probably the Chinese Peoples Liberation Army (PLA), hacked into computer files at the U.S. Office of Personnel Management and stole sensitive information on 30 million federal employees and U.S. citizens.

Russia apparently made a cyber attack on the U.S. Joint Chiefs of Staff in July 2015 that crippled an unclassified e-mail communications network used by the Joint Chiefs. "The U.S. military believes hackers connected to Russia are behind the recent intrusion into a key, unclassified e-mail server used by the office of the Joint Chiefs," according to a CNN report ("Official: Russia Suspected In Joint Chiefs E-mail Server Intrusion" August 7, 2015), "Military officials assessed the attack had a sophistication that indicates it came from a state-associated actor." The widely reported Russian cyber attack on the Joint Chiefs disrupted e-mail communications for 4,000 users at the Defense Department for over 10 days.

The same CNN report noted that in April 2015 another Russian cyber attack penetrated "sensitive parts of the White House computer system."

Few Americans make any connection between cyber theft and EMP attacks on the grid that would threaten the existence of our society. But when you understand China and Russia's military doctrine on Total Information Warfare, these cyber thefts and intrusions look less like isolated cases of theft and hacking and more like probing U.S. defenses and gauging Washington reactions--perhaps in preparation for an all-out cyber offensive that would include physical sabotage, radiofrequency weapons, and nuclear EMP attack. In Nazi Germany's blitzkrieg strategy, the massed onslaught of heavy armored divisions was always preceded by scouting and probing by their motorcycle corps. The same principle may be at work here in cyber space with probing attacks on the U.S. from China, Russia, North Korea and Iran.

On March 31, 2015, Turkey's national electric grid was temporarily blacked-out, briefly causing widespread chaos to businesses and society in a member of NATO and crucial U.S. ally in the Middle East. Reportedly, Iran caused the blackout by a cyber attack. But Turkey has not officially confirmed that Iran was the culprit. If so, it will be the first time in history that a nationwide blackout is confirmed as resulting from cyber warfare.

States Should EMP Harden Their Grids
Cyber warfare is an existential threat to the United States, not because of computer viruses and hacking alone, but as envisioned in the military doctrines of potential adversaries whose plans for an all-out Cyber Warfare Operation include the full spectrum of military capabilities--including EMP attack. In 2011, a U.S. Army War College study *In The Dark: Planning for a Catastrophic Critical Infrastructure Event* warned U.S. Cyber Command that U.S. doctrine should not overly focus on computer viruses to the exclusion of EMP attack and the full spectrum of other threats, as planned by potential adversaries.

Reinforcing the above, a Russian technical article on cyber warfare by Maxim Shepovalenko (*Military-Industrial Courier* July 3, 2013), notes that a cyber attack can collapse "the system of state and military control...its military and economic infrastructure" because of "electromagnetic weapons...an electromagnetic pulse acts on an object through wire leads on infrastructure, including telephone lines, cables, external power supply and output of information."

Resilient Military Systems and the Advanced Cyber Threat, a January 2013 study by the Defense Science Board, recommends that it may be necessary for the U.S. to respond to an all-out cyber warfare operation with nuclear deterrence--or nuclear war. The Defense Science Board warns that while operationally "a nuclear and cyber attack are very different" in terms of the consequences "the existential impact to the United States is the same."

The Defense Science Board is the Defense Department's brain trust of blue ribbon scientists and strategic experts who advise the Department on the most complex and important scientific and technical matters bearing on national security. The Defense Science Board's *Advanced Cyber Threat* report is among the most in depth DSB studies, having been 18 months in the making by a panel of 24 experts whose research included 50 Defense Department and Intelligence Community briefings.

The Congressional EMP Commission warned in 2004 and again in 2008 that cyber warfare doctrine among potential adversaries includes nuclear EMP attack--an existential threat to the United States. Former Director of Central Intelligence, R. James Woolsey, reiterated this warning in testimony on cyber threats before the House Energy and Commerce Committee in May 2013 and again before the Senate Homeland Security Committee in July 2015. .

The Defense Science Board likewise warns that cyber warfare is not only about computer viruses and hacking, but becomes an existential threat "from a sophisticated and well-resourced opponent utilizing cyber capabilities in combination with all of their military and intelligence capabilities (a 'full spectrum' adversary)."

Cyber warriors who think narrowly in terms of computer hacking and viruses invariably propose anti-hacking and anti-viruses as solutions. Such a solution will result in an endless virus versus anti-virus software arms race that may ultimately prove unaffordable and futile.

States can protect themselves from the worst case cyber scenario by following the "all hazards" strategy recommended by the Congressional EMP Commission. The worst case scenario envisions a computer virus infecting the SCADAS that regulate the flow of electricity into EHV transformers, damaging the transformers with overvoltage, and causing a protracted national blackout.

But if the transformers are protected with surge arrestors against the worst threat--nuclear EMP attack--they would be unharmed by the worst possible overvoltage that might be system generated by any computer virus. This EMP hardware solution would provide a permanent and relatively inexpensive fix to what is the extremely expensive and apparently endless virus versus anti-virus software arms race that is ongoing in the new cyber defense industry.

EMP Attack

High-altitude nuclear electromagnetic pulse attack is the most severe threat to the electric grid and other critical infrastructures. A nuclear EMP attack would likely be more damaging than a geomagnetic super-storm, the worst case of severe weather, sabotage by kinetic attacks, or cyber attack.

Contrary to non-experts sometimes cited in the press, there is more empirical data on nuclear EMP and more analysis and a better understanding of EMP effects on electronic systems and infrastructures than almost any other threat, except severe weather. In addition to the 1962 STARFISH PRIME high-altitude nuclear test that generated EMP that damaged electronic systems in Hawaii and elsewhere, the Department of Defense has decades of atmospheric and underground nuclear test data relevant to EMP. And defense scientists have for over 50 years studied EMP effects on electronics in simulators. Most recently, the Congressional EMP Commission made its threat assessment by testing a wide range of modern electronics crucial to critical infrastructures in EMP simulators.

There is a scientific and strategic consensus behind the Congressional EMP Commission's assessment that a nuclear EMP attack would have catastrophic consequences for the United States, but that "correction is feasible and well within the Nation's means and resources to accomplish." Every major U.S. Government study to examine the EMP threat and solutions concurs with the EMP Commission, including the Congressional Strategic Posture Commission (2009), the U.S. Department of Energy and North American Electric Reliability Corporation (2010), the U.S. Federal Energy Regulatory Commission interagency report, coordinated with the White House, Department of Defense, and Oak Ridge National Laboratory (2010), and numerous other studies.

Not one major U.S. Government study dissents from the consensus that nuclear EMP attack would be catastrophic, and that protection is achievable and necessary.

Russian Nuclear EMP Tests
STARFISH PRIME is not the only high-altitude nuclear EMP test.

The Soviet Union (1961-1962) conducted a series of high-altitude nuclear EMP tests over what was then its own territory--not once but seven times--using a variety of warheads of different designs. The EMP fields from six tests covered Kazakhstan, an industrialized area larger than Western Europe. In 1994, during a thaw in the Cold War, Russia shared the results from one of its nuclear EMP tests, that used their least efficient warhead design for EMP--it collapsed the Kazakhstan electric grid, damaging transformers, generators and all other critical components.

The USSR during the Kazakhstan high-altitude EMP experiments tested some low-yield warheads, at least one probably an Enhanced Radiation Warhead that emitted large quantities of gamma rays, that generate the E1 EMP electromagnetic shockwave. It is possible that the USSR developed their Super-EMP Warhead early in the Cold War as a secret super-weapon.

Perhaps the most important lesson to be learned from the USSR's unconscionable and evil nuclear EMP tests against their own people is that there is no excuse to be vulnerable to EMP. The Soviets apparently quickly repaired the damage to Kazakhstan's electric grid and other critical infrastructures, thereby proving definitively that with smart planning and good preparedness it is possible to survive and recover from an EMP catastrophe.

Super-EMP Weapons and Low-Tech EMP Attacks by Missile, Aircraft and Balloon
A nuclear weapon detonated at an altitude of 300 kilometers over the geographic center of the U.S. would create an EMP field potentially damaging to electronics over all 48 contiguous United States. The Congressional EMP Commission concluded that virtually any nuclear weapon, even a crude first generation atomic bomb having a low yield, could potentially inflict an EMP catastrophe.

However, the EMP Commission also found that Russia, China, and probably North Korea have nuclear weapons specially designed to generate extraordinarily powerful EMP fields-- called by the Russians Super-EMP weapons--and this design information may be widely proliferated: "Certain types of relatively low-yield nuclear weapons can be employed to generate potentially catastrophic EMP effects over wide geographic areas, and designs for variants of such weapons may have been illicitly trafficked for a quarter-century."

Nor is a sophisticated long-range missile required to make an EMP attack.

Any short-range missile or other delivery vehicle that can deliver a nuclear weapon to an altitude of 30 kilometers or higher can make a potentially catastrophic EMP attack on the United States. Although a nuclear weapon detonated at 30 kilometers altitude could not cover the entire continental U.S. with an EMP field, the field would still cover a very large multi-state region--and be more intense. Lowering the height-of-burst (HOB) for an EMP attack decreases field radius, but increases field strength.

An EMP attack at 30 kilometers HOB anywhere over the eastern half of the U.S. would cause cascading failures far beyond the EMP field and collapse the Eastern Grid, that generates 75 percent of U.S. electricity. The nation could not survive without the Eastern Grid.

A Scud missile launched from a freighter could perform such an EMP attack. Over 30 nations have Scuds, as do some terrorist groups and private collectors. Scuds are available for sale on the world and black markets.

Any aircraft capable of flying Mach 1, such as a small civilian jetliner, could probably do a zoom climb to 30 kilometers altitude to make an EMP attack, if the pilot is willing to commit suicide.

Even a meteorological balloon could be used to loft a nuclear weapon 30 kilometers high to make an EMP attack. During the period of atmospheric nuclear testing in the 1950s and early 1960s, more nuclear weapons were tested at altitude by balloon than by bombers or missiles.

Nuclear EMP Effects on Critical Infrastructures

Nuclear EMP is like super-lightning. The electromagnetic shockwave unique to nuclear weapons, called E1 EMP, travels at the speed of light, potentially injecting into electrical systems thousands of volts in a nanosecond--literally a million times faster than lightning, and much more powerful. Russian open source military writings describe their Super-EMP Warhead as generating 200,000 volts/meter, which means that the target receives 200,000 volts for every meter of its length. So, for example, if the cord on a PC is two meters long, it receives 400,000 volts. An automobile 4 meters long could receive 800,000 volts, unless it is parked underground or protected in some other way.

No other threat can cause such broad and deep damage to all the critical infrastructures as a nuclear EMP attack. A nuclear EMP attack would collapse the electric grid, blackout and directly damage transportation systems, industry and manufacturing, telecommunications and computers, banking and finance, and the infrastructures for food and water.

Jetliners carry about 500,000 passengers on over 1,000 aircraft in the skies over the U.S. at any given moment. Many, most or virtually all of these would crash, depending upon the strength of the EMP field. Satellite navigation and communication systems would be knocked out, as would ground and air traffic control systems, necessitating that any surviving aircraft land "blind."

Cars, trucks, trains and traffic control systems would be damaged. In the best case, even if only a few percent of ground transportation vehicles are rendered inoperable, massive traffic jams would result. In the worst case, most vehicles of all kinds exposed to the EMP field would be rendered inoperable. In any case, all vehicles would stop operating when they run out of gasoline. The blackout would render gas stations inoperable and paralyze the infrastructure for synthesizing and delivering petroleum products and fuels of all kinds.

Industry and manufacturing would be paralyzed by collapse of the electric grid. Damage to SCADAS and safety control systems would likely result in widespread industrial accidents, including gas line explosions, chemical spills, fires at refineries and chemical plants producing toxic clouds.

Seven days after the commencement of blackout, emergency generators at nuclear reactors would run out of fuel. The reactors and nuclear fuel rods in cooling ponds would likely meltdown and catch fire, as happened in the nuclear disaster at Fukushima, Japan. The 104 U.S. nuclear reactors, located mostly among the populous eastern half of the United States, could cover vast swaths of the nation with dangerous plumes of radioactivity.

Cell phones, personal computers, the internet, and the modern electronic economy that supports personal and big business cash, credit, debit, stock market and other transactions and record keeping would cease operations. The Congressional EMP Commission warns that society could revert to a barter economy.

Worst of all, there will be no running water, and about 72 hours after the commencement of blackout, when emergency generators at the big regional food warehouses cease to operate, the nation's food supply will begin to spoil. Supermarkets are resupplied by these large regional food warehouses that are, in effect, the national larder, collectively having enough food to sustain the lives of 320 million Americans for about one month, at normal rates of consumption. The Congressional EMP Commission warns that as a consequence of the collapse of the electric grid and other critical infrastructures, "It is possible for the functional outages to become mutually reinforcing until at some point the degradation of infrastructure could have irreversible effects on the country's ability to support its population."

The EMP Commission estimates that a nationwide blackout lasting one year could kill up to 9 of 10 Americans through starvation, disease, and societal collapse.

Nuclear EMP Threat Is Real
The nuclear EMP threat is not merely theoretical, but real.

"China and Russia have considered limited nuclear attack options that, unlike their Cold War plans, employ EMP as the primary or sole means of attack," according to the Congressional EMP Commission, "Indeed, as recently as May 1999, during the NATO bombing of the former Yugoslavia, high-ranking members of the Russian Duma, meeting with a U.S. congressional delegation to discuss the Balkans conflict, raised the specter of a Russian EMP attack that would paralyze the United States."

Russia has made many nuclear threats against the U.S. since 1999, which are reported in the western press only rarely. On December 15, 2011, Pravda, the official mouthpiece of the Kremlin, gave this advice to the United States in "A Nightmare Scenario For America":

No missile defense could prevent...EMP...No one seriously believes that U.S. troops overseas are defending "freedom" or defending their country....Perhaps they ought to close the bases, dismantle NATO and bring the troops home where they belong before they have nothing to come home to and no way to get there.

On June 1, 2014, Russia Today, a Russian television news show, also broadcast to the West in English, predicted that the United States and Russia would be in a nuclear war by 2016.

Iran, the world's leading sponsor of international terrorism, openly writes about making a nuclear EMP attack to eliminate the United States. An Iranian military textbook, recently translated by the intelligence community, refers to nuclear EMP attack no less than 20 times, according to Rep. Trent Franks at a December 2014 congressional hearing. Iran has practiced missile launches that appear to be training and testing warhead fusing for a high-altitude EMP attack--including missile launching for an EMP attack from a freighter, according to the EMP Commission. An EMP attack launched from a freighter could be performed anonymously, leaving no fingerprints, to foil deterrence and escape retaliation.

"What is different now is that some potential sources of EMP threats are difficult to deter--they can be terrorist groups that have no state identity, have only one or a few weapons, and are motivated to attack the U.S. without regard for their own safety," cautions the EMP Commission in its 2004 report, "Rogue states, such as North Korea and Iran, may also be developing the capability to pose an EMP threat to the United States, and may also be unpredictable and difficult to deter."

On April 16, 2013, North Korea apparently simulated a nuclear EMP attack against the United States, orbiting its KSM-3 satellite over the U.S. at the optimum trajectory and altitude to place a peak EMP field over Washington and New York and blackout the Eastern Grid, that generates 75 percent of U.S. electricity. On the very same day, as described earlier, parties unknown executed a highly professional commando-style sniper attack on the Metcalf transformer substation that is a key component of the Western Grid. Blackout of the Western Grid, or even of just San Francisco, would cripple U.S. power projection capabilities against North Korea.

These events happened amidst the worst ever nuclear crisis with North Korea, in the aftermath of Pyongyang's third illegal nuclear test, when the North's new dictator Kim Jong-Un was threatening to make nuclear missile strikes against the U.S. and its allies. The White House and Department of Defense took these threats so seriously that they beefed-up the National Missile Defense and conducted bombing exercises with B-2s just outside the Demilitarized Zone, as demonstrations to deter North Korean aggression.

A few months later, in July 2013, North Korean freighter *Chon Chong Gang* transited the Gulf of Mexico carrying nuclear-capable SA-2 missiles in its hold on their launchers. The missiles had no warheads, but the event demonstrated North Korea's capability to execute a ship-launched nuclear EMP attack from U.S. coastal waters anonymously, to escape U.S. retaliation. The missiles were only discovered, hidden under bags of sugar, because the freighter tried returning to North Korea through the Panama Canal and inspections.

What does all this signify?

Connect these dots: North Korea's apparent practice EMP attack with its KSM-3 satellite; the simultaneous "dry run" sabotage attack at Metcalf; North Korea's possible practice for a ship-launched EMP attack a few months later; and cyber attacks from various sources were happening all the time, and are happening every day. These suggest the possibility that in 2013 North Korea may have deliberately provoked a crisis with its third illegal nuclear test in order to practice against the United States an all-out combined arms operation aimed at targeting U.S. critical infrastructures--the Blackout War.

Or are these coincidences merely accidental?

Is it also mere happenstance that Metcalf services the Silicon Valley, that reportedly developed the Stuxnet Worm that attacked Iran's nuclear program, for which transgression the Iranian Revolutionary Guard swore revenge? Iran and North Korea are by treaty strategic partners and closely cooperate in their scientific and military programs. With North Korean help, Iran too has orbited satellites on trajectories consistent with practicing a surprise nuclear EMP attack on the United States.

Non-Nuclear EMP Weapons

Radio-Frequency Weapons (RFWs) are non-nuclear weapons that use a variety of means, including explosively driven generators, to emit an electromagnetic pulse similar to the E1 EMP from a nuclear weapon, except less energetic and of much shorter radius. The range of RF Weapons is rarely more than one kilometer.

RF Weapons can be built relatively inexpensively using commercially available parts and design information available on the internet. In 2000 the Terrorism Panel of the House Armed Services Committee conducted an experiment, hiring an electrical engineer and some students to try building an RFW on a modest budget, using design information available on the internet, made from parts purchased at Radio Shack.

They built two RF Weapons in one year, both successfully tested at the U.S. Army proving grounds at Aberdeen. One was built into a Volkswagen bus, designed to be driven down Wall Street to disrupt stock market computers and information systems and bring on a financial crisis. The other was designed to fit in the crate for a Xerox machine so it could be shipped to the Pentagon, sit in the mailroom, and burn-out Defense Department computers.

EMP simulators that can be carried and operated by one man, and used as an RF Weapon, are available commercially. For example, one U.S. company advertises for sale an "EMP Suitcase" that looks exactly like a metal suitcase, can be carried and operated by one man, and generates 100,000 volts/meter over a short distance. The EMP Suitcase is not intended to be used as a weapon, but as an aid for designing factories that use heavy duty electronic equipment that emit electromagnetic transients, so the factory does not self-destruct.

But a terrorist or criminal armed with the EMP Suitcase, could potentially destroy electric grid SCADAS or an EHV transformer and blackout a city. Thanks to RF Weapons, we have arrived at a place where the technological pillars of civilization for a major metropolitan area could be toppled by a single madman.

The EMP Suitcase can be purchased without a license by anyone.

Terrorists armed with RF Weapons might use unclassified computer models to duplicate the U.S. FERC study and figure out which nine crucial transformer substations need to be attacked in order to blackout the entire national grid for weeks or months.

RFWs would offer significant operational advantages over assault rifles and bombs. Something like the EMP Suitcase could be put in the trunk of a car, parked and left outside the fence of an EHV transformer or SCADA colony, or hidden in nearby brush or a garbage can, while the bad guys make a leisurely getaway. Or a single RFW could be driven from one transformer substation to another (the substations are unguarded) to knock-out enough SCADAS and transformers to cause a regional or even national protracted blackout.

If the EMP fields are strong enough, an RFW could be more effective, and far less conspicuous, than dropping a big bomb to destroy the whole transformer substation. Since all electronics within the field of the RFW could be damaged, precision targeting would be unnecessary, as is the case for firearms and explosives. Unlike firearms and bombs, damage inflicted by RFWs might be mistaken as a freak accident or unusual systemic failure.

Some documented examples of successful attacks using Radio Frequency Weapons, and accidents involving electromagnetic transients, are described in the Department of Defense *Pocket Guide for Security Procedures and Protocols for Mitigating Radio Frequency Threats* (Technical Support Working Group, Directed Energy Technical Office, Dahlgren Naval Surface Warfare Center):

--"In the Netherlands, an individual disrupted a local bank's computer network because he was turned down for a loan. He constructed a Radio Frequency Weapon the size of a briefcase, which he learned how to build from the Internet. Bank officials did not even realize that they had been attacked or what had happened until long after the event."
--"In St. Petersburg, Russia, a criminal robbed a jewelry store by defeating the alarm system with a repetitive RF generator. Its manufacture was no more complicated than assembling a home microwave oven."
--"In Kzlyar, Dagestan, Russia, Chechen rebel commander Salman Raduyev disabled police radio communications using RF transmitters during a raid."
--"In Russia, Chechen rebels used a Radio Frequency Weapon to defeat a Russian security system and gain access to a controlled area."
-- "Radio Frequency Weapons were used in separate incidents against the U.S. Embassy in Moscow to falsely set off alarms and to induce a fire in a sensitive area."
--"March 21-26, 2001, there was a mass failure of keyless remote entry devices on thousands of vehicles in the Bremerton, Washington, area...The failures ended abruptly as federal investigators had nearly isolated the source. The Federal Communications Commission (FCC) concluded that a U.S. Navy presence in the area probably caused the incident, although the Navy disagreed."
--"In 1999, a Robinson R-44 news helicopter nearly crashed when it flew by a high frequency broadcast antenna."
--"In the late 1980s, a large explosion occurred at a 36-inch diameter natural gas pipeline in the Netherlands. A SCADA system, located about one mile from the naval port of Den Helder, was affected by a naval radar. The RF energy from the radar caused the SCADA system to open and close a large gas flow-control valve at the radar scan frequency, resulting in pressure waves that traveled down the pipe and eventually caused the pipeline to explode."
--"In June 1999 in Bellingham, Washington, RF energy from a radar induced a SCADA malfunction that caused a gas pipeline to rupture and explode."

--"In 1967, the *USS Forrestal* was located at Yankee Station off Vietnam. An A4 Skyhawk launched a Zuni rocket across the deck. The subsequent fire took 13 hours to extinguish. 134 people died in the worst U.S. Navy accident since World War II. EMI [Electro-Magnetic Interference, Pry] was identified as the probable cause of the Zuni launch."

--North Korea used an Radio Frequency Weapon, purchased from Russia, to attack airliners and impose an "electromagnetic blockade" on air traffic to Seoul, South Korea's capitol. The repeated attacks by RFW also disrupted communications and the operation of automobiles in several South Korean cities in December 2010; March 9, 2011; and April-May 2012 as reported in "Massive GPS Jamming Attack By North Korea" (*GPSWORLD.COM*, May 8, 2012).

Protecting the electric grid and other critical infrastructures from nuclear EMP attack will also protect them from the lesser threat posed by Radio Frequency Weapons.

States Should EMP Harden Their Grids

States should harden their electric grids against nuclear EMP attack because there is a clear and present danger, because protecting against nuclear EMP will mitigate all lesser threats, and because both the federal government in Washington and the electric power industry have failed to protect the people from the existential peril that is an EMP catastrophe.

In the U.S. Congress, bipartisan bills with strong support, such as the GRID Act and the SHIELD Act, that would protect the electric grid from nuclear and natural EMP, have been stalled for a half-decade, blocked by corruption and lobbying by powerful utilities.

The U.S. Federal Energy Regulatory Commission has published interagency reports acknowledging that nuclear EMP attack is an existential threat against which the electric grid must be protected. But U.S. FERC claims to lack legal authority to require the North American Electric Reliability Corporation and the electric utilities to protect the grid.

"Given the national security dimensions to this threat, there may be a need to act quickly to act in a manner where action is mandatory rather than voluntary and to protect certain information from public disclosure," said Joseph McClelland, Director of FERC's Office of Energy Projects, testifying in May 2011 before the Senate Energy and Natural Resources Committee. "The commission's legal authority is inadequate for such action."

Others think U.S. FERC has sufficient legal authority to protect the grid, but lacks the will to do so because of an incestuous relationship with the NERC.

NERC and the electric power industry deny that it is their responsibility to protect the grid from nuclear EMP attack. NERC and the utilities have even argued, absurdly, that they should not protect the grid from nuclear EMP because it is the worst case threat!

NERC also thinks it is not their job, but the job of the Department of Defense, to protect the United States from nuclear EMP attack, so argued NERC President and CEO, Gerry Cauley, in his May 2011 testimony before the Senate Energy and Natural Resources Committee. Mark Lauby, NERC's reliability manager, is quoted by Peter Behr in his *EENEWS* article (August 26, 2011) that "...the terrorist scenario--foreseen as the launch of a crude nuclear weapon on a version of a SCUD missile from a ship off the U.S. coast--is the government's responsibility, not industry's."

But the Defense Department can protect the grid only by waging preventive wars against countries like Iran, North Korea, China and Russia, or by vast expansion and improvement of missile defenses costing tens of billions of dollars--none of which may stop the EMP threat.

Preventive wars would make an EMP attack more likely, perhaps inevitable. It is not worth spending thousands of lives and trillions of dollars on wars, just so NERC and the utilities can avoid a small increase in electric bills for EMP hardening the grid. U.S. FERC estimates EMP hardening would cost the average ratepayer an increase in their electric bill of 20 cents annually.

The Department of Defense has no legal authority to EMP harden the privately owned electric grid. Such protection is supposed to be the job of NERC and the utilities.

Most alarming, NERC and the utilities do not appear to know their jobs, and are already in panic and despair over the challenges posed by severe weather, cyber threats, and geomagnetic storms. Peter Behr in an article published in *Energy Wire* (September 12, 2014) reports that at an electric grid security summit, Gary Leidich, Board Chairman of the Western Electricity Coordinating Council--which oversees reliability and security for the Western Grid--appears overwhelmed, as if he wants to escape his job, crying: "Who is really responsible for reliability? And who has the authority to do something about it?"

"The biggest cyber threat is from an electromagnetic pulse, which in the military doctrines of our potential adversaries would be part of an all-out cyber war.", writes former Speaker of the House, Newt Gingrich, in his article "The Gathering Cyber Storm" (*CNN*, August 12, 2013). Gingrich warns that NERC "should lead, follow or get out of the way of those who are trying to protect our nation from a cyber catastrophe. Otherwise, the Congress that certified it as the electric reliability organization can also decertify it."

Much to their credit, a few in the electric power industry understand the necessity of protecting the grid from nuclear EMP attack, have broken ranks with NERC, and are trying to meet the crisis. John Houston of Centerpoint Energy in Texas; Terry Boston of PJM, the largest grid in North America (located in the midwest); and Con Ed in New York--all are trying to protect their grids from nuclear EMP.

State Governors and State Legislatures need to come to the rescue. States have a duty to their citizens to fill the gap in homeland security and public safety when the federal government, and the utilities, fail.

State governments and their Public Utility Commissions have the legal authority and the moral obligation to, where necessary, compel the utilities to secure the grid against all hazards. State governments have an obligation to help and oversee and ensure that grid security is being done right by those utilities that act voluntarily.

Failing to protect the grid from nuclear EMP attack is failing to protect the nation from all hazards.

JULY 23, 2012

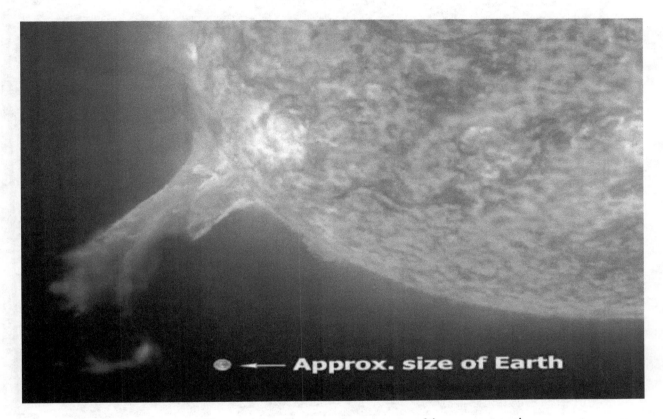

Coronal Mass Ejection (CME) capable of generating catastrophic geomagnetic super-storm narrowly missed Earth on July 23, 2012. NASA estimates the likelihood of such a storm hitting Earth to be 12 percent over the next decade--which virtually guarantees a natural EMP catastrophe will happen in our lifetimes or that of our children.

APRIL 16, 2013

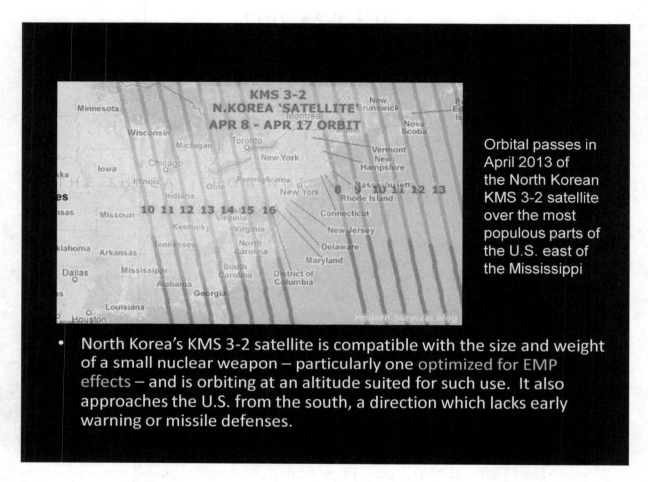

Orbital passes in April 2013 of the North Korean KMS 3-2 satellite over the most populous parts of the U.S. east of the Mississippi

- North Korea's KMS 3-2 satellite is compatible with the size and weight of a small nuclear weapon – particularly one optimized for EMP effects – and is orbiting at an altitude suited for such use. It also approaches the U.S. from the south, a direction which lacks early warning or missile defenses.

February-April 2013, North Korea's Kim Jong-Un threatened a nuclear missile strike against the U.S. mainland in retaliation for new sanctions imposed for the North's third illegal nuclear test in February. North Korea's KSM-3 satellite flew on the classic trajectory and altitude for a surprise nuclear EMP attack executed by a Fractional Orbital Bombardment System (FOBS)--a secret weapon invented by the USSR during the Cold War. The FOBS is designed to disguise a satellite launch as an EMP attack, and further surprise the U.S. by flying the satellite over the South Pole. The U.S. has no ballistic missile early warning radars or missile interceptors looking South, and is blind from that direction.

JULY 2013

IS AN EMP-FROM-THE-SEA THREAT REALISTIC?

The *Chong Chon Gang*, a tramp steamer owned by Iran's ally, North Korea, and its secret cargo, hidden under 10,000 tons of sugar

Two full-up, nuclear-capable SA-2 missiles on their launchers were discovered in Panama on a North Korean-flagged vessel under sugar bags in July 2013

The Congressional EMP Commission's nightmare scenario is an EMP attack launched off a freighter operating near the U.S. coast. Such an attack could not be intercepted by missile defense and could be performed anonymously, so the U.S. would not know against whom to retaliate. North Korea's freighter *Chong Chon Gang* carried two nuclear capable SA-2 missiles, on their launchers, into the Gulf of Mexico, a few months after Kim Jong-Un threatened a nuclear missile strike against the United States.

OCTOBER 27, 2013

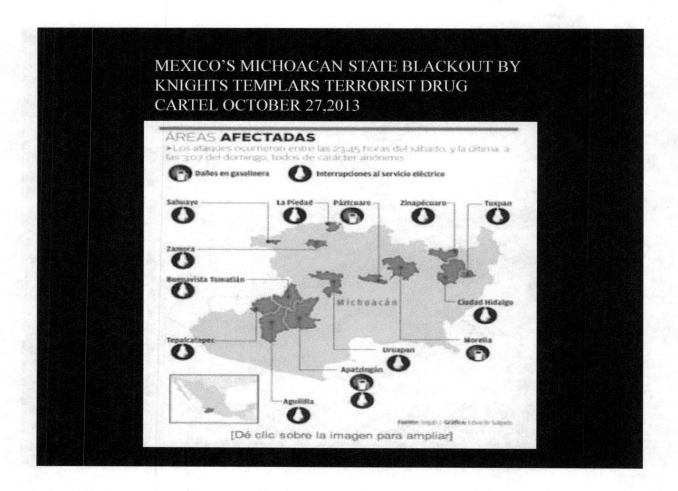

The Knights Templars, a terrorist drug cartel, used small arms and explosives to blackout Mexico's Michoacan State, putting 420,000 people in the dark and isolating them from help from federal police, so they could publicly assassinate town and village leaders. Surely the drug lords, who are targets of the U.S. war on drugs, have noticed that the United States border is undefended.

JUNE 9, 2014

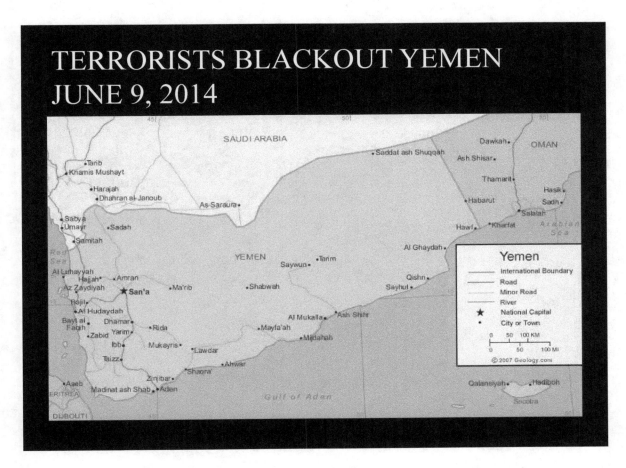

TERRORISTS BLACKOUT YEMEN
JUNE 9, 2014

For the first time in history, a terror attack has blacked-out an entire nation.
While ISIS was conquering northern Iraq, Al Qaeda in the Arabian Peninsula (AQAP) blacked-out the nation of Yemen--an unprecedented event little noted by western media. ISIS, AQAP and other terror groups work together. ISIS has threatened to attack the United States. A U.S. Federal Energy Regulatory Commission study warns that a coordinated attack on just 9 transformer substations could blackout the U.S. for weeks or months.

NUCLEAR HEMP AREA COVERAGE

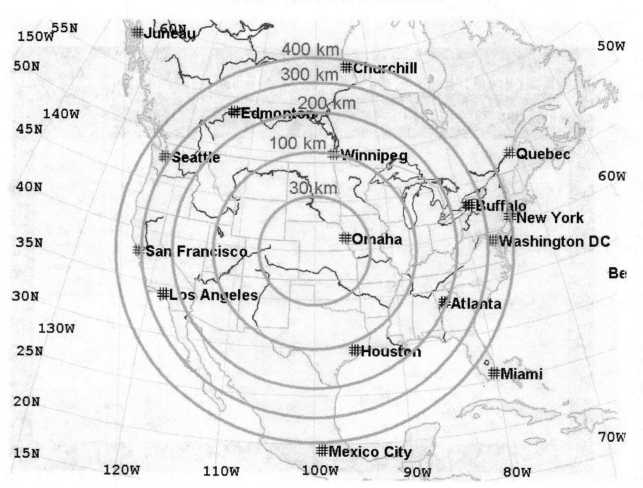

EMP field coverage increases with increasing height-of-burst. A balloon or jet aircraft could loft a nuclear warhead to an altitude of 30 kilometers which, targeted over New York City, would also cover Washington, D.C., New York State, New Jersey, Pennsylvania, Virginia, Maryland, Delaware, and most of New England.

II

THE BLACKOUT WAR

A Failure of Strategic Imagination

Russia, China, North Korea and Iran in their military doctrines advocate using combined attacks by EMP, cyber and sabotage against electric grids and other civilian critical infrastructures as a "Revolution in Military Affairs" that could prove decisive in war, enabling a small power to surprise and humble a great power, much as Nazi Germany nearly conquered the western democracies in World War II by the surprise use of the "Blitzkrieg" ("Lightning War") strategy.

A Defense Science Board study *Resilient Military Systems and the Advanced Cyber Threat* (January 2013) equates an all-out cyber attack on the United States with the consequences of a nuclear attack, and concludes that a nuclear response is justified to deter or retaliate for cyber warfare: "While the manifestation of a nuclear and cyber attack are very different, in the end, the existential impact to the United States is the same."

The Congressional EMP Commission found that the military doctrines of potential adversaries for Information Warfare or Cyber Warfare include, not only computer viruses and hacking, but nuclear EMP attack.

The Defense Science Board, which is the braintrust of top scientists and strategists for the Department of Defense, agrees with the EMP Commission.

The DSB study *Resilient Military Systems and the Advanced Cyber Threat* likewise concludes that cyber warfare is an existential threat not because of computer viruses alone: "...the cyber threat is serious and the United States cannot be confident that our critical Information Technology (IT) systems will work under attack from a sophisticated and well resourced opponent utilizing cyber capabilities in combination with all of their military and intelligence capabilities (a 'full spectrum' adversary)."

Dangerously for the West, U.S. political and military leaders continue to think of cyber threats narrowly, as largely or entirely limited to hacking and computer bugs. This failure of strategic imagination is a major catastrophe in the making. It is akin to the blindness that afflicted nearly everyone in the West, and made possible World War II, from a failure of strategic imagination among most Western elites to foresee and understand Nazi Germany's Blitzkrieg strategy.

A Revolution in Military Affairs

The Blitzkrieg revolutionized warfare by using the new technologies of airpower, armored divisions, and mobile infantry and artillery in closely coordinated combined arms operations to rapidly outmaneuver and overwhelm with superior firepower the antiquated Western strategy, tactics and technologies of static trench warfare. Nazi Germany developed the Blitzkrieg secretly in experiments, during military exercises, and tested the new strategy in a low profile way during the Spanish Civil War (1936-1939) to keep the West in the dark.

Winston Churchill, Major General J.F.C. Fuller and a few others saw the Blitzkrieg coming --but their warnings were ignored. When Nazi Germany sprang the Blitzkrieg on their unprepared victims in 1939-1941, they routed the Allies and nearly won World War II.

The Blitzkrieg is an example of a "Revolution in Military Affairs"--an epoch shattering moment in history when new military technology and strategy inflicts such decisive defeat that it threatens to overthrow and replace one civilization with another.

Soviet General P.A. Zhilin, in his classic *The History of Military Art*, a Cold War era textbook still used in Russia's Voroshilov General Staff Academy, describes history as a series of Revolutions in Military Affairs. For example, according to Zhilin:

--The Agricultural Revolution makes possible the rise of the first kingdoms and armies that are conquered and unified into the first Empires by Egypt and the Hittites whose greater productivity enables them to field bigger armies, the first equipped with massed chariots.
--The Persian Empire falls to Alexander the Great and his new Macedonian Phalanx enabling Greek civilization to conquer the Near East and inaugurating the Hellenistic Age.
--Hellenism is conquered by the Roman Empire with its numerically and organizationally superior Roman Legions, military roads, catapults, ballistas and other early war engines.
--Feudal Europe with its castles, mounted knights, and semi-autonomous baronies is shattered by the invention of gunpowder, artillery, and the longbow and is dominated by kings and kingdoms.
--Kingdoms are eclipsed by early nation states, rising nationalism, and the early Industrial Revolution that invents mass citizen armies of the Napoleonic Era and Total War.
--World War I, the first scientific Total War, harnesses the machine gun, poison gas, and industrial mass production to slaughter million man armies, destroying the old world order dominated by Western Europe.
--Nazi Germany nearly wins World War II with the Blitzkrieg, but is defeated by the USSR's "scientific socialism" that supposedly enables the Soviets to out-produce and outfight the Nazis with a better Blitzkrieg.
--Zhilin ends *The History of Military Art* with the Revolution in Military Affairs that is the Nuclear Missile Age, which Zhilin predicts will enable the USSR to defeat the West.

The Nazis and Soviets were right that their Revolutions in Military Affairs would change history. Fortunately, they were wrong that their RMAs would make history go their way. Blitzkrieg strategy and tactics were learned by the Allies at an enormous cost in blood, and ultimately used to destroy the Nazis. Soviet nuclear war plans were deterred, by an enormously expensive and deadly nuclear arms race and decades-long Cold War, that ended with the USSR's disintegration.

The costly lesson of World War II and the Cold War, that left 100 million dead, is that the United States and the Western democracies cannot be surprised by the next Revolution in Military Affairs--or we risk annihilation.

Russian General Vladimir Slipchenko, picking up where General Zhilin's history of the evolution of warfare left off, advances in his military textbook *No Contact Wars* the theory of a new Revolution in Military Affairs, the greatest in history, that he calls No Contact Warfare or Sixth Generation Warfare. It is a Blitzkrieg, not against enemy armies, but in cyberspace and against electric grids and other civilian critical infrastructures, combining and coordinating attacks by cyber, precision weapons, and EMP weapons that could defeat a rival nation, or an entire civilization, in a matter of hours.

Russian theories about the Revolution in Military Affairs represented by attacking electric grids and other civilian critical infrastructures with cyber and EMP appears also in the military doctrines and exercises of China, North Korea, and Iran.

For example, an Iranian military textbook recently translated by the Defense Intelligence Agency's National Intelligence University, ironically titled *Passive Defense* (2010), describes nuclear EMP effects in detail, and recommends EMP attack to defeat decisively an adversary over 20 times.

The official Iranian military textbook advocates a revolutionary new way of warfare that combines coordinated attacks by nuclear and non-nuclear EMP weapons, physical and cyber attacks against electric grids to black out and collapse entire nations. Iranian military doctrine makes no distinction between nuclear EMP weapons, non-nuclear radiofrequency weapons and cyber operations--they regard nuclear EMP attack as the ultimate cyber weapon. EMP is most effective at blacking-out critical infrastructures, while EMP also does not directly damage the environment or harm human life, according to Iran's *Passive Defense*:

As a result of not having the other destructive effects that nuclear weapons possess, among them the loss of human life, weapons derived from electromagnetic pulses have attracted attention with regard to their use in future wars...The superficiality of secondary damage sustained, as well as the avoidance of human casualties, serves as a motivation to transform this technology into an advanced and useful weapon in modern warfare.

Because EMP kills electronics directly, but people indirectly, EMP is regarded by Iran as Shariah compliant use of a nuclear weapon. "Passive Defense" and other Iranian military writings are well aware that nuclear EMP attack is the most efficient way of killing people, through secondary effects, over the long run. The rationale appears to be that people starve to death, not because of EMP, but because they live in materialistic societies so dependent upon modern technology that materialism and technology have been elevated to the status of a false God. People die of their sins. EMP is divine justice.

The new Revolution in Military Affairs is called many things by many nations. Official Russian military doctrine calls it by inconspicuous names like: Cyber Warfare Operation, Information Warfare, or Electronic Warfare. Chinese military doctrine calls it all these things and Total Information Warfare. Some at the U.S. Army War College call the new Revolution in Military Affairs "Cybergeddon."

Unprecedented Threat to Civilization

Here we have called this latest Revolution in Military Affairs the New Blitzkrieg, the New Lightning War, and the Blackout War, hoping to communicate by these labels the gravity of the threat facing the United States and Western Civilization.

Our potential adversaries have planned and practiced combined operations using computer viruses and hacking, sabotage and kinetic attacks, and nuclear EMP attack to blackout electric grids, collapse critical infrastructures, to defeat--or render extinct--entire nations.
Like the Nazis, they have planned and practiced the New Blitzkrieg in secret, experimenting with bits and pieces to keep a low profile, intending, when zero hour comes, that we will be surprised.

The Blackout War is potentially the greatest and most decisive Revolution in Military Affairs in history:

--The New Blitzkrieg literally strikes with super-lightning and other new technologies against the technological Achilles Heel of our electronic civilization, and in *hours, minutes or seconds* could blackout our entire nation, possibly for years, which is really the same as saying possibly forever.

--The New Lightning War strikes against the societal Achilles Heel of our civilization, going around our armed forces to attack civilians in the utilities and our families that depend upon them for survival. Our civilian critical infrastructures are outside of our national security culture, and are the least prepared for the speedy massed onslaught from the best warriors and best technology of the adversary. *It is a mismatch unique in history.*

--*For the first time in history,* the Blackout War enables the least successful society on Earth, like a North Korea that cannot even feed its own people, or even atavistic non-state actors like ISIS or Al Qaeda, to destroy the most successful societies, including the United States. Retaliation may not even be an option since the U.S. military relies for 99 percent of its electricity for operations and power projection upon the civilian electric grid.

Ambassador R. James Woolsey, former Director of the Central Intelligence Agency, in writings and testimony to Congress, warns that an all-out Cyber Warfare Operation as planned in the military doctrines of potential adversaries would not be limited to computer viruses and hacking, but would include physical sabotage and nuclear EMP attack.

Unfortunately, like Churchill's warnings about the impending Nazi Blitzkrieg, few appear to be listening.

Maine, Virginia, and Arizona have heard the warning, and other States are listening. When Washington is failing, all is not lost. The States, like the Minutemen and colonial militias of old, can and should lead the way.

Former CIA Director Woolsey points the way forward below, warning:

Administratively, a coherent and effective answer will not likely arise from uncoordinated decisions made independently by the thousands of individual industries at risk. Because cyber preparedness should encompass EMP preparedness--and since EMP is an existential threat--it is imperative that Government play a supervisory and coordinating role to achieve protection against these threats swiftly. (Hearing on Cyber Threats, House Committee on Energy and Commerce, May 21, 2013)

AMBASSADOR R. JAMES WOOLSEY
FORMER DIRECTOR OF CENTRAL INTELLIGENCE
HEARING ON CYBER THREATS
TESTIMONY BEFORE THE
HOUSE COMMITTEE ON ENERGY AND COMMERCE
May 21, 2013

This hearing is about cyber threats and solutions. But I am going to talk about a dimension of the cyber threat that is not usually considered a cyber threat in Western doctrine, but is in the playbooks for an Information Warfare Operation of Russia, China, North Korea, and Iran. These potential adversaries in their military doctrines include as a dimension of cyber warfare a wide spectrum of operations beyond computer viruses, including sabotage and kinetic attacks, up to and including nuclear electromagnetic pulse (EMP) attack.

It is vitally important that we understand that a nuclear EMP attack is part of cyber and information warfare operations as conceived by our potential adversaries. Our cyber doctrine must be designed to deter and defeat the cyber doctrines of our potential adversaries by anticipating how they plan to attack us--but our doctrine currently does not.

Our cyber and information warfare doctrines are dangerously blind to the likelihood that a potential adversary making an all-out information warfare campaign designed to cripple U.S. critical infrastructures would include an EMP attack.

The assessment that nuclear EMP attack is included in the cyber and information warfare doctrine of potential adversaries, and the effects of an EMP attack described here, are based on the work of the Congressional EMP Commission that analyzed this threat for nearly a decade (2001-2008). The Congressional Strategic Posture Commission and several other major U.S. Government studies independently arrived at similar conclusions, and represent collectively a scientific and strategic consensus that nuclear EMP attack upon the United States is an existential threat.

What is EMP?

A nuclear weapon detonated at high-altitude, above 30 kilometers, will generate an electromagnetic pulse that can be likened to a super-energetic radio wave, more powerful than lightning, that can destroy and disrupt electronics across a broad geographic area, from the line of sight from the high-altitude detonation to the horizon.

For example, a nuclear weapon detonated at an altitude of 30 kilometers would project an EMP field with a radius on the ground of about 600 kilometers, that could cover all the New England States, New York and Pennsylvania, damaging electronics across this entire region, including electronics on aircraft flying across the region at the time of the EMP attack. The EMP attack would blackout at least the regional electric grid, and probably the entire Eastern Grid that generates 75 percent of U.S. electricity, for a protracted period of weeks, months, possibly years. The blackout and EMP damage beyond the electric grid in other systems would collapse all the other critical infrastructures--communications, transportation, banking and finance, food and water--that sustain modern civilization and the lives of millions.

Such an EMP attack, a nuclear detonation over the U.S. East Coast at an altitude of 30 kilometers, could be achieved by lofting the warhead with a meteorological balloon.

A more ambitious EMP attack could use a freighter to launch a medium-range missile from the Gulf of Mexico, to detonate a nuclear warhead over the geographic center of the United States at an altitude of 400 kilometers. The EMP field would extend to a radius of 2,200 kilometers on the ground, covering all of the contiguous 48 United States, causing a nationwide blackout and collapse of the critical infrastructures everywhere.

All of this would result from the high-altitude detonation of a single nuclear warhead.

The Congressional EMP Commission warned that Iran appears to have practiced exactly this scenario. Iran has demonstrated the capability to launch a ballistic missile from a vessel at sea. Iran has also several times practiced and demonstrated the capability to detonate a warhead on its medium-range Shahab III ballistic missile at the high-altitudes necessary for an EMP attack on the entire United States. The Shahab III is a mobile missile, a characteristic that makes it more suitable for launching from the hold of a freighter.

Launching an EMP attack from a ship off the U.S. coast could enable the aggressor to remain anonymous and unidentified, and so escape U.S. retaliation.

The Congressional EMP Commission warned that Iran in military doctrinal writings explicitly describes making a nuclear EMP attack to eliminate the United States as an actor on the world stage as part of an Information Warfare Operation. For example, various Iranian doctrinal writings on information and cyber warfare make the following assertions:

- "Nuclear weapons...can be used to determine the outcome of a war...without inflicting serious human damage [by neutralizing] strategic and information networks."
- "Terrorist information warfare [includes]...using the technology of directed energy weapons (DEW) or electromagnetic pulse (EMP)."
- "...today when you disable a country's military high command through disruption of communications you will, in effect, disrupt all the affairs of that country....If the world's industrial countries fail to devise effective ways to defend themselves against dangerous electronic assaults, then they will disintegrate within a few years."

China's premier military textbook on information warfare, written by China's foremost expert on cyber and information warfare doctrine, makes unmistakably clear that China's version of an all-out Information Warfare Operation includes both computer viruses and nuclear EMP attack. According to People's Liberation Army textbook *World War, the Third World War--Total Information Warfare*, written by Shen Weiguang, "Therefore, China should focus on measures to counter computer viruses, nuclear electromagnetic pulse...and quickly achieve breakthroughs in those technologies...":

With their massive destructiveness, long-range nuclear weapons have combined with highly sophisticated information technology and information warfare under nuclear deterrence....Information war and traditional war have one thing in common, namely that the country which possesses the critical weapons such as atomic bombs will have "first strike" and "second strike retaliation" capabilities....As soon as its computer networks come under attack and are destroyed, the country will slip into a state of paralysis and the lives of its people will ground to a halt. Therefore, China should focus on measures to counter computer viruses, nuclear electromagnetic pulse...and quickly achieve breakthroughs in those technologies in order to equip China without delay with equivalent deterrence that will enable it to stand up to the military powers in the information age and neutralize and check the deterrence of Western powers, including the United States.

North Korea appears to be attempting to implement the information warfare doctrine described above by developing a long range missile capable of making a catastrophic nuclear EMP attack on the United States. In December 2012, North Korea demonstrated the capability to launch a satellite on a polar orbit circling the Earth at an altitude of 500 kilometers. An altitude of 500 kilometers would be ideal for making an EMP attack that places the field over the entire contiguous 48 United States, using an inaccurate satellite warhead for delivery, likely to miss its horizontal aimpoint over the geographic center of the U.S. by tens of kilometers.

North Korea appears to have borrowed from the Russians their idea for using a so-called Space Launch Vehicle to make a stealthy nuclear attack on the United States. During the Cold War, Moscow developed a secret weapon called a Fractional Orbital Bombardment System (FOBS) that looked like a Space Launch Vehicle, but was designed to launch a nuclear warhead southward, away from the United States initially, but deliver the warhead like a satellite on a south polar orbit, so the nuclear attack comes at the U.S. from the south. The United States has no Ballistic Missile Early Warning (BMEW) radars or missile interceptors facing south. We might not even see the attack coming.

Miroslav Gyurosi in *The Soviet Fractional Orbital Bombardment System* describes Moscow's development of the FOBS:

The Fractional Orbital Bombardment System (FOBS) as it was known in the West, was a Soviet innovation intended to exploit the limitations of U.S. BMEW radar coverage. The idea behind FOBS was that a large thermonuclear warhead would be inserted into a steeply inclined low altitude polar orbit, such that it would approach CONUS from any direction, but primarily from the southern hemisphere, and following a programmed braking maneuver, re-enter from a direction which was not covered by BMEW radars.

"The first warning the U.S. would have of such a strike in progress would be the EMP...," writes Gyurosi.

The trajectory of North Korea's satellite launch of December 12, 2012 looked very much like a Fractional Orbital Bombardment System for EMP attack. The missile launched southward, away from the United States, sent the satellite over the south polar region, approaching the U.S. from the south, at the optimum altitude for EMP attack.

North Korea appears to have borrowed from Russia more than the FOBS. In 2004, a delegation of Russian generals met with the Congressional EMP Commission to warn that design information for a Super-EMP nuclear warhead had leaked from Russia to North Korea, and that North Korea might be able to develop such a weapon "in a few years." A few years later, in 2006, North Korea conducted its first nuclear test, of a device having a very low yield, about 3 kilotons. All three North Korean nuclear tests have had similarly low yields. A Super-EMP warhead would have a low-yield, like the North Korean device, because it is not designed to create a big explosion, but to produce gamma rays, that generate the EMP effect.

According to several press reports, South Korean military intelligence concluded independently of the EMP Commission that Russian scientists are in North Korea helping develop a Super-EMP nuclear warhead. In 2012, a military commentator for the People's Republic of China stated that North Korea has Super-EMP nuclear warheads.

One design of a Super-EMP warhead would be a modified neutron bomb, more accurately an Enhanced Radiation Warhead (ERW) because it produces not only large amounts of neutrons but large amounts of gamma rays, that cause the EMP effect. One U.S. ERW warhead (the W-82) deployed in NATO during the Cold War weighed less than 50 kilograms. North Korea's so-called Space Launch Vehicle, which orbited a satellite weighing 100 kilograms, could deliver such a warhead against the U.S. mainland--or against any nation on Earth.

Iran may already have a FOBS capability, as it has successfully launched several satellites on polar orbits, assisted by North Korean missile technology and North Korean technicians. Iranian scientists were present at all three North Korean nuclear tests, according to press reports.

What is to be done about the Cyber and EMP threats?

Technically, it is important to understand that surge arrestors and other hardware designed to protect against EMP can also protect against the worst-case cyber scenarios that, for example, envision computer viruses collapsing the national power grid. For example, surge arrestors that protect Extra High Voltage transformers from EMP can also protect transformers from damaging electrical surges caused by a computer virus that manipulates the grid Supervisory Control And Data Acquisition Systems (SCADAS).

Administratively, a coherent and effective answer will not likely arise from uncoordinated decisions made independently by the thousands of individual industries at risk. Because cyber preparedness should encompass EMP preparedness--and since EMP is an existential threat--it is imperative that Government play a supervisory and coordinating role to achieve protection against these threats swiftly.

AMBASSADOR R. JAMES WOOLSEY
FORMER DIRECTOR OF CENTRAL INTELLIGENCE
STATEMENT FOR THE RECORD
BEFORE THE
SENATE HOMELAND SECURITY AND
GOVERNMENTAL AFFAIRS COMMITTEE
July 22, 2015

Heading Toward An EMP Catastrophe*

For over a decade now, since the Congressional EMP Commission delivered its first report to Congress eleven years ago in July of 2004, various Senate and House committees have heard from numerous scientific and strategic experts the consensus view that natural and manmade electromagnetic pulse (EMP) is an existential threat to the survival of the American people, that EMP is a clear and present danger, and that something must be done to protect the electric grid and other life sustaining critical infrastructures--immediately.

Yet this counsel and the cost-effective solutions proposed to the looming EMP threat have been ignored. Continued inaction by Washington will make inevitable a natural or manmade EMP catastrophe that, as the Congressional EMP Commission warned, could kill up to 90 percent of the national population through starvation, disease, and societal collapse.

Indeed, some actions taken by the Congress, the White House, and the federal bureaucracy are impeding solutions, making the nation more vulnerable, and helping the arrival of an EMP catastrophe. More about that later.

Why has Washington failed to act against the EMP threat? A big part of the problem is that policymakers and the public still fail to understand that EMP, and the catastrophic consequences of an EMP event, are not science fiction.

The EMP threat is as real as the Sun and as inevitable as a solar flare.

The EMP threat is as real as nuclear threats from Russia, China, North Korea, and Iran. Nuclear EMP attack is part of the military doctrines, plans and exercises of all of these nations for a revolutionary new way of warfare that focuses on attacking electric grids and civilian critical infrastructures--what they call Total Information Warfare or No Contact Wars, and what some western analysts call Cybergeddon or Blackout Wars.

The nuclear EMP threat is as real as North Korea's KSM-3 satellite, that regularly orbits over the U.S. on the optimum trajectory and altitude to evade our National Missile Defenses and, if the KSM-3 were a nuclear warhead, to place an EMP field over all 48 contiguous United States.

The EMP threat is as real as non-nuclear radiofrequency weapons that have already been used by terrorists and criminals in Europe and Asia, and no doubt will sooner or later be used here against America.

A Clear And Present Danger

EMP, while still inadequately understood by policymakers and the general public, has been the subject of numerous major scientific and strategic studies. All of these warn by consensus that a natural or nuclear EMP, in the words of the Congressional EMP Commission, "Is one of a small number of threats that has the potential to hold our society seriously at risk" and "Is capable of causing catastrophe for the nation." Such is the warning not only of the Congressional EMP Commission, but of studies by the

Congressional Strategic Posture Commission, the National Academy of Sciences, the Department of Energy, the National Intelligence Council, a U.S. Federal Energy Regulatory Commission report coordinated with the Department of Defense and Oak Ridge National Laboratory, and numerous other reports.

Yet a recent Wall Street Journal article (May 1, 2015) on NORAD moving back into Cheyenne Mountain and spending $700 million to further harden the mountain against a nuclear EMP attack from North Korea, received hundreds of comments from shocked readers, half of whom still think that EMP is science fiction.

Nuclear EMP. We know that EMP is not science fiction but an existential threat that would have catastrophic consequences for our society because of high-altitude nuclear tests by the U.S. and Russia during the early Cold War, decades of underground nuclear testing, and over 50 years of tests using EMP simulators. For example, in 1961 and 1962, the USSR conducted several EMP tests in Kazakhstan above its own territory, deliberately destroying the electric grid and other critical infrastructures over an area larger than Western Europe. The Congressional EMP Commission based its threat assessment partially on using EMP simulators to test modern electronics--which the Commission found are over one million times more vulnerable than the electronics of the 1960s.

One prominent myth is that a sophisticated, high-yield, thermonuclear weapon is needed to make a nuclear EMP attack. In fact, the Congressional EMP Commission found that virtually any nuclear weapon--even a primitive, low-yield atomic bomb such as terrorists might build--would suffice. The U.S. electric grid and other civilian critical infrastructures--for example, communications, transportation, banking and finance, food and water--have never been hardened to survive EMP. The nation has 18 critical infrastructures--all 17 others depend upon the electric grid.

Another big myth is that a sophisticated long-range missile is needed to deliver an EMP attack. The iconic EMP attack detonates a single warhead about 300 kilometers high over the center of the U.S., generating an EMP field over all 48 contiguous United States.

However, any warhead detonated 30 kilometers high anywhere over the eastern half of the U.S. would collapse the Eastern Grid. The Eastern Grid generates 75 percent of U.S. electricity and supports most of the national population. Such an attack could be made by a short-range Scud missile launched off a freighter, by a jet fighter or small private jet doing a zoom climb, or even by a meteorological balloon.

According to a February 2015 article by President Ronald Reagan's national security brain trust--Dr. William Graham who was Reagan's Science Advisor and ran NASA, Ambassador Henry Cooper who was Director of the Strategic Defense Initiative, and Fritz Ermarth who was Chairman of the National Intelligence Council--North Korea and Iran have both practiced the iconic nuclear EMP attack against the United States. Both nations have orbited satellites on south polar trajectories that evade U.S. early warning radars and National Missile Defenses. North Korea and Iran have both orbited satellites at altitudes that, if the satellites were nuclear warheads, would place an EMP field over all 48 contiguous United States.

Dr. Graham and his colleagues in their article warn that Iran should already even be regarded as having nuclear weapons and missiles capable of making an EMP attack against the U.S., or against any nation on Earth.

North Korea and Iran have also apparently practiced making a nuclear EMP attack using a short-range missile launched off a freighter. Such an attack could be conducted anonymously to escape U.S. retaliation--thus defeating nuclear deterrence.

Natural EMP. We know that natural EMP from the Sun is real. Coronal mass ejections traveling over one million miles per hour strike the Earth's magnetosphere, generating geomagnetic storms every year. Usually these geo-storms are confined to nations at high northern latitudes and are not powerful enough to have catastrophic consequences. In 1989, the Hydro-Quebec Storm blacked-out half of Canada for a day causing economic losses amounting to billions of dollars.

However, we are most concerned about the rare solar super-storm, like the 1921 Railroad Storm, which happened before American civilization became dependent for survival upon electricity and the electric grid. The National Academy of Sciences estimates that if the Railroad Storm were to recur today, there would be a nationwide blackout with recovery requiring 4-10 years, if recovery is possible at all.

The most powerful geomagnetic storm on record is the 1859 Carrington Event. Estimates are that Carrington was about 10 times more powerful than the 1921 Railroad Storm and 100 times more powerful than the 1989 Hydro-Quebec Storm. The Carrington Event was a worldwide phenomenon, causing forest fires from flaring telegraph lines, burning telegraph stations, and destroying the just laid intercontinental telegraph cable at the bottom of the Atlantic Ocean.

If a solar super-storm like the Carrington Event recurred today, it would collapse electric grids and life-sustaining critical infrastructures worldwide, putting at risk the lives of billions.

NASA in July 2014 reported that two years earlier, on July 23, 2012 , the Earth narrowly escaped another Carrington Event. A Carrington-class coronal mass ejection crossed the path of the Earth, missing our planet by just three days. NASA assesses that the resulting geomagnetic storm would have had catastrophic consequences worldwide.

We are overdue for recurrence of another Carrington Event. The NASA report estimates that likelihood of such a geomagnetic super-storm is 12 percent per decade. This virtually guarantees that Earth will experience a catastrophic geomagnetic super-storm within our lifetimes or that of our children.

Radio-Frequency Weapons (RFWs). Just as nuclear and natural EMP are not science fiction, we also know that the EMP threat from non-nuclear weapons, commonly called Radio-Frequency Weapons, is real. Terrorists, criminals, and even disgruntled individuals have already made localized EMP attacks using RFWs in Europe and Asia. Probably sooner rather than later, the RFW threat will come to America.

RFWs typically are much less powerful than nuclear weapons and much more localized in their effects, usually having a range of one kilometer or less. Reportedly, according to the Wall Street Journal, a study by the U.S. Federal Energy Regulatory Commission warns that a terrorist attack that destroys just 9 key transformer substations could cause a nationwide blackout lasting 18 months.

RFWs offer significant advantages over guns and bombs for attacking the electric grid. The EMP field will cause widespread damage of electronics, so precision targeting is much less necessary. And unlike damage from guns and bombs, an attack by RFWs is much less conspicuous, and may even be misconstrued as an unusual accident arising from faulty components and systemic failure.

Some documented examples of successful attacks using Radio Frequency Weapons, and accidents involving electromagnetic transients, are described in the Department of Defense *Pocket Guide for Security Procedures and Protocols for Mitigating Radio Frequency Threats* (Technical Support Working Group, Directed Energy Technical Office, Dahlgren Naval Surface Warfare Center):

--"In the Netherlands, an individual disrupted a local bank's computer network because he was turned down for a loan. He constructed a Radio Frequency Weapon the size of a briefcase, which he learned how to build from the Internet. Bank officials did not even realize that they had been attacked or what had happened until long after the event."

--"In St. Petersburg, Russia, a criminal robbed a jewelry store by defeating the alarm system with a repetitive RF generator. Its manufacture was no more complicated than assembling a home microwave oven."

--"In Kzlyar, Dagestan, Russia, Chechen rebel commander Salman Raduyev disabled police radio communications using RF transmitters during a raid."

--"In Russia, Chechen rebels used a Radio Frequency Weapon to defeat a Russian security system and gain access to a controlled area."

-- "Radio Frequency Weapons were used in separate incidents against the U.S. Embassy in Moscow to falsely set off alarms and to induce a fire in a sensitive area."

--"March 21-26, 2001, there was a mass failure of keyless remote entry devices on thousands of vehicles in the Bremerton, Washington, area...The failures ended abruptly as federal investigators had nearly isolated the source. The Federal Communications Commission (FCC) concluded that a U.S. Navy presence in the area probably caused the incident, although the Navy disagreed."

--"In 1999, a Robinson R-44 news helicopter nearly crashed when it flew by a high frequency broadcast antenna."

--"In the late 1980s, a large explosion occurred at a 36-inch diameter natural gas pipeline in the Netherlands. A SCADA system, located about one mile from the naval port of Den Helder, was affected by a naval radar. The RF energy from the radar caused the SCADA system to open and close a large gas flow-control valve at the radar scan frequency, resulting in pressure waves that traveled down the pipe and eventually caused the pipeline to explode."

--"In June 1999 in Bellingham, Washington, RF energy from a radar induced a SCADA malfunction that caused a gas pipeline to rupture and explode."

--"In 1967, the *USS Forrestal* was located at Yankee Station off Vietnam. An A4 Skyhawk launched a Zuni rocket across the deck. The subsequent fire took 13 hours to extinguish. 134 people died in the worst U.S. Navy accident since World War II. EMI [Electro-Magnetic Interference] was identified as the probable cause of the Zuni launch."

--North Korea used an Radio Frequency Weapon, purchased from Russia, to attack airliners and impose an "electromagnetic blockade" on air traffic to Seoul, South Korea's capitol. The repeated attacks by RFW also disrupted communications and the operation of automobiles in several South Korean cities in December 2010; March 9, 2011; and April-

May 2012 as reported in "Massive GPS Jamming Attack By North Korea" (*GPSWORLD.COM*, May 8, 2012).

All Hazards Strategy. The Congressional EMP Commission recommended an "all hazards" strategy to protect the nation by addressing the worst threat--nuclear EMP attack. Nuclear EMP is worse than natural EMP and the EMP from RFWs because it combines several threats in one. Nuclear EMP has a long-wavelength component like a geomagnetic super-storm, a short-wavelength component like Radio-Frequency Weapons, a mid-wavelength component like lightning--and is potentially more powerful and can do deeper damage than all three.

Thus, protecting the electric grid and other critical infrastructures from nuclear EMP attack will also protect against a Carrington Event and RFWs. Moreover, protecting against nuclear EMP will also protect the grid and other critical infrastructures from the worst over-voltages that may be generated by severe weather, physical sabotage, or cyber attacks.

EMP--The Ultimate Cyber Weapon

Ignorance of the military doctrines of potential adversaries and a failure of strategic imagination is setting America up for an EMP Pearl Harbor that could easily be avoided--if we would only heed that terrorist sabotage of electric grids and cyber attacks are early warning indicators. In fact, in the military doctrines, planning, and exercises of Russia, China, North Korea and Iran, nuclear EMP attack is the ultimate weapon in an all-out cyber operation aimed at defeating nations by blacking-out their electric grids and other critical infrastructures.

For example, Russian General Vladimir Slipchenko in his military textbook *No Contact Wars* describes the combined use of cyber viruses and hacking, physical attacks, non-nuclear EMP weapons, and ultimately nuclear EMP attack against electric grids and critical infrastructures as a new way of warfare that is the greatest Revolution in Military Affairs (RMA) in history. Like Nazi Germany's Blitzkrieg ("Lightning War") Strategy that coordinated airpower, armor, and mobile infantry to achieve strategic and technological surprise that nearly defeated the Allies in World War II, the New Blitzkrieg is, literally and figuratively an electronic "Lightning War" so potentially decisive in its effects that an entire civilization could be overthrown in hours. According to Slipchenko, EMP and the new RMA renders obsolete modern armies, navies and air forces. For the first time in history, small nations or even non-state actors can humble the most advanced nations on Earth.

China's military doctrine sounds an identical theme. According to People's Liberation Army textbook *World War, the Third World War--Total Information Warfare*, written by Shen Weiguang (allegedly the inventor of Information Warfare), "Therefore, China should focus on measures to counter computer viruses, nuclear electromagnetic pulse...and quickly achieve breakthroughs in those technologies...":

With their massive destructiveness, long-range nuclear weapons have combined with highly sophisticated information technology and information warfare under nuclear deterrence....Information war and traditional war have one thing in common, namely that the country which possesses the critical weapons such as atomic bombs will have "first strike" and "second strike retaliation" capabilities....As soon as its computer networks come under attack and are destroyed, the country will slip into a state of paralysis and the lives of its people will ground to a halt. Therefore, China should focus on measures to counter computer viruses, nuclear electromagnetic pulse...and quickly achieve breakthroughs in those technologies in order to equip China without delay with equivalent deterrence that will enable it to stand up to the military powers in the information age and neutralize and check the deterrence of Western powers, including the United States.

Iran in a recently translated military textbook endorses the theories of Russian General Slipchenko and the potentially decisive effects of nuclear EMP attack some 20 times. An Iranian political-military journal, in an article entitled "Electronics To Determine Fate Of Future Wars," states that the key to defeating the United States is EMP attack and that, "If the world's industrial countries fail to devise effective ways to defend themselves against dangerous electronic assaults, then they will disintegrate within a few years.":

Advanced information technology equipment exists which has a very high degree of efficiency in warfare. Among these we can refer to communication and information gathering satellites, pilotless planes, and the digital system....Once you confuse the enemy communication network you can also disrupt the work of the enemy command and decision-making center. Even worse, today when you disable a country's military high command through disruption of communications you will, in effect, disrupt all the affairs of that country....If the world's industrial countries fail to devise effective ways to defend themselves against dangerous electronic assaults, then they will disintegrate within a few years....American soldiers would not be able to find food to eat nor would they be able to fire a single shot. (Tehran, *Nashriyeh-e Siasi Nezami*, December 1998 -January 1999)

North Korea appears to have practiced the military doctrines described above against the United States--including by simulating a nuclear EMP attack against the U.S. mainland. Following North Korea's third illegal nuclear test in February 2013, North Korean dictator Kim Jong-Un repeatedly threatened to make nuclear missile strikes against the U.S. and its allies. In what was the worst ever nuclear crisis with North Korea, that lasted months, the U.S. responded by beefing-up National Missile Defenses and flying B-2 bombers in exercises just outside the Demilitarized Zone to deter North Korea. On April 9, 2013, North Korea's KSM-3 satellite orbited over the U.S. from a south polar trajectory, that evades U.S. early warning radars and National Missile Defenses, at the near optimum altitude and location to place an EMP field over all 48 contiguous United States. On April 16, 2013, the KSM-3 again orbited over the Washington, D.C.-New York City corridor where, if the satellite contained a nuclear warhead, it could project the peak EMP field over the U.S. political and economic capitals and collapse the Eastern Grid, which generates 75 percent of U.S. electricity. On the same day, parties unknown used AK-47s to attack the Metcalf transformer substation that services San Francisco, the Silicon Valley, and is an important part of the Western Grid. Blackout of the Western Grid, or of just San Francisco, would impede U.S. power projection capabilities against North Korea. In July 2013, a North Korean freighter transited the Gulf of Mexico with two nuclear capable SA-2 missiles in its hold, mounted on their launchers hidden under bags of sugar, discovered only after the freighter tried to return to North Korea through the Panama Canal. Although the missiles were not nuclear armed, they are designed to carry a 10 kiloton warhead, and could execute the EMP Commission's nightmare scenario of an anonymous EMP attack launched off a freighter. All during this period, the U.S. electric grid and other critical infrastructures experienced various kinds of cyber attacks, as they do every day and continuously.

North Korea appears to have been so bold as to use the nuclear crisis it deliberately initiated to practice against the United States an all-out cyber warfare operation, including computer bugs and hacking, physical sabotage, and nuclear EMP attack.

Just as Nazi Germany practiced the Blitzkrieg in exercises and during the Spanish Civil War (1936-1939), before surprising the Allies in World War II, so terrorists and state actors appear to be practicing now. For example:

62

--On October 27, 2013, the Knights Templars, a criminal drug cartel, blacked-out Mexico's Michoacan state and its population of 420,000, so they could terrorize the people and paralyze the police. The Knights, cloaked by the blackout, entered towns and villages and publicly executed leaders opposed to the drug trade.

--On June 9, 2014, Al Qaeda in the Arabian Peninsula used mortars and rockets to destroy transmission towers, plunging into darkness all of Yemen, a country of 16 cities and 24 million people. It is the first time in history that terrorists put an entire nation into blackout, and an important U.S. ally, whose government was shortly afterwards overthrown by terrorists allied to Iran.

--In July 2014, according to press reports, a Russian cyber-bug called Dragonfly infected 1,000 electric power-plants in Western Europe and the United States for purposes unknown, possibly to plant logic bombs in power-plant computers to disrupt operations in the future.

--On January 25, 2015, terrorists blacked-out 80 percent of the electric grid in Pakistan, a nation of 185 million people, and a nuclear weapons state.

--On March 31, 2015, most of Turkey's 75 million people experienced a widespread and disruptive blackout, the NATO ally reportedly victimized by a cyber attack from Iran.

On June 20, 2015, the New York Times reported that administration officials in a classified briefing to Congress on a cyber attack from China, that stole sensitive U.S. Government data on millions of federal employees, was information warfare "on a scale we've never seen before from a traditional adversary." Yet this and the other ominous threats described above are already forgotten, or relegated to back page news, as policymakers and the public stumble on, seemingly shell-shocked and uncomprehending, to the latest cyber crisis.

We as a nation are not "connecting the dots" through a profound failure of strategic imagination. Like the Allies before the Blitzkrieg of World War II, we are blind to the unprecedented existential threat that is about to befall our civilization--figuratively and literally, from the sky, like lightning.

Washington Dysfunction

The Congressional EMP Commission recommended a plan to protect the national electric grid from nuclear EMP attack, that would also mitigate all lesser threats--including natural EMP, RFWs, cyber bugs and hacking, physical sabotage, and severe weather--for about $2 billion, which is what the U.S. gives away every year in foreign aid to Pakistan. About $10-20 billion would protect all the critical infrastructures from nuclear EMP attack and other threats.

There are other plans that cost much less, and much more, because there are different technologies and strategies for protecting against EMP, and to different levels of risk. Any or all of these plans are commendable. There is no such thing as being over-prepared for an existential threat.

Unfortunately, none of these plans has been implemented. The U.S. electric grid and other civilian critical infrastructures remain utterly vulnerable to EMP because of lobbying by the electric utilities in Congress, the federal bureaucracy, and the White House.

Lobbying by the electric power industry and their North American Electric Reliability Corporation (NERC) has, so far, thwarted every bill by the U.S. Congress to protect the grid from EMP. For example, in 2010, the House passed unanimously the GRID Act--which was denied a vote in the Senate, because a single Senator on the Energy and Natural

Resources Committee put a hold on the bill. If the GRID Act passed in 2010, the national electric grid would already be protected from EMP, a process the EMP Commission estimated would take about 3-5 years.

The SHIELD Act, another bipartisan bill to protect the electric grid, has been stalled in the House Energy and Commerce Committee for years, due to lobbying by the electric utilities.

Even worse, the U.S. Federal Energy Regulatory Commission, which has a too deferential and too cozy relationship with NERC, has approved a NERC proposed standard for protecting the grid from solar storms that has been condemned by the best scientific experts. Dr. William Radasky and John Kappenman, who both served on the Congressional EMP Commission, and other independent experts have written scientific critiques proving that the NERC standard for natural EMP (also called GMD for Geo-Magnetic Disturbance) is based on "junk science" that grossly underestimates the threat from natural EMP.

For example, Kappenman and Radasky, who are among the world's foremost scientific and technical experts on geomagnetic storms and grid vulnerability, warn that NERC's GMD Standard consistently underestimates the natural EMP threat from geo-storms: "When comparing...actual geo-electric fields with NERC model derived geo-electric fields, the comparisons show a systematic under-prediction in all cases of the geo-electric field by the NERC model."

Dr. Radasky, who holds the Lord Kelvin Medal for setting standards for protecting European electronics from natural and nuclear EMP, and John Kappenman, who helped design the ACE satellite upon which industry relies for early warning of geomagnetic storms, conclude that the NERC GMD Standard so badly underestimates the natural EMP threat that "its resulting directives are not valid and need to be corrected." Kappenman and Radasky:

These enormous model errors also call into question many of the foundation findings of the NERC GMD draft standard. The flawed geo-electric field model was used to develop the peak geo-electric field levels of the Benchmark model proposed in the standard. Since this model understates the actual geo-electric field intensity for small storms by a factor of 2 to 5, it would also understate the maximum geo-electric field by similar or perhaps even larger levels. Therefore, the flaw is entirely integrated into the NERC Draft Standard and its resulting directives are not valid and need to be corrected.

The excellent Kappenman-Radasky critique of the NERC GMD Standard represents the consensus view of all the independent observers who participated in the NERC GMD Task Force.

Perhaps most revelatory of U.S. FERC's failures, by approving the NERC GMD Standard that grossly underestimates the natural EMP threat from geo-storms--U.S. FERC abandoned its own much more realistic estimate of the natural EMP threat from geo-storms. It is incomprehensible why U.S. FERC would ignore the findings of its own excellent interagency study, one of the most in depth and meticulous studies of the EMP threat ever performed, that was coordinated with Oak Ridge National Laboratory, the Department of Defense, and the White House.

U.S. FERC's preference for NERC's "junk science" over U.S. FERC's own excellent scientific assessment of the geo-storm threat is indefensible.

The White House has not helped matters by issuing a draft executive order for protecting the national grid from natural EMP--but that trusts NERC and the electric utilities to set the standards.

Nor has the White House or the U.S. FERC challenged NERC's assertion that it has no responsibility to protect the electric grid from nuclear EMP or Radio-Frequency Weapons.

Nor has the White House or the U.S. FERC done anything to prevent NERC and the utilities from misinforming policymakers and the public about the EMP threat and their lack of preparedness to survive and recover from an EMP catastrophe.

Consequently, policymakers in the States who are alarmed by the lack of progress in Washington on EMP preparedness, find themselves seriously disadvantaged in efforts to protect their State electric grids by the utilities and their well-funded lobbyists who falsely claim Washington and the utilities are making great progress partnering on the EMP problem. So far in 2015, State initiatives to protect their electric grids have been defeated by industry lobbyists in Maine, Colorado, and Texas.

Texas State Senator Bob Hall, a former USAF Colonel and himself an EMP expert, characterizes as "equivalent to treason" the behavior of the electric utilities and their lobbyists:

As a Texas State Senator who tried in the 2015 legislative session to get a bill passed to harden the Texas grid against an EMP attack or nature's GMD, I learned first hand the strong control the electric power company lobby has on elected officials. We did manage to get a weak bill passed in the Senate but the power companies had it killed in the House. A very deceitful document which was carefully designed to mislead legislators was provided by the power company lobbyist to legislators at a critical moment in the process. The document was not just misleading, it actually contained false statements. The EMP/GMD threat is real and it is not "if" but WHEN it will happen. The responsibility for the catastrophic destruction and wide spread death of Americans which will occur will be on the hands of the executives of the power companies because they know what needs to be done and are refusing to do it. In my opinion power company executives, by refusing to work with the legislature to protect the electrical grid infrastructure are committing an egregious act that is equivalent to treason. I know and understand what I am saying. As a young US Air Force Captain, with a degree in electrical engineering from The Citadel, I was the project officer who lead the Air Force/contractor team which designed, developed and installed the modification to "harden" the Minuteman Strategic missile to protect it from an EMP attack. The American people must demand that the power company executives that are hiding the truth stop deceiving the people and immediately begin protecting our electrical grid so that life as we know it today will not end when the terrorist EMP attack comes.

Ironically, while electric power lobbyists are fighting against EMP protection in Washington, Texas, Maine, Colorado and elsewhere, the Iranian news agency MEHR recently reported that Iran is violating international sanctions and going full bore to protect itself from a nuclear EMP attack:

Iranian researchers...have built an Electromagnetic Pulse (EMP) filter that protects country's vital organizations against cyber attack. Director of Kosar Information and Communication Technology Institute Saeid Rahimi told MNA correspondent that the EMP (Electromagnetic Pulse) filter is one of the country's boycotted products and until now procuring it required considerable costs and various strategies. "But recently Kosar

ICT...has managed to domestically manufacture the EMP filter for the very first time in this country," said Rahimi. Noting that the domestic EMP filter has been approved by security authorities, Rahimi added "the EMP filter protects sensitive devices and organizations against electromagnetic pulse and electromagnetic terrorism." He also said the domestic EMP filter has been implemented in a number of vital centers in Iran. (MEHR News Agency, "Iran Builds EMP Filter For 1st Time" June 13, 2015)

What Is To Be Done?

Congress should pass the Critical Infrastructure Protection Act (CIPA), which requires the Department of Homeland Security to adopt a new National Planning Scenario focused on EMP; to develop plans to protect the critical infrastructures; and for emergency managers and first responders to plan and train to protect and recover the nation from an EMP catastrophe. CIPA will enable DHS to draw upon the deep expertise within the Department of Defense and the Intelligence Community to help protect the critical infrastructures from EMP. Do not let the electric power lobby defeat CIPA or weaken its provisions, as they are presently trying to do.

Reestablish the Congressional EMP Commission. The greatest progress was being made when the EMP Commission existed to advance EMP preparedness. Progress stopped when the EMP Commission terminated in 2008. Currently, the struggle to advance national EMP preparedness is being carried on by a handful of patriotic individuals and Non-Government Organizations who have no official standing and extremely limited resources. Bring back the EMP Commission with its deep expertise to advise Congress, government at all levels, and the private sector on how best to protect the nation, and to serve as a watchdog and leader for national EMP preparedness.

Pass the SHIELD Act or the GRID Act to establish adequate regulatory authority within the U.S. Government to achieve timely protection of the electric grid--and watch U.S. FERC like a hawk to make sure that regulatory authority is exercised.

Include in the National Defense Authorization Act the simple two-sentence provision below, that could rapidly reverse the trend of America's increasing vulnerability to EMP, by directing the Secretary of Defense to help State governments and the electric utilities protect themselves from an EMP catastrophe:

Energy Security For Military Bases And Critical Defense Industries

Whereas 99 percent of the electricity used by CONUS military bases is supplied by the national electric grid; whereas the Department of Defense has testified to Congress that DoD cannot project power overseas or perform its homeland security mission without electric power from the national grid; whereas the Congressional EMP Commission warned that up to 9 of 10 Americans could die from starvation and societal collapse from a nationwide blackout lasting one year; therefore the Secretary of Defense is directed to urge governors, state legislators, public utility commissions of the 50 states, the North American Electric Reliability Corporation (NERC) and the utilities that supply electricity to CONUS military bases and critical defense industries, to protect the electric grid from a high-altitude nuclear electromagnetic pulse (EMP) attack, from natural EMP generated by a solar super-storm and from other EMP threats including radiofrequency weapons, and to help the states, NERC, public utilities commissions, and electric utilities by providing DoD expertise on EMP and other such support and resources as may be necessary to protect the national electric grid from natural and manmade EMP threats. The Secretary of Defense is authorized to spend up to $2 billion in FY2017 to help protect the national electric grid from EMP.

Ambassador R. James Woolsey is former Director of Central Intelligence and is Chairman of the Foundation for Defense of Democracies.

*I am highly indebted to my friend and colleague, Dr. Peter Vincent Pry, who served on the Congressional EMP Commission and is Executive Director of the EMP Task Force on National and Homeland Security, for assistance in drafting this testimony.

BLACKOUT WAR

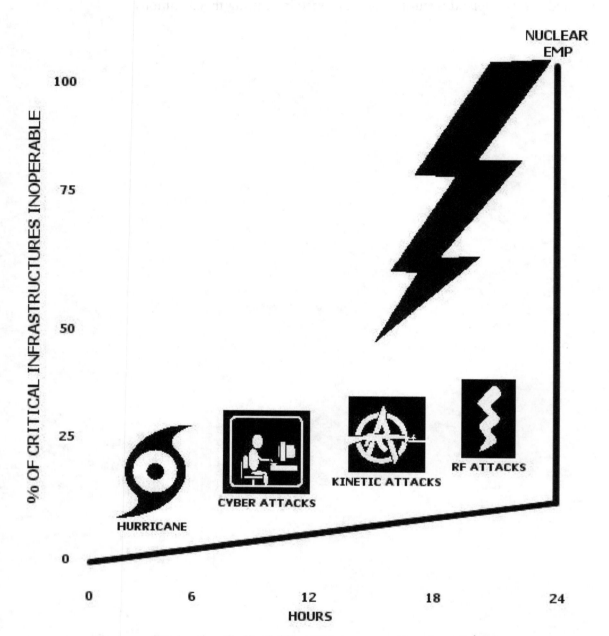

Severe weather, cyber attack, sabotage, RF weapons, and nuclear EMP attack used in coordinated operation to collapse the electric grid and other critical infrastructures.
Source: Dr. Peter Vincent Pry

III

THE STATES TO THE RESCUE

The States may succeed where the Federal Government has failed to protect the national electric grid and the American people. State legislatures and public utility commissions have the legal authority to require utilities to protect their assets from EMP and other hazards. Governors have legal authority, including under their emergency powers and responsibilities for homeland security, to launch initiatives to secure their State electric grids from EMP and all hazards that constitute a threat to the peoples of their State.

Washington Is Broken

After a half decade of trying in Washington, Congress and the Administration have failed to protect the national electric grid from EMP. For example, in Congress since 2008, strong bipartisan efforts to pass bills to protect the grid, first the GRID Act and then the SHIELD Act, have failed repeatedly, despite majority support for these bills, thwarted in both cases by a single member of Congress. The SHIELD Act has been introduced again, but may well remain bottled up in the House Energy and Commerce Committee without coming to a vote.

The book *Apocalypse Unknown: The Struggle To Protect America From An Electromagnetic Pulse Catastrophe* (2013) examines in great detail various institutional impediments in Washington obstructing progress on national EMP preparedness. It explains how almost every major institution in Washington has tried--the White House, the Congress, the Department of Defense, and the Department of Homeland Security--but failed to protect the American people from an EMP catastrophe.

For example, one big problem is that U.S. CYBER COMMAND is run by the National Security Agency (NSA), that is fixated on computer bugs and hacking to the exclusion of greater cyber threats--like EMP attack--that are planned by our adversaries.

Another problem is whether NSA and the Department of Defense are constitutionally and legally allowed to undertake the kind of intrusive policies and operations necessary to protect civilian critical infrastructures. Even if NSA and DOD were able and willing, their protection is unwelcome from the private sector and average citizens.

"Depending on your point of view, U.S. General Keith Alexander [the chief of CYBER COMMAND--Pry] is either an Army four-star trying to stave-off a cyber Pearl Harbor attack, or an overreaching spy chief who wants to eavesdrop on the private e-mails of every American," Reuters accurately reports in "Four-Star General In Eye Of U.S. Cyber Storm" (May 26, 2013). The same story quotes Ira Winkler, President of the Information Systems Security Organization, explaining that CYBER COMMAND's General Alexander "basically has to defend U.S. cyberspace which requires securing commercial websites and infrastructures, but no one wants him to have access to those networks, since he's also in charge of NSA."

Another problem is that the private sector industries and utilities that run the civilian critical infrastructures do not want to spend money on security. "I'm not sure you understand how the corporate world works, they are de facto capable of protecting themselves but won't, that costs money," opines an anonymous industry insider in an online article "Cybersecurity: Can U.S. Civilian Agencies Protect American Citizens in Cyberspace?"

(toinformistoinfluence.com August 7, 2011), "It is a calculation that they won't lose money by not investing in proper cybersecurity. It will usually take a very large boot to the teeth and continuing down the throat before they get energized."

Calls for State Leadership

Thomas Popik and William Harris, leaders of the watchdog Foundation for Resilient Societies, the nation's foremost independent authority on the federal regulatory process for electric grid security--warn that Washington and industry have both failed, and grid security should be managed by the States. Highlights from their important article "Weak Security For America's Electric Grid Makes Us Vulnerable" (*Investor's Business Daily* September 26, 2014) follow:

--"Overseas military action is not enough to protect the public. We also need effective defensive measures for our critical infrastructures, starting with the grid upon which modern life depends.. Unfortunately, electric grid security is weak, and the regulatory process is broken."

--"The federal process to regulate electric grid security is badly broken. Responsibility for setting grid security standards has been delegated to an industry self-regulatory organization, the North American Electric Reliability Corporation (NERC)."

--"The vulnerability of America's electric grid is well known. In March 2014, a leaked staff analysis from the Federal Energy Regulatory Commission (FERC) revealed that an attack on only nine critical transformer substations could bring down our continental grid for 18 months....an attack on just four substations could black out the grid from the Rocky Mountains to the East Coast. An attack on just three could black out California and 10 other Western states."

--"**In May, 2013, only three weeks after the Metcalf attack, a key NERC committee voted to cancel its project for a physical security standard. Hamstrung by inadequate legislative authority and influenced by industry lobbying, federal regulator FERC waited a year after Metcalf before reinitiating a standard for grid security.**" [Boldface-Pry]

--"Protecting key grid facilities would greatly reduce the threat from terrorists and be cost effective. According to former FERC chairman Jon Wellinghoff, about 100 critical, high-voltage substations need protection from physical attack. Just 16 regional control centers supervise daily grid operations and manage power restoration. There are 50 large-generation plants with capacity of two gigawatts or more."

--"**All of these facilities need mandatory physical protection, but the pending physical security standard [proposed by NERC--Pry] exempts all generation plants and three major control centers supervising power for 100 million Americans.**" [Boldface--Pry]

The bottom line from experts Popik and Harris and their Foundation is that the States should take over management of electric grid security: "State governments retain authority to assure the safety and reliability of their grids."

Ambassador Henry Cooper, former Director of the Strategic Defense Initiative and one of our nation's foremost defense scientists, concurs with Popik and Harris and endorses their recommendation that grid security be managed by the States. Ambassador Cooper in his online article "Wake UP: ISIS Is Here!" (Message 141001 October 1, 2014) writes "...the Washington establishment--both the Executive and Legislative Branches--is not dealing effectively with the vulnerability of the grid, the loss of which would be catastrophic."

Highlights from Ambassador Cooper's article include these recommendations for State leadership on electric grid security:

--"State governments retain authority to assure the safety and reliability of their grids. Some States have already begun to act without waiting for the federal government."
--"To deter those who might attack our grid, police and National Guard troops should conduct rapid-deployment drills. At times of severe threat, government authorities must protect critical grid facilities; experience has already shown that private security is not enough."

In this article, and in every one of his newsletters, Ambassador Cooper praises "the excellent work of Maine and Virginia" for passing legislation to protect their electric grids from EMP. "The time to protect our electric grid is now, not after the first successful attack is executed," warns the former SDI Director and chief nuclear arms negotiator, "While America dawdles, foreign adversaries study our grid and make war plans."

Washington may be so broken that progress is currently impossible through the Congress, the White House, or the departments and agencies of jurisdiction--unless the States and the people bring pressure to bear.

Maine Leads The Way

Bypassing Washington, in February 2013, the Task Force on National and Homeland Security made common cause with Maine State Representative Andrea Boland (D) to educate the Maine State Legislature on the EMP threat and its solutions. After five months, February-June 2013, of meetings with and briefings to the Maine Joint Energy Committee, the Maine Public Utilities Commission, the Maine House and Senate, and the Governor's Office, in June 2013 they passed into law LD-131--a binding Resolution to protect the Maine electric grid from EMP.

Maine may be the first State in the union to achieve protection of its electric grid. Maine achieved in five months what Washington has not been able to accomplish in five years, and appears to have finally found a path toward national EMP preparedness--through the States.

If the States could be persuaded to protect their grids, then national EMP preparedness could be achieved eventually. Hopefully, State initiatives for EMP protection might bring added pressure to bear on Washington, break the logjam in Congress over the SHIELD Act, move the U.S. government to act, and thus by "attacking the bridge from both ends"--from the Federal and State levels--achieve EMP protection of the grid on an accelerated basis.

Islanding A State Grid

Technically, although most States are part of a larger regional electric grid, it is possible to "island" a State grid by hardening its key assets so that the electric generating and distribution systems within the protected State would survive an EMP event.

For example, Extra-High Voltage (EHV) transformers and big generators can be protected from EMP by installing blocking devices, surge arrestors, faraday cages, and other proven technologies. There are many ways to harden the grid. For example, the book *Apocalypse Unknown* describes three different plans for protecting electric grids, so States enjoy flexibility in technological alternatives to meet their varied grid security needs and budgets.

Controversy still rages over whether higher priority should be given to protecting the grid from severe weather, geomagnetic storms, sabotage, cyber attacks, or nuclear EMP. The controversy should have been settled by the blue ribbon Congressional EMP Commission. The EMP Commission--that dedicated more time and resources and had greater scientific and technical expertise focused on the problem than any other study--recommends protecting against nuclear EMP attack, as this is the worst threat and will mitigate all lesser hazards, including cyber threats, kinetic attacks, severe weather, and geomagnetic storms.

The EMP Commission recommends "islanding" the national electric grid into smaller subsystems, such as State grids, protected with surge arrestors, blocking devices, and other proven technologies, which would secure the grid not just against EMP but against all hazards: **"Breaking the larger electrical system into subsystem islands...will enhance what now exists to minimize the impact, decrease the likelihood of broad system-wide collapse, and provide for more rapid and widespread recovery. It is just as useful for normal reliability against random disturbances or natural disasters in reducing size and time for blackouts. Thus, it is critical for protection and restoration coming from any type of attack, not just EMP."**

"Islanding" a State electric grid, as recommended by the EMP Commission, will not change the normal operations of the grid, will not isolate the grid from importing electricity from other States, and will not interfere with exporting electricity to other States. Hardware for grid hardening is a passive defense that only activates when the grid is under attack.

A State grid that can survive EMP and other threats will also benefit neighboring States by enabling their more rapid recovery. There may be no recovery if everyone is in blackout.

Cost

The Congressional EMP Commission estimated that protecting the national electric grid to survive a nuclear EMP attack, and all lesser threats, would cost about $2 billion dollars. The U.S. FERC calculates that paying for grid protection against an EMP catastrophe can be accomplished painlessly by increasing the electric bill of the average ratepayer by merely 20 cents annually.

For the 50 States, their share of $2 billion dollars to protect their grids for each State is $40 million dollars on average.

However, this average cost is generally inaccurate. The primary driver of cost for grid protection is the number of EHV transformers in a State. The more EHV transformers that need to be protected, the higher the cost. There are many more EHV transformers concentrated in a few big States, like Pennsylvania, New York, California and Texas, while most States have far fewer EHV transformers.

Maine, for example, instead of spending $40 million to protect its grid, will really have to spend about $6-12 million, depending on the level of security desired.

According to EMPrimus, a contractor who does electric grid protection against EMP, "the total protective cost per transformer will be in the range of $85,000 to $130,000 installed" (see *Apocalypse Unknown* p. 296). So a State can roughly calculate the *upper cost* of protecting its grid from EMP and lesser threats by multiplying the number of EHV transformers in the State grid by $130,000.

The actual cost is likely to be less, perhaps much less, than $130,000 per transformer. EMPrimus offers less costly options. And there are other technologies and plans far less costly, including one that is $10,000 per transformer. See *Apocalypse Unknown* Part II "Affordable Plans To Protect The Grid" for a detailed analysis of several example plans and their costs for protecting electric grids against EMP.

Appended to this chapter is a memo "Quick Fix EMP Protection" that describes inexpensive steps that could be undertaken immediately by any State. These quick fixes are no substitute for EMP hardening EHV transformers with blocking devices and surge arrestors and hardening other critical nodes, but they would significantly improve grid resilience against EMP and other threats at very little cost and in the near term.

Political Strategies for Grid Protection

The primary purpose of this book is to serve as a guide for State legislators and citizens on how to advance public policy initiatives for protecting electric grids and advancing EMP preparedness in their States.

Valuable lessons have been learned so far from experience in several States that there is more than one public policy pathway to protect the grid and advance EMP preparedness in the States:

The State Legislature: The most obvious path is to copy the Congress and introduce a bill to protect the electric grid in the Energy Committee of the State Legislature, just as Congress has introduced a bill, the SHIELD Act, in the House Energy and Commerce Committee. Maine State Rep. Andrea Boland (D) pioneered this strategy in 2013. Whereas the SHIELD Act has been stalled in Congress for five years, Rep. Boland's bill passed the Maine State Legislature in five months, garnering unanimous votes in the Joint Energy Committee and State House, and near unanimity in the State Senate (just 3 dissenting votes).

The Governor: EMP preparedness in a State may be by Executive Order from the Governor. Governors in every state have broad emergency powers to provide for public safety and homeland security. Research accomplished so far indicates a majority of Governors, and probably all Governors, have the power to order electric and other utilities within their State to protect their assets from an EMP catastrophe. Florida State Rep. Michelle Rehwinkel Vasilinda (D) is pioneering this strategy, with a petition to Florida Governor Scott to invoke his executive powers to protect the Florida grid.

The State Emergency Management Agencies: Another pathway is to enlist the State emergency management agency or agencies by educating them on the EMP threat so that they can then begin preparing to survive and recover the State in their emergency planning, training, and resource allocation. In Pennsylvania, Professor Cindy Ayers of the U.S. Army War College, and in Utah, Mr. Michael Suflita, an emergency management official with the State Water Authority, are pioneering this strategy.

Additionally or alternatively, the State Legislature could amend the charter of the State Emergency Management Agency to require the Agency to protect and recover the State from an EMP catastrophe. In Arizona, Senator David Farnsworth and in Florida, Rep. Rehwinkel Vasilinda pioneered this strategy with bills requiring EMP preparedness in Arizona and in the charter of the Florida Division of Emergency Management.

Popular Referendum: State legislatures can go to the people directly for a vote on whether or not they want their grid protected by including the issue on the ballot for a popular referendum. This strategy entails the opportunity, and the necessity, of educating the general public on the EMP threat and solutions. In Oklahoma, State Senator Ralph Shortey and Mr. Michael Hoehn pioneered this strategy. Their proposed popular referendum would have asked voters if they are willing to fund, by a small increase in their electric rates for example, protection of the State electric grid from an EMP catastrophe.

Presidential Policy Directive 8

Finally, the White House itself wants the States to protect themselves and their people from catastrophic "acts of terrorism, cyber attacks, pandemics, and catastrophic natural disasters."

President Barak Obama, one of the most ardent champions of Federal power and prerogatives to ever occupy the White House, on March 30, 2011, signed PPD-8 "National Preparedness" that in its first paragraph declares: "This directive is aimed at strengthening the security and resilience of the United States through systematic preparation for the threats that pose the greatest risk for the security of the Nation, including acts of terrorism, cyber attacks, pandemics, and catastrophic natural disasters. Our national preparedness is the shared responsibility *of all levels of government*, the private and non-profit sectors, and individual citizens." [Italics--Pry]

Chapters that follow provide examples and case studies of actual State initiatives to achieve preparedness against an EMP catastrophe in Maine, Virginia, Arizona, Florida, and Oklahoma that may be emulated, or improved upon, by other States.

Chapter IX provides a generic bill that could be introduced by any State Senator or State Representative, and a generic Executive Order that could be issued by any Governor, to advance EMP preparedness.

Quick Fix Low Cost EMP Protection

The memo that follows was drafted for Maine State Representative Andrea Boland at the request of the Maine State Legislature's Joint Committee on Energy, Utilities and Technology that queried whether there was anything Maine could do to protect the State electric grid immediately.

The recommendations in the memo, as acknowledged in the memo, are no substitute for a good plan that would give highest priority to EMP hardening EHV transformers and other critical nodes, a plan "designed for implementation in affordable stages, so that the most important EMP protection can be purchased early-on." However, the recommendations in the memo would significantly increase grid resilience against EMP and other threats at no cost or very little cost, and quickly.

The recommendations could be implemented by any State.

MEMO

TO: Rep. Andrea Boland, Maine State Legislature

FROM: Dr. Peter Vincent Pry, Executive Director, Task Force on National and Homeland Security

SUBJECT: "Quick Fix" EMP Protection for the Maine Electric Grid

---

Highest priority for protecting the Maine electric grid from natural and manmade electromagnetic pulse should be development of a plan for the most robust, cost-effective protection of the grid, especially the high-value hard to replace grid components, particularly Extra-High Voltage (EHV) transformers and generators. There is no substitute for a good plan, which will optimize protection, keep costs to a minimum, and should be designed for implementation in affordable stages, so that the most important EMP protection can be purchased early-on.

However, there are near-term, low-cost "quick fixes" that can very significantly increase the security of the Maine electric grid, or of any electric grid, and that are of such obvious benefit that they could be implemented immediately, without waiting for development of a master plan. For example:

Metal Sheds for SCADAS. Supervisory Control And Data Acquisition Systems (SCADAS) are small computers or modems of which there are many thousands in an electric grid and are indispensable to its operation. Protection of SCADAS is just as important as protection of EHV transformers and generators--as EMP-induced malfunction of SCADAS can damage or destroy EHV transformers and generators. Indeed, some analysts believe that damage to EHV transformers and other critical grid components is more likely to be caused by EMP-induced SCADAS malfunction than by the direct effects of EMP itself. Typically, SCADAS at a facility are collected together and housed in a single shed for ease of maintenance. So EMP protection of SCADAS can be achieved relatively easily and inexpensively by housing them in a metal shed with no window and a metal door. Almost any metal shed, with some simple modifications, can be designed to serve as a faraday cage to provide EMP protection for SCADAS. With new grid construction, as is happening in Maine, the additional cost of this method for providing EMP protection for SCADAS should be little or nothing--since the new SCADAS have to be housed in some kind of structure anyway. Nor would it be very costly to retrofit existing SCADAS sheds to convert them into faraday cages. If the existing sheds are made of wood or other material transparent to EMP, they could be lined with metalized insulation or wire mesh, and windows covered with metal shutters or wire mesh, to convert existing structures into a functional faraday cage, at low cost.

Metal Sheds and More Fuel for Emergency Generators. Critical nodes in the electric grid will be equipped with an emergency generator to maintain power through a temporary blackout--but not for the protracted blackout likely to be caused by an EMP. The capability to sustain emergency power to these critical nodes for as long as possible increases grid resiliency by preventing the whole system from crashing into blackout, and making it easier to resurrect the grid. As discussed above for providing EMP protection to SCADAS, emergency generators too could be protected by housing them in metal sheds. Moreover, the utility of emergency generators in an EMP scenario could be greatly increased by increasing their fuel supply to cope with a protracted blackout. Unfortunately, over the years, fire codes have tended to discourage the storage of large quantities of flammable fuels on-site, steadily reducing the on-site fuel supplies for emergency electric generation from about two weeks in the 1960s to about 72 hours today. This is also true for emergency electricity generation at hospitals, police, fire and emergency services. Increasing the on-site fuel supply for electric grid emergency generators--and for emergency generators at hospitals, police, fire and emergency services--would increase their utility and overall system resilience during an EMP event. In many cases, the fuel storage tanks for accommodating a two-week fuel supply for emergency generators is still there, just no longer used. Simply parking a truck-hauled tanker full of fuel on-site would dramatically increase the fuel supply for emergency generation from 72 hours to weeks or months.

Set Emergency Generators On "Manual" Start. Natural and nuclear EMP can damage or destroy emergency generators by traveling down power lines, through the wiring of a building, and into its emergency generator. Damage is more likely to happen if the emergency generator is set for "automatic" start, in which mode the generator is always connected to the building it services and starts itself automatically as soon as a blackout is detected, so that there is no interruption in electrical power. Most people and institutions prefer automatic start because of its convenience. However, because the emergency generator is always connected to the building electrical system when in automatic start mode, it is more vulnerable to EMP. Most emergency generators also have a "manual" start mode, which requires a person to start the generator by pressing a button which simultaneously connects the generator to the building electrical system. Simply by setting emergency generators on manual start, it makes them less vulnerable to EMP. However, this is not a perfect solution, because the gap between the poles on the generator manual control switch may be small enough for an EMP to flashover, and so damage the generator. The ideal solution would be to install between the emergency generator and the building electrical system a robust lever switch, with a gap between the poles of several inches. By this means, the generator would be disconnected from the building electrical system until needed, protected by a robust switch not susceptible to EMP flashover, and can be brought into service when needed manually by closing the lever switch and pressing the manual start button. The cost of setting emergency generators on manual start is nothing. The material cost of installing a lever switch is about $50.

Metal Garages for Utility Vehicles and Vehicle Hardening. Utility vehicles are necessary for maintaining and repairing the electric grid and will be in high demand after an EMP. Natural EMP does not directly threaten vehicles because the wavelength is too long, but manmade nuclear and non-nuclear EMP can damage and destroy vehicles. These can be protected, as with SCADAS and emergency generators above, by garaging vehicles in a structure designed or modified to serve as a faraday cage. Also or alternatively, EMP effects against vehicles can be mitigated by hardening the vehicles themselves. The wavelengths of nuclear EMP and non-nuclear radiofrequency weapons are not sufficiently short to couple directly into microchips and small electronic components that are the chief vulnerability of modern vehicles. The EMP couples into the wires and finds these vulnerable components by following the wires. So the vehicle can be EMP hardened by insulating the wires against EMP. This can be accomplished by covering the vehicle wiring--especially the longest wires--with ferrite tubes. Ferrite tubes are insulators resistant to electromagnetic transients, like EMP, and can be purchased at Radio Shack or any electronics store. The material cost for EMP hardening a typical car with ferrite tubes should be less than $100.

Food and Water for Workforce and Families. In the aftermath of a natural or nuclear EMP, the electric utility workforce will be needed around the clock for a protracted period to effect repairs and restore full electric power as soon as possible. Utilities should have on hand, stored at their facilities, sufficient supplies of food and water to sustain their workforce through a protracted crisis that could last weeks or months. Utility emergency planning for an EMP event should not assume that workers will be able to find food and water in the field, available from restaurants and grocery stores. Moreover, utilities should provide, or educate their workforce to provide, workers' families with an adequate supply of food and water to survive a protracted EMP event. The Congressional EMP Commission found that during severe natural disasters, as in the aftermaths of hurricanes Katrina and Andrew, these crises were made significantly worse because many utility crews and other emergency workers--including police and fire--did not report for duty, out of concern for the safety of their families.

Educate the Workforce and Learn From Them. The Congressional EMP Commission recommended educating the workforce of the electric utilities and other critical infrastructures about the EMP threat as an important part of the solution. Lack of situation awareness about the EMP threat could very well lead workers to make mistakes in responding to an EMP event that will make the catastrophe worse. This is especially so since the electric power industry tends to prefer operational procedures to deal with emergencies, yet such procedures are dependent upon electronic information systems and controls that are vulnerable to EMP. Educating the workforce about EMP immediately empowers them to become part of the solution. For example, awareness of SCADAS vulnerability could conceivably enable workers to save EHV transformers and generators from damage induced by malfunctioning SCADAS. Nor should we underestimate the capacity of an educated workforce to help us find the best solutions to EMP preparedness. Just as all solutions do not come from Washington, the best ideas do not always come from scientists. Technicians and workers who labor every day in the electric grid may well provide some of the best ideas about how to cope with EMP--once they are educated about the threat. Education of their workforce could be easily accomplished by the electric utilities at low or no cost by requiring workers as a routine part of their training to watch the National Geographic DVD "Electronic Armageddon" (available for free from EMPact America) and by making available technical materials on the characteristics of EMP and basic protection systems, available for free on the internet.

A Design For Survival. Crucial to the survival of the people of Maine is simply an accounting of those vital services necessary to the sustenance and safety of the people, the physical location of these services, and their electric power requirements. For example, where are the water purification plants, the main pumps servicing the major population areas, and how much electricity is required to supply cities with pure running water? Where are the regional food warehouses that supply grocery stores, and how much electricity do they need to preserve and distribute the food supply? Where are the most important hospitals, that service the most people, and what are their electricity needs? Where are the most important police, fire and emergency services, and what are their electricity needs? From the answers to these basic questions will emerge a design for survival for the State of Maine. This accounting should cost nothing, and could begin immediately, as there must be several existing departments and agencies in the government of Maine for public safety and homeland security that could be assigned this project. Collection of this data will raise situation awareness for public officials and the electric utilities, and will inform and accelerate the development of a master plan to protect the Maine electric grid.

Diesel Electric Locomotives. General Electric, the chief manufacturer of diesel electric locomotives, reports that some 8,000 of these have been retired from service, are warehoused, and available for purchase or loan. Diesel electric locomotives can be used as mobile generators capable of producing up to 1 Megawatt, enough to power a small town. Diesels are used in Canada precisely for this purpose. Such locomotives have been exported to Iraq to serve as generators in the aftermath of the Iraq War, that destroyed the national electric grid. Maine might consider purchasing or taking on loan diesel electric locomotives as a "quick fix" to any shortfalls in emergency generating power needed at facilities crucial to survival and public safety--such as water purification and pumping plants, regional food warehouses, hospitals, police, fire and emergency services. If the electric power industry proves reluctant or slow to protect the Maine grid from EMP, the government of Maine might consider purchasing diesel electric locomotives as a partial "quick fix" toward grid security--and bill ISO New England for the cost to incentivize them to do their duty for public safety.

Economic Opportunities For Maine. EMP preparedness is entirely about survival and public safety. But there will be potentially significant economic opportunities generated by EMP preparedness. From the perspective of major corporations, international businesses and manufacturers, it will be no small thing that the Maine electric grid is the most secure from EMP, Cyber, and other threats in the entire Free World. Likewise, the various departments and agencies of the U.S. Government--and especially the Department of Defense, that is currently spending $30 million annually on electric power security experiments alone--will find Maine a most attractive location for offices and facilities that need secure electricity. The Maine contractor who builds metal sheds configured as faraday cages to protect SCADAS and other grid components will have a skill and experience almost unique in the world, and be much in demand nationally and internationally. The Maine contractor who hardens electric utility vehicles against EMP will have a skill and experience almost unique in the world, and be much in demand nationally and internationally. What survivalist, what prudent person, would not want their family car EMP protected for a couple hundred bucks? EMP protection also protects against the worst consequences of a Cyber attack. EMP and Cyber are the defense industries of the future. EMP preparedness is a ticket for Maine to get in on the ground floor and benefit from the financial rewards that will flow from this new industry. The financial opportunity for Maine is enormous.

IV

MAINE

State Representative Andrea Boland

Summary

Representative Andrea Boland succeeded in passing LD-131 in 2013, making Maine the first State in the Union en route to hardening its electric power grid against EMP. LD-131 requires the Maine Public Utilities Commission (PUC) to protect the Maine grid from EMP, beginning with a study examining the feasibility and cost of various options. The original version of LD-131 is appended to this chapter, followed by the more comprehensive and more aggressive version of LD-131 designed by the Joint Standing Committee on Energy, Utilities and Technology that passed on an emergency basis.

Also appended to this chapter is a rebuttal to the "final draft" of the Public Utilities Commission report on LD-131. The PUC final draft report essentially followed the advice of the utilities and the North American Electric Reliability Corporation recommending that Maine do nothing, but wait for Washington to protect the grid. Rep. Boland credits the appended rebuttal with reversing the PUC's position in its final report and testimony delivered to the energy committee. The PUC Chairman, Thomas Welch, recommended investigating technical options for protecting the Maine electric grid from EMP.

Representative Boland's Narrative

I first learned about electromagnetic pulse (EMP) in 2011 when conferring with my science advisor, Hawkins Kirk. At the time, I was asking him about electromagnetic fields (EMF) of high-voltage power lines, and safety concerns they posed for people living very near them. I introduced the first legislation in the nation to ask for health and safety warning labels on cell phones, because of their electromagnetic radiation emissions. Kirk noticed my interest in EMF, and introduced himself to me to offer help.

I became more and more involved in issues around electromagnetic fields, partly because others identified me as a resource. I learned I could rely on Kirk for guidance. His scientific knowledge was extraordinary. After he answered my power line question, he added that there was something more serious to look at about power lines. They could all be taken out by a bad solar storm or a nuclear weapon detonated high above the Earth interacting with the Earth's electromagnetic fields.

What?

Kirk then introduced me to the incredible phenomenon of EMP and the appalling magnitude of its existential threat to our civilization. I was stunned by the enormity of the problem.

How could this situation have been allowed to develop? Under what crazy policy-making scheme was it being allowed to continue to exist? Whether by an extreme solar storm, known as a GMD (for geomagnetic disturbance) or natural EMP, or an intentional man-made electromagnetic pulse (EMP), often together referred to as just EMP, a single event could cause a nationwide blackout from which it could take years to recover, if, in fact, we could at all. We would lose 65- 90 percent of our population within the first year due to starvation, exposure, and societal collapse. Maine is one of the most vulnerable states to solar storms, due to its high northerly latitude, geology, and proximity to the ocean.

The EMP threat seemed overwhelming.

At first, I thought Kirk was kidding when he said I should take it on. I had taken on a lot of tough issues that challenged big interests, and did not think I really wanted to take on this breathtaking assignment. After all, it was truly a national issue, and I was a State Representative. It even sounded a little ridiculous to imagine that I could do something about EMP as an individual State Representative. Kirk knew me well enough to ask the right question: "Why wouldn't you want to protect Maine?"

My answer: "Of course, I had to try."

I had learned to trust Kirk's counsel. He recommended that I start by contacting Dr. Peter Vincent Pry, a national leader working on protecting America from the EMP threat. Dr. Pry served in the CIA, the House Armed Services Committee, and the Congressional EMP Commission.

I gave him a call.

It seemed like a stretch to expect to get Pry on the phone very easily, but Peter picked up on the first try. Great! He's real. He was impressive, dynamic, compelling and welcoming.

Peter introduced me to his colleague, Dr. Cynthia Ayers, formerly with the National Security Agency for many years, and now an adjunct professor at the U.S. Army War College, and Peter's deputy on the Task Force for National and Homeland Security. Kirk had spoken of her, also. She was also impressive and engaging, and quietly disarming.

Peter encouraged me to become part of their crusade for national EMP preparedness. I felt as though I already had. He invited me to be a guest on his EMP radio show, and allowed me to bring Kirk on, too. Kirk's remarks are usually brief and often startling. Together with Peter and the military man that was also participating, we put on what sounded to me like a show pretty full of intriguing observations. It was fun to be among them. Sobering, too. My role was to bring the legislator's perspective.

It was remarkable to me that Peter was so enthusiastic about hearing from me, a state legislator in Maine only proposing to protect one state, when his scope was national. What he saw in me, though, was a person who could meet a practical need – I could introduce legislation that would allow for expert testimony to take place at a hearing before a legislative body with the power to make law. He could imagine that Maine might just be the place where a breakout of EMP legislation might occur. If other states then followed, perhaps Congress would also finally be moved to act, and drive protection from the national level.

That vision would power the team of national experts who came to Maine, magnificently supported my legislation, and ultimately brought in a great victory for Maine, and hope for the country.

Peter, a history scholar, further educated me, bringing to bear his CIA and congressional experience, to add policy foundation context. He had been committed to this mission for many years. He referred me to Congressman Roscoe Bartlett, the Member of Congress who was then the top leader of the national EMP movement.

Bartlett's office connected me with several other national experts who were deeply concerned about the EMP threat, notably Richard Andres of the National Defense University, Joseph McClelland of the U.S. Federal Energy Regulatory Commission (FERC), John Kappenman of Storm Analysis Consultants, and Avi Schnurr and Chris Beck of the Electric Infrastructure Security Council (EISC).

All greeted me cordially, with interest and generous offerings of time, research, and insights.

I felt I was being pulled into an elite corps of very high level performers on the national stage. Each, in his or her own way reinforced Peter's initial message that the EMP threat was the greatest threat to our electronic civilization and must urgently be addressed. The inevitable geomagnetic solar storm would take out our electricity, and a hostile and crazy enemy's EMP weapon could do the same, and burn out all our electronics, as well.

Every conversation increased my confidence in following this strange and compelling path, lighted as it was by luminiferous guides. But it was clearly going to be work. I needed to educate myself more, and pay close attention to my guides.

The SHIELD Act

Peter recommended, as an immediate first step, that I help him try to pass the SHIELD Act through Congress.

The SHIELD Act, a bipartisan bill co-sponsored by Congressman Trent Franks (R-AZ) and Congresswoman Yvette Clark (D-NY), would empower the U.S. Federal Energy Regulatory Commission (FERC) to require the electric utilities to protect the national electric grid from a natural or nuclear EMP catastrophe. The legislation had gotten stalled in committee.

To help Peter, I set up a meeting in Washington, D.C. for Maine's two U.S. Senators: Senator Susan Collins, Ranking Member of the House Homeland Security Committee, and Senator Olympia Snow – and Maine Congressman Mike Michaud. I briefed Congresswoman Chellie Pingree separately.

Their legislative staffs and professional staff from the Senate Homeland Security Committee met with Peter, Chris Beck, and me, while Kirk joined us by phone. Chris, President of the Electric Infrastructure Security Council, and a physicist, was formerly the Science Advisor to Congressman Bennie Thompson (D-MS), Chairman of the House Homeland Security Committee. EISC is an international organization trying to save the planet from EMP. Kirk is an astrophysicist and national weapons consultant.

We all made our introductions and Peter took the lead on the briefing. The small conference room was packed. I could recognize in some the familiar feeling I experienced when hearing this stunning new information for the first time. All were very attentive to what Peter, Chris and I had to say, but a number of our politely restrained questions seeking signs of buy-in received only vague and unsatisfying answers.

In frustration, Kirk vigorously interjected over the conference phone and ended up telling the staffers from the Senate Homeland Security Committee that their boss, Senator Bingaman, was not doing his job, and that it was unforgiveable that he had failed to pass the GRID Act, the previous year's version of the SHIELD Act. Kirk's plain speaking provoked the staffer chairing our meeting to anger, and a tense exchange ensued, while everyone else held their silence. The moment of suspended animation was interesting; it seemed to give everyone in the room a chance to contemplate what truth had been uttered. We moved on.

On the whole, the meeting was cordial, and seemed positive and promising. I remember stopping downstairs afterwards with Peter and Chris, and asking them, "OK, What do I do now?" In the pause that followed, it occurred to me that my question was maybe a bit concerning to them. The question might have been partly rhetorical because I knew what I had to do--just follow up, keep in touch, and move forward with my work in Maine.

I kept after my congressional delegation a bit, but principally my focus shifted necessarily to what I could do in my own state legislature. The federal delegation had expressed interest and taken it all seriously, so I felt we had positioned them well to understand the issue. I could push them a little harder later, if things in Washington started moving--they never did.

The First State EMP Bill

Back in Maine, in the fall of 2011, I proposed introducing legislation for the upcoming short session of the Maine State Legislature. It was a long shot, but I felt it was important to try to introduce legislation to protect the Maine electric grid from EMP as soon as possible.

In order to get any legislation to move forward in a short session, however, the concept of the bill needed to be approved as an emergency measure by the Legislative Council, a body composed of leaders of both parties of the Senate and House. If they approved, I could proceed with drafting a bill and introducing it.

There was not a lot of time to educate my colleagues, who had never heard of EMP, so I filled their emails with information, stopped them in the halls, and left messages on their phones. Peter Pry orchestrated phone calls, e-mails, and letters from national experts, including from Congressman Roscoe Bartlett. I sent them the link to the excellent National Geographic documentary film, "Electronic Armageddon," which is based on Peter's book, *Electric Armageddon*. I also kept up outreach to all the other legislators, so they would be prepared for the bill, if it was allowed in. It had to be seen as an emergency measure.

Sometimes I started to cry as I drove the long way from my home in Sanford to the Capitol in Augusta.

Admiring the peaceful landscape and thinking of all the unknowing, good Maine people whose world could go away as a result of the untended threat that loomed over them, and all the work it would take to change that, crushed my spirit and outraged me. That those we entrusted with such a critical asset to the sustainability of life were so willing to allow it to be imperiled to the point of utter collapse and national, cataclysmic disaster was beyond negligence and incompetence. It was criminal. It was such a bleak, unexpected, yet not uncommon story of the disinterest, denial, greed, inertia, and ethical and moral depravity so much at work in the halls of state houses, complicating governance "of, by and for the people."

The Council, had, as usual, a lot of bills before them, and little time to select the few that would be allowed to proceed.

Admittedly, our bill was startling and big. Not surprisingly, it failed to gain the Council's vote.

Only Assistant Democratic House Leader Terry Hayes grasped the import of the bill, and voted in support of it. The bill was not going forward in 2012. But Peter and I had exploited the opportunity well to provide a strong foundation for building our case for legislation in the following (long) session, 2013, when no vote of the Legislative Council would be required to submit it and have it heard. Meanwhile, I had more to do to prepare myself.

The London and Washington EMP Summits

In the spring of 2012, I was invited to London by members of Congress and members of Parliament as a U.S. delegate to the Electric Infrastructure Security Council's annual international summit, organized by Avi Schnurr and Chris Beck. That invitation struck me with the apparent confidence and hope they had in me to help accomplish something meaningful. By participating in this meeting as a U. S. delegate, I hoped to further the work of informing myself.

The Summit met in the House of Commons, Westminster Palace, in Parliament. We met amidst the impressive trappings of a grand history. To look out on the Thames through the soaring, leaded windows of the meeting rooms, in the company of distinguished statesmen from over 20 countries, assembled there to work on the survival of the planet, was, by turns, humbling, thrilling and sobering.

Avi Schnurr, a scientist and missile defense expert, Chairman of the EIS Council, told us to look around the room, and consider that we gathered there comprised most of the people in the world that were working on preventing EMP disaster.

There were 80 of us.

I met my hosts, the Right Honorable Lord Arbuthnot, Chairman of the Defense Committee of the House of Commons and Congressman Trent Franks, Chairman of the U.S. Congressional EMP Caucus and author of the SHIELD Act. General Shlomo Wald, from Israel, very memorably told us to, "Face it. We are an endangered species."

Lord Arbuthnot advised us that the United Kingdom had made the EMP threat a top defense priority. Not so the United States. You die a little bit inside when you hear something like that.

Avi Schnurr reminded us that our work, if successful, would be a monumental accomplishment – but, also, very likely turn out to be, "the greatest story never told." We could not expect to get credit for it. The EMP threat remained largely unknown. What was done to neutralize it would probably also be largely left unknown.

If we fail to succeed, the result will be terrible.

I met Tom Popik there for the first time, but, unbelievably, did not remember it afterwards. He would end up becoming the rock upon which I could lean for intellectual support, research and analysis of technical data, and distinguished presentations in the grueling hours of preparation and committee sessions to come.

Peter Pry spoke at the summit. His knowledge, vision and eloquence always strikes to the heart, fires up the crowd and makes everyone determined to do something.

Britain's Home Secretary, responsible for the homeland security of the United Kingdom, made newspaper headlines at the Summit by warning about the grave threat posed by EMP. The headlines came and went without follow-up from the press: a negligence that has burdened progress on this effort both here and abroad.

In December of 2012, I was invited to the DuPont Summit in Washington, D.C, sponsored by the Carnegie Foundation and put on by Chuck Manto's Infragard/EMP Special Interest Educational Group affiliated with the FBI. Dr. Peter Vincent Pry was the opening speaker. Others followed.

Thomas Popik spoke. He was the founder and President of the Foundation for Resilient Societies, a small non-profit dedicated to EMP research and education, and other critical infrastructure issues. He was succinct, clear, and intriguing, and, very exciting to me at the time, was located in the neighboring state of New Hampshire. He brought with him William Harris, the organization's Secretary, a brilliant lawyer of Rand Corporation and White House background, who understood the intricacies of the legal and regulatory environment within which we had to operate. This time he drew my attention, and I reached out to him. It was the beginning of a wonderful, productive partnership.

John Kappenman, premier U.S. space weather analyst, James Woolsey, former CIA Director, and Cynthia Ayers, cybersecurity expert were there, too, and would also be champions for Maine. I met Yuki Karakawa, of Japan, and Chuck Manto, of course, who spoke urgently of the need for preparedness. Yuki compared our status on EMP to that of Japan's unpreparedness for the nuclear meltdown at Fukushima that resulted from the loss of electric power to cool it.

The net effect of these summits was to buoy me for the fight to come and cement my resolve to make protecting Maine from EMP catastrophe my highest priority for the 2013 session of the Maine State Legislature.

LD-131: EMP Breakthrough

On February 19, 2013, I introduced LD-131, to the Joint Standing Committee on Energy, Utilities, and Technology (EUT) of the Maine legislature. It was the first EMP bill ever presented to a state legislature.

Representative Barry Hobbins, House Chair of the Committee, and a member of the former session's Legislative Council, chaired the hearing on the bill. The team of experts that Peter Pry assembled were all there. So was Kirk. It was a great honor to have them there with me, and to present the bill.

The team Peter had mobilized was an impressive array of experts from diverse backgrounds, who heard his call, caught his vision, and volunteered to follow him to Maine, at their own expense, to brief the over-burdened Energy, Utilities and Technology Committee on what was knowingly anticipated to be for them a very challenging issue.

The night before the public hearing, our small group met at The Senator Inn, a local hotel, to plan our strategy. A small contingent of interested legislators joined us.

Among the briefers were: Bronius Cikotas, one of our nation's top EMP scientists, known as "the Father of GWEN" for designing the Ground Wave Emergency Network to protect military and strategic forces communications from an EMP attack; Professor Cynthia Ayers, a veteran of the National Security Agency who teaches counter-terrorism and cyber-security at the U.S. Army War College, and Peter's deputy on the Task Force for National and Homeland Security; Mike Maloof, a counter-terrorism expert and former Department of Defense official who had just published a book warning about the EMP threat. Also joining us was Kirk, astrophysicist, academician, weaponeer, consultant to elite scientific research organizations, and my loyal science advisor..

I invited my daughter, Michaela, to serve as "companion pony" to me in my new racehorse status, to help steady me among them and have the opportunity to observe what made them national champions.

Tom Popik, apparently as minimally interested in me as I had been in him in London, had to be persuaded by Peter that coming to Maine was more important than going to Atlanta,

Georgia, to battle the North American Reliability Corporation (NERC). NERC was then in the process of producing a "junk science" report to justify their doing nothing to protect the national grid from extreme solar storms (GMD), or natural EMP.

Peter thought that Maine offered better prospects for Tom's attention. Tom was not totally on board yet, but he was listening. Peter and Tom had been closely tracking NERC for some time, trying to induce them to set robust reliability standards against EMP, so this would be a complete change of focus.

NERC is responsible for the United States being ill-prepared to endure a GMD or EMP. They are the organization of private electric utility owners that dominate the entire national grid. They have sole authority to set "reliability standards," by which their performance is measured, and they are the national lobbyists for the industry. This is a blatant conflict of interest, because they succeed in keeping reliability standards low for GMD (as a weather problem) and don't accept any responsibility at all for protecting against manmade EMP. They say that EMP is a defense issue, so should be handled by the military. But when I ask their representatives if they want to release control or ownership of their grid to the military for EMP work, they don't answer.

Tom Popik's decision to come to Augusta to participate in the EMP briefings before Maine's EUT Committee proved extremely fortuitous. He has an engineering background from the Massachusetts Institute of Technology (MIT) and the U.S. Air Force, and was to share with the Committee his Foundation's technical research on disturbing specifics of the Maine grid. After stunning testimony from one expert after another, his presentation near the end of the hearing would bring it all squarely home to the riveted committee members.

By accident or fate, Tom's close proximity to Maine (the other experts were mostly located around Washington, D.C.), his Foundation's developing research, now further enhanced by John Kappenman's solar storm analysis, and his combined research, analytic and presentation skills made him the perfect partner for me in advancing LD131, my EMP bill, through the Committee and on to the full legislature.

I briefed Committee members beforehand on the EMP issue via emails and conversations, but nothing could have prepared them for the breakthrough EMP hearing that was to unfold before them. Chair Barry Hobbins told me he would allow my experts all the time they needed: a welcome accommodation, and great relief, we had only hoped to secure. There was so much to tell. The door had been opened and the experts invited in. I was so pleased and proud to introduce them.

My brief introduction gave an overall review of the issue: the 100 percent probability of a devastating geomagnetic solar storm; the potential attack by hostile enemies; the 1989 case of our neighbor Quebec's solar storm blackout that lasted 9 hours and cost them $2 billion dollars in direct costs ($10 billion in lost economic activity), the national studies; available low-cost mitigations and protections; the promise of economic, as well as societal, benefit to Maine by providing safe refuge for sophisticated businesses seeking power reliability; and our own duties as legislators to protect the public.

It was clear the message was having an impact when EUT Committee members asked why I had not asked to protect the whole grid?

My bill only asked for EMP protection for work currently under construction, especially the $1.4 billion expansion by electric utility Central Maine Power (CMP), and for protections to be designed into future construction. I did not want to overreach and discourage them from at least doing something. In fact, I hoped that, in leaving room for them to broaden it themselves, they would take that opportunity and take more ownership of the bill.

I explained my strategy to the experts during our meeting at The Senator the night before, because I knew they'd think it was less than needed. So in that moment, we could enjoy the import of the question: we had the beginning of buy-in from the Energy, Utilities and Technology Committee.

I answered the question, introduced Dr. Peter Vincent Pry, and left the lectern.

Peter shocked the Committee with his depiction of this truly unimaginable, existential threat to civilization. They listened with rapt attention. Having served with distinction in the CIA and on the Congressional EMP Commission, he focused mostly on defense and national security implications of EMP.

The others followed, each testimony as precise and as compelling as the one before. Their years of experience, research, and consulting in science, defense, intelligence, industry, academia, and policy making was undeniable.

Bron Cikotas described the effects of an extended loss of power on all our other infrastructures (water, transportation, banking, heating, etc.) the sparking of electrical outlets and widespread fires. Mike Maloof talked about his experiences in terrorism work in other countries and at home. Cynthia Ayers talked about cybersecurity issues, and their connection to EMP in taking down the grid. Tom Popik presented specific information about Maine's electric grid and the New England grid, which gave great definition to the local threat.

The testimony of Peter's EMP Task Force astounded the Committee. In a single meeting, they became convinced of the urgency of this legislation

Advanced Fusion Systems, the developer of EMP testing and protective equipment, showed the Committee a catalog of various protective products, and explained how they worked. Kirk made remarks about fixes that could be accomplished in weeks. Deputy Fire Chief Mike Laracy, of Walpole, Massachusetts, described his own research that showed he might not even be able to respond to an EMP emergency. A legislator and Vietnam War veteran, Representative David Cotter, understood the technology from his military experience. Representative Ralph Chapman, a physicist, backed up the science. Bettie Harris-Howard, a nurse and nursing home administrator, described implications for medical response. Legislators and Maine residents expressed their own knowledge and concerns. Experts who could not attend submitted testimony in writing ahead of the hearing.

The hearing lasted, without interruption, for almost 5 hours.

Representative Hobbins, who opposed introduction of my EMP bill when he was part of the prior session's Legislative Council, now ended the meeting by saying, "I don't know what we are going to do, but I can promise you right now, that we are going to do something."

The EUT Committee scheduled the customary follow-on work session to decide what action should be taken. Hobbins commented that he was dismayed that the utility companies had not sent anyone except their lobbyists to the hearing, and said he hoped to hear more from them. Their lobbyist representatives from ISO New England, Central Maine Power, and Emera (formerly Bangor Hydro) had been blown away by the experts at this meeting, their arguments all trite obfuscations parroting talking points from the North American Electric Reliability Corporation (NERC).

NERC, of course, is supposed to be protecting the grid, but in reality is the national lobby for the electric power industry. People ask why they wouldn't want to protect their own business, their assets. They never give a clear answer, but there is ample cause for speculation.

Work Session I: Widening The Breach

On February 28, 2013, the Energy, Utilities and Technology Committee convened their first formal Work Session on LD-131. It opened with the usual review of the public hearing by the committee analyst.

Prior to this Work Session, Tom Popik and John Kappenman, the latter perhaps our nation's foremost expert on the effects of geomagnetic storms on electric grids, provided the Committee with technical questions they suggested the EUT Committee pose to the utilities. Tom and John also provided copies of the questions to the utilities, along with their own answers.

When it comes to solar storms, Maine is one of the nation's most vulnerable states. There have been many instances of solar storm impacts, including tripping of high-capacity transmission lines, complaints about power quality from ratepayers, melting of transformer components at the Seabrook nuclear plant just over the Maine border, and a catastrophic transformer fire at the now-closed Maine Yankee nuclear plant.

All of these incidents were legitimate areas of inquiry for the EUT Committee.

The February 2013 public hearing in Maine had been a crucial event for consideration of solar storm risks to electric grids, because it was a rare instance of the utilities' not being able to control the forum. In previous inquiries at the NERC Geo-Magnetic Disturbance (GMD) Task Force, the process was disturbingly scripted in such a way as to produce the industry-desired outcome. Likewise, in previous testimony before the U.S. Congress, Senators and Representatives asked generally bland questions, suggesting they might be overly mindful of the outsized political influence of this industry they were confronting.

But now, our independent-minded Maine legislators had the opportunity to ask commonsense questions that should have been asked and answered years before. The representatives for the electric utilities had to admit that they did not know the answers, even though the questions, with their own answers, had been provided to the electric utilities in advance by Tom and John.

In fact, the representatives from ISO New England and Central Maine Power were confounded by the preparation of the experts testifying on behalf of the public, and by the newfound knowledge of the EUT Committee members. The utilities were unable to provide satisfying technical answers to the questions. Many times they could supply no answers at all. Their responses were lightweight, mostly vague assurances that industry had been coping with EMP from solar storms for years, and that everything was fine

The EUT Committee members, who had been anticipating a robust presentation by the utilities were astonished. Their performance in committee demonstrated that everything was clearly not fine.

The Committee was particularly disappointed that the utilities failed to provide any historic data on the effects of solar storms on the Maine electric power grid.

In contrast, Tom Popik provided an excellent briefing to the Committee, including some very discouraging data on the vulnerability of the Maine-New England electric grid to solar storms. Tom's modest, respectful attitude, and obvious competence, won the trust of the Committee.

The bottom line from the first Work Session was that now the Committee was asking the same question of the utilities as were Tom Popik and John Kappenman: "Where is the data?" Critically, Central Maine Power had agreed to research this data and make the results public.

A new work session was scheduled.

Work Session II: Rout

The second official Work Session of the Energy, Utilities and Technology Committee convened on March 5, 2013. Here, the utilities fared even worse.

The extra time allowed the advocates for the public to further refine their research. The Foundation for Resilient Societies authored a research paper specifically on the situation for Maine, "Solar Storm Risks for Maine and the New England Electric Grid and Potential Protective Measures."

The paper exposed the grave risk to the people of Maine. On several past occasions, solar storms tripped critical equipment and could have caused a protracted blackout. It became clear that if the Maine grid was not protected, eventually luck would run out.

The EUT Committee was listening and waiting with growing alarm at the continuing inability of ISO New England and Central Maine Power to answer questions about the EMP threat from solar storms and their plans for protecting the Maine grid. They could not even respond to roughly a third to a half of the questions the EUT had given them.

Those questions the utilities could answer appeared to confirm the worst fears of the Committee: that Maine was unprotected from a solar storm catastrophe.

The utilities confirmed that they have only two instruments, GIC (Geomagnetically Induced Current) monitors, deployed to monitor solar storms, and that one of these monitors is 25 years old. Chair Hobbins interjected here, aghast, as he described how far just cell phone technology had advanced since he got his first brick-sized one 25 years ago. And we were not even talking so much about what happened in the last 25 years. We were talking about the 150-year solar storm that would not, essentially, be survivable, and was known to be 100 percent probable. Their two GIC monitors are also inadequate because of their limited scope of coverage.

Prudently, Tom Popik and John Kappenman, before Work Session II, visited Tom Welch, Chairman of the Public Utilities Commission (PUC). They introduced themselves and talked to him about the EMP issue, so that he would not be taken by surprise or ill at ease at the upcoming work session. Consequently, Welch did not try to defend the utilities, or criticize Tom and John, during testimony. They were able to form a cordial working relationship.

At Work Session II, Tom Popik and John Kappenman did a masterful job exposing to the EUT Committee the limitations of the expertise and candor of the utilities on the EMP threat. They earned the Committee's trust and are regarded as friendly expert advisors.

In contrast, the pretensions of the utilities as the only legitimate source of expertise on all matters related to the electric grid were exposed as hollow. Their representative, Kevin Clarke, of ISO New England, was tense and sweating profusely as he slowly and painfully let out the truth to the Committee that they did not have answers to their questions. The robust response the Committee had sought and expected from the utilities was not there.

ISO New England's plan for protection relied on an operations manual with many communications steps to share information and confer on what decisions to take. One could only imagine how difficult, under the pressure of terrifying circumstances, it would be to make the very hard choices that would be required.

ISO New England's Clarke was forced to admit that they would not have enough time to implement their solar storm operating procedures in all circumstances. Could they respond with 15 minutes warning? No. A solar storm might not give them even that much time. 30 minutes warning? Yes, well, probably. The committee members looked incredulous.

It was as if the veil protecting the mysteries of the electric grid had been pulled away, and its operations revealed to be threatened by the ill-equipped guardians entrusted to protect it. At the close of the session, Chairman Hobbins, looking utterly dismayed, exclaimed, "I feel if we ask you one more question, you will throw up your hands and declare yourself guilty."

Chairman Hobbins proposed that, whereas the Energy, Utilities and Technology Committee was not professionally able to tell the utilities or the Public Utilities Commission (PUC) how to protect the grid (and the Committee clearly did not know themselves) the Committee would amend LD131, to direct the PUC to compile specific information on Maine's grid and return a report to them the following January. The PUC was to investigate: grid vulnerabilities to GMD and EMP; options for mitigation; costs (low, medium and high) and who should pay them; policy implications; time frame for deploying protections.

The full committee supported the Hobbins plan. They directed Jeanne Guzzetti, the EUT Committee analyst, to draft the necessary legislation.

Work Session II came to a close.

Work Session III

In preparation for Work Session III, I arranged a teleconference among Joseph McClelland, Director of the Office of Energy Infrastructure Security, a department within the U.S. Federal Energy Regulatory Commission (FERC); Tom Welch, Chairman of the Maine Public Utilities Commission; and me. I figured that Tom Welch might be understandably uneasy about being tasked to protect the Maine grid from EMP. McClelland's office could help. I was there to facilitate conversation and make sure I had first-hand understanding of the possibilities.

Joe McClelland reassured Tom Welch that FERC would be there to help him draft his report, and that his office was mandated to help the States with energy security. He told Tom that his office had all the studies, staff and expertise to assist them. All Tom had to do was call and ask. Although McClelland's office could not initiate any intrusion into the State's process, they could respond if asked: U.S. FERC would be there to help.

Tom asked Joe if FERC might disapprove of their actions down the line, and if it might cause them to have a hard time getting cost recovery allowed. Joe assured him he should not have any real worries about either.

I also tracked the drafting of the bill, because it was likely the PUC or the industry might try to influence its wording.

Checking in with the analyst, Jeanne Guzzetti, I found that she had drafted the amended bill to direct both the Public Utilities Commission and the electric utilities to do the study, which was not what the EUT decided. It was to be independent of industry influence. She changed it. She had also drafted the study to just address GMD and not EMP. I advised her of that error, too. She was so surprised, she went to the committee chairs to check on it. That got fixed, too.

Without these corrections, the bill could have been critically compromised. The North America Electric Reliability Corporation (NERC), representing the nation's electric utilities, had been lobbying against man-made EMP protection for years, arguing that it is the responsibility of the military. We could not allow them the opportunity to obstruct the will of the legislature here in Maine.

Meanwhile, Peter Pry was doing preparatory work leading up to the third Work Session. He and his EMP Task Force were providing long distance "air support" from Washington, DC.

Peter had several highly prominent national security experts associated with his Task Force call Chairman Hobbins and other key EUT Committee members to urge them to pass my legislation to protect the Maine grid. These included Ambassador R. James Woolsey, former Director of the CIA; Ambassador Henry Cooper, former Director of the Strategic Defense Initiative and lead negotiator with the USSR on missile and defense treaties; and Vice Admiral Robert Monroe, former Director of the U.S. Defense Nuclear Agency.

They reinforced the message that Peter had come to Maine to deliver, one he had so earnestly and vigorously been delivering for so many years: the EMP threat is real, possibly imminent. The particular message for Maine was that it urgently needed to protect itself and set an example for other states to follow. The broader vision was that if Maine and some other states were to protect their electric grids from EMP, we might break through the bureaucratic logjam in Washington, and lead the way for passage of congressional legislation.

We did radio interviews in Maine. Peter published articles in national journals to encourage Maine to lead the way. One of his articles was re-published in Israel National News. Committee members commented to each other on who had contacted them. To me, it was deeply moving to see the faith and hope and confidence he placed in Maine.

The third official Work Session of the Energy, Utilities and Technology Committee convened on April 10, 2013. I was there alone this time, without the familiar presence of Tom Popik for support in facing any late surprise challenges from the utilities, the PUC, or even the EUT Committee. Any questions not handled well here could disturb Committee equilibrium and threaten passage of my bill. I knew Tom was listening online as both a support and a quick witness to any slip-up. Others around the country would be anxiously awaiting the outcome.

No challenge came.

My original bill called for protecting only current and future construction on the electric grid. The EUT Committee decided to do a lot more.

Jeanne Guzzetti brought in the draft of the more ambitious bill. The new LD-131 directed the Public Utilities Commission to investigate the EMP threat and the range of cost-effective options for protecting not just current and new construction, but the entire Maine electric power grid, old and new, and authorized the EUT to report out permanent legislation in the next (short) session, thereby bypassing the need for Legislative Council approval.

The Committee's amended version of my bill made protecting the Maine grid a high priority and urgent mission. It was drafted as "emergency legislation." The PUC was to report back an initial study in 5-6 weeks, and the final study by the following January 20, 2014.

Public Utilities Commission Chairman, Tom Welch, agreed to get started right away.

What I remember most about Work Session III was a moment of high drama. Chairman Hobbins polled all the involved parties in the room, pointing at them and addressing them one by one – Central Maine Power, Bangor Hydro/Emera, ISO New England, Thomas Welch, the Public Advocate, and finally, me: asking if all were supportive of this proposed bill. Each one answered, "Yes."

Hobbins then asked for a vote of the Energy, Utilities and Technology Committee. LD-131 passed unanimously, as emergency legislation.

It was on to the Legislature, and then to the Governor.

Sailing Through

I met with Governor Paul LePage and his aide, Patrick Woodcock, in anticipation of questions from other legislators wanting to know whether he would sign the bill, if passed. Governor LePage listened with surprised interest. He especially responded to the promise of potential economic benefits from attracting new business. He asked where Tom Welch stood on it. I told him he was on board. The Governor said he would confer with Tom.

Governor LePage is known for vetoing lots of bills, so this looked reasonably good. There still was no certainty, however, of his support.

On May 7 and 8, 2013, the EMP bill passed its first and second readings in Maine's House of Representatives: unanimously.

The bill then went to the Senate. I followed it down there to lobby the senators. Because this was "emergency legislation," it required a two-thirds vote for passage.

On May 9th, the bill passed its first reading in the Senate: unanimously.

On May 14, LD-131 passed its second reading, and headed back to the House for final passage. LD-131 finally completed its journey through the House, passing there on its final vote on May 14.

LD-131, nearly finished with the round robin of multiple votes before both houses that we have here in the Maine State Legislature, then headed back to the Senate for the final vote. The bill could have been acted upon quickly, but 5 days later there was still no final vote on LD-131.

I interpreted this as a bad sign. Many tricks can be played on the way to passage.

On May 19th, I headed down to the 2013 international summit of the Electric Infrastructure Security Council in Washington, DC. Just one year after I first met the international community at the 2012 EISC Summit in London, I was invited to speak at the 2013 EISC Summit convening in Washington.

How far I had traveled, from knowing nothing about EMP, to sponsoring the first bill to protect, for the first time, an entire state (that hopefully would lead to protection of all 50 states) from the existential threat that is EMP.

I hoped to tell everyone at the EISC Summit in Washington that my legislation finally passed into law. They were all so jubilant about the introduction of LD-131. But now I could only hope that it would pass.

Senator Linda Valentino kept in touch with me about the status of LD-131. On May 21, the second day of the Summit, she texted to say that the Minority Leader was having the bill tabled. He was going to fight it.

I had to leave the Summit without knowing more.

I waited longer when I got home, still getting text updates from the Senate while I sat in the House. On May 28, Senate President Alfond took it off the table and LD- 131 finally passed the Senate: nearly unanimously 32-3. Only the Minority Leader and two chums were holdouts.

LD-131 was through the House and Senate. Now it had to survive a governor who was not at all reluctant to brandish his veto pen.

The Governor

The bill went to Governor Paul LePage. Peter teleconferenced with Governor LePage and his staff to explain the EMP threat and the importance of protecting the grid. LePage still made no commitments. He had 10 days to decide whether to sign the bill, veto it, or let it pass into law without his signature.

On June 10, 2013, the Governor sent his Energy Aide, Patrick Woodcock, to speak to me in the House. Patrick, typically inscrutable, smiled and told me the Governor had allowed the bill to pass into law without his signature: the last day he could do it voluntarily.

Wow! The first legislative victory for EMP protection! A landmark victory for Maine, the expert advocates, Kirk's initiative, Peter's great vision, a single committed state legislature, and, hopefully, the nation.

I credit Governor LePage with showing great wisdom and making the right decision on short notice, the excellent work of the experts, my own wisdom to both follow and lead, the careful analysis and drafting by Jeanne Guzzetti, and the smart attention of the legislators. After the U.S. Congress tried unsuccessfully to pass a bill to protect the national grid from EMP for five years, Maine passed a bill to protect its grid from EMP in just four months – the first EMP law in the nation.

It is a profound pleasure for me to have sponsored and lead that effort in Maine, and helped bring a victory to those extraordinary veteran EMP experts who had worked so diligently for years to protect the nation, and so generously shared their intellectual and experiential bounty with us in Maine. It was a pleasure, too, to witness the participation at the hearing of many Maine people, legislators, and first responders who understood and came to testify. They solidified the presentation.

But the work was not over. The report mandated by LD-131 had to get done satisfactorily. Big interests did not want it to be.

Pushback from the Public Utilities Commission

Public Utilities Commission Chairman Tom Welch opted to provide an online docket for the study. All input of experts and others was to be deposited there, and anyone who wished could read it or comment. The PUC would review the submissions and work independent of any other parties. Everyone was to have equal access to the docket.

Welch's plan for the study sounded good, which was reassuring. The deadline for remarks was in October 2013, so there was plenty of time to prepare them. Very significant papers were submitted. In an effort to make sure the PUC did not overlook work already done by the Energy, Utilities and Technology Committee, I submitted all the legislative file documents. Meanwhile, the preliminary report was due in mid-June 2013.

The first disappointment, and sign of future trouble, came from the Public Utilities Commission.

Tom Welch and his PUC were supposed to deliver a preliminary report in mid-June. From the great one-hour phone conversation we had earlier with Joe McClelland, I expected Tom Welch to quickly reach out to Joe, take advantage of the expertise offered by the FERC (the U.S. Federal Energy Regulatory Commission) and make fast progress on the report. But Tom did not.

The preliminary report, which the Public Utilities Comission had agreed to commence upon passage of LD-131 through the EUT Committee on April 10th, turned out to be a short, one-page letter outlining their plan and citing a few resources they intended to use.

Six weeks had produced little.

This raised suspicions that we would be subjected to the kind of delay tactics that have been typical of Washington, DC and NERC. We worried that the Maine Public Utilities Commission might also be too close with the power companies to convincingly regulate them, a phenomenon known as "regulatory capture." I feared Tom Welch and the PUC were going to rely on the spotty "expertise" of the reluctant utilities, which would block progress toward a finished and satisfactory report. Four months earlier, the Energy, Utilities and Technology Committee public hearing had shown that the utilities knew little about EMP, had no interest in effectively shielding Maine's grid and people from its wrath, and were under a lot of influence from NERC to resist compliance with the law.

On December 8, 2013, the Public Utilities Commission issued its draft report for public scrutiny and comment. The draft report recommended against protecting Maine's power grid against GMD (natural EMP), and had not even studied manmade EMP, using the old NERC argument that grid security against manmade EMP is a national defense problem, to be solved in Washington. Of course, nuclear EMP is a defense problem. But the power companies are a monopoly. They own the electric grid, have control over it, and own responsibility for it: while the military does not.

There was still no evidence of input from McClelland's office at the U.S. Federal Energy Regulatory Commission. The PUC had sent a copy of their draft report to Joe McClelland and asked him to critique it, seven months after he had offered his assistance. It was too late. His office does not critique reports for the states. U.S. FERC only assists in developing them. That opportunity had been missed.

The PUC allowed eight working days for responses to their report: a very short response time for busy people at that time of year, just before the Christmas holidays.

The Public Utilities Commission's recommendation to kick the problem down to Washington was a grating echo of the well-worn advisories of the North America Electric Reliability Corporation (NERC) in their fights against grid protection. It was clearly heavily influenced by the electric companies. The PUC recommendation to defer to decisions to Washington was industry code for doing nothing.

Reaction to the PUC draft report was condemnation.

Tom Popik and Peter Pry were both bitterly disappointed with what they read, as were we all, and quickly responded in an effort to rescue the report. They drafted rebuttals exposing the PUC draft report's mistakes, oversights, and misinformation. Tom and his Foundation for Resilient Societies coolly and meticulously detailed the factual errors.

Peter's rebuttal delivered a severe criticism of the draft report, exposing incompetence and, most devastating, dishonesty. His analysis was searing, demonstrating that there could be no doubt that the PUC draft report "cherry picked" favored information and chose to ignore evidence that contradicted their recommendation to do nothing.

Peter's expose bravely risked continued collegiality with the Public Utilities Commission, but the tone and substance of such a rebuttal was the necessary remedy to wake them up to the requirements of their job. In fact, it did temporarily hurt his relationship with Chairman Welch, but it also might well have been, along with Tom's technical detail, a decisive factor in causing the Public Utilities Commission to quickly reverse course and get back on track with protecting the Maine electric grid.

Back On Track

The final report was due back to the Energy, Utilities and Technology Committee by January 20, 2014. It was scheduled for hearing on January 30th.

On January 29th, Peter Pry and Cynthia Ayers returned to Augusta to brief State legislators on the EMP threat and attend the final Work Session of the EUT Committee's work on LD-131.

During a dinner at The Senator Inn, Peter described an important new development.

The U.S. Congress tasked the Department of Defense for a plan to build a new anti-missile defense site somewhere on the east coast, and Maine had been identified as one of the possible locations. If Maine wanted to seek that base, and all the ancillary business development that would accompany it, protecting Maine's electric grid from EMP would provide it a competitive advantage over other states.

Some legislators were uneasy about the notion of an anti-missile defense site in Maine, but Peter's point had been made – investment in sophisticated, robust economic development is increasingly aware of electric infrastructure weaknesses, and attracted to sites with secure, reliable electric power.

Across the wide table, Professor Cynthia Ayers was quietly engaging with a knowledgeable tribal representative and a few other legislators about preparedness and technology. We lingered a while over our conversations with her. Peter, Cynthia, and I lingered even longer in the lounge afterwards, meandering through various subjects, including cyber security and intelligence (Cynthia's field) and its interplay with EMP.

Final Report--Not Really

On January 30, 2014, the Energy, Utilities and Technology Committee convened to receive Tom Welch's presentation of the PUC's "Report Relating to Geomagnetic Disturbance (GMD) and Electromagnetic Pulse (EMP)."

The report did not answer several specific key questions mandated in the law, and the PUC was requesting more time to complete the study, this time to include the study of EMP. The Public Utilities Commission plan was written up on Iberdrola stationery! Iberdrola is the multinational corporation based in Spain that owns Central Maine Power. A "study task force" was to be convened for another year of study, under the direction of CMP. This all threatened more industry manipulation of data and heavy NERC influence.

However, the Public Utilities Commission had performed an amazing reversal of its earlier "do nothing" recommendation of the previous month. To his credit, Chairman Welch now admitted to the Energy, Utilities and Technology Committee that both natural (GMD) and manmade EMP are a clear and present danger to the Maine electric grid. Instead of "doing nothing," his new recommendation was to proceed to examine both GMD and EMP for cost-effective plans for protecting the Maine electric power grid against collapse.

Peter pointed out that Chairman Welch seemed to have learned from his and Tom's rebuttals to their draft report and responded positively. To so completely reverse course, and now head in the right direction, Peter averred, was rare and highly commendable for any government bureaucracy.

To recommend that they do more work dismayed me, though, because the Public Utilities Commission was already mandated to deliver a report on cost-effective options for protecting the grid against GMD and EMP. Theirs was not an original idea, but the purpose of LD-131, which the PUC had so far failed to implement.

While Peter and Tom were thrilled to hear Welch's newfound commitment, I was angry that the PUC had wasted months not doing what the law already required. The Energy, Utilities and Technology Committee members already recognized the EMP problem: they did not need the PUC to tell them there was one.

I understood that we were seeing important progress, but, meanwhile, we were still without a completed report. When invited to speak, I expressed my displeasure with all the delays and omissions, and failure to access, in a timely way, Director Joseph McClelland's FERC Office of Energy Infrastructure Security for help, and have it completed by now. I reminded the Committee that this was "emergency" legislation.

As I spoke, Welch upset the room, barking out his angry objections from his seat. Hobbins chastised me for my critical remarks, denigrated me for acting like there was an impending threat (while at that very moment, the Sun was boiling with big solar flares pointed directly at us), gaveled me out of order, and dismissed me.

He gently and sympathetically invited Welch back up to respond. Hobbins was very solicitous of him. Welch was shaking with anger. He was outraged at my purportedly criticizing his staff, proclaiming how hard working they were. Of course, I was criticizing the report and the management of the study, not the staff personally. The PUC had not done the work the law required of it.

The session ended tumultuously as Hobbins marched out of the room without inviting remarks by the Committee or recognizing anyone else. It was quite upsetting to Peter, Tom and Cynthia, startling to the Committee, and probably embarrassing to my daughter. In my estimation, it was most likely just legislative theater by a deft politician seizing the opportunity to assure Welch of a pre-arranged outcome. He escaped stage left without having to address the irregularities of the meeting: no vote of the Committee to approve the report, draft any legislation, or even adjourn

Tom Popik and Peter generously congratulated Tom Welch on his new commitment to complete a good plan. It was sincere and gracious of them, but seemed a bit lame to me. Tom Popik had been given one opportunity to speak, Peter and Cynthia, who had traveled hours and miles to attend, were given none, I was rudely dismissed, and the report only tacitly left to default to acceptance.

It was still also true, however, that under Welch's leadership, the Public Utilities Commission was committing to more serious and complete work on answering questions on how to protect the grid from EMP as well as GMD. For years, the industry had argued it was not their responsibility to protect against hostile attack. What we could all agree on was that he had changed that message. This was progress.

Good relations were now needed to move forward productively. What threatened failure was that the plan included the proviso that the task force be convened and directed by Central Maine Power, which had lobbied against LD-131 at the outset and was subject to the influence of NERC. We were moving, though.

Enter Central Maine Power

As directed by the legislature in LD-131, the Maine Public Utilities Commission did a general study on protecting the grid -- but only against GMD, the natural EMP from solar storms, not nuclear EMP as was also required. However, the detailed work of determining specific equipment needing protection, including hard-to-replace extra high voltage transformers, still needed to be done for both.

Central Maine Power convened the task force to conduct a year-long project for a "Maine GMD/EMP Risk Analysis." Tom Welch had agreed to invite public and private stakeholders into the working group: ISO-New England; electric utilities Emera Maine, Brookfield Power, NextEra; EMPrimus, a vendor for protective equipment; and two consulting firms, Metatech and John Kappenman's Storm Analysis Consultants. Significantly, the non-profit Foundation for Resilient Societies was allowed to participate as a public observer. I did not ask to be included.

While the threat from solar storms has been obvious since the March 1989 Hydro Quebec blackout, no U.S. electric utility had yet protected their transmission network from GMD. A prerequisite for any protection must be detailed modeling of geomagnetically-induced currents in transmission lines and cost proposals for protective hardware. EMPrimus offered to fund a well-known independent firm to do that. Central Maine Power accepted, and, with the encouragement of the Maine PUC, engaged their own modeling firm, as well. They began their hard work. While other utilities have modeled their networks, the results of the modeling have been kept hidden. CMP was the first utility to conduct this work as part of a public process. As a result, CMP benefited from the significant involvement of outside experts.

LD-131 mandated study of both GMD -- the long pulse from solar storms, or E3, and the short pulse from nuclear weapons, EMP, or E1. (We already protect against E-2, effects such as lightning.) To its credit, Central Maine Power agreed to taking on study of E1 EMP vulnerability, including cost aspects. This was in compliance with LD-131, but, of course, unusual for electric power companies. When this study is completed, Maine will be the first state in the nation to have studied how E1 EMP protection can be implemented for an electric utility.

We Are Not Out of the Woods Yet

As the study group progressed, I relied on updates from Tom Popik and others. Their news sounded pretty good, but we all worried that ISO-New England, NERC, or Central Maine Power might sabotage the study by, for example, low-balling the solar threat, or exaggerating the costs for EMP protection, and thereby again arrive at a recommendation to "do nothing."

Disturbingly, the September 2014 meeting of the study task group was canceled on short notice. The director of the study group had left Central Maine Power. It was to be the final meeting before the draft report was released. Many questions floated around us.

As a member of the Government Oversight Committee, I questioned Tom Welch about it at our next meeting, because I understood they might once again leave EMP out of the LD-131 study. Again he burst out from his seat, angrily denying the suggestion. He said that EMP would definitely be included in the report, and the report would be out by the end of the year. Astoundingly, later that day, he announced his early retirement, to become effective at the end of the year.

Wow, that raised new questions in my mind that I knew he'd never answer.

I just hoped that his promise was good and, before he left would manage to get this job done.

Then, the October 27, 2014 meeting of the study group was scheduled as the final one. Tom Popik was one of the members. For this one, his Secretary and Foundation counsel, Bill Harris, and I attended with him.

It was alarming.

EMPrimus, a research and development licensing company for EMP protective devices, and well respected for its work, presented their findings, using the outside modeling firm's results and their own research and analysis. They included data from CMP records. It was very clear and concise, hitting all the key points. It focused on GMD because their products mostly protect against the natural EMP.

Then, Central Maine Power gave their presentation. It was filled with NERC-generated assumptions that floored the rest of us. NERC assumptions were what had brought the country to this precipice of disaster, and what our legislation was intended to overcome. The NERC benchmarks they used were from a different country, recorded from a period of quiet solar activity. They had not studied manmade EMP.

A new young replacement for the former project manager ran the briefing, which concluded that Maine did not need any protection. He said that he would write up their report as presented. He dismissed the EMPrimus report by just ignoring it. It was a very cold and upsetting experience.

Central Maine Power deliberately omitted the historical real-world data that they shared with the legislature in hearings, data which proved Maine needs protection from natural and nuclear EMP. CMP did not even want to add monitors to see how the grid is performing during solar storms, and definitely did not intend to release to the public what any monitoring showed.

Central Maine Power intended to give the Energy, Utilities and Technology Committee their recommendations. I reminded them that LD131 did not call for their recommendations, but for options available to the legislature for them to consider in choosing a plan of protection. They said they did not include manmade EMP because there was not enough research yet – totally wrong. They denied they had to post the work to the online docket for scrutiny by independent experts and the public: we soon changed that.

We somberly awaited the Final Report.

Where We Are Now

Nothing much changed. The EMPrimus report to Central Maine Power showed very promising solutions at minimal cost. The Central Maine Power report still showed skewed data, more expensive solutions, but they claim that nothing needed to be done. We have promises from CMP to do more study. As of this date, they are still in denial, and the new Energy, Utilities and Technology Committee, composed of mostly new members from the 2014 election, gave experts limited time to testify about the reports. The follow-up 2015 legislation to enact protections failed by a single vote, in the State Senate, along party lines.

Maine could have been the first state in the nation to protect itself against the terror and societal collapse that is the EMP threat. It is not. But we have blown open the door to other states to go forward with their own efforts. That is happening, and the heat is building, now even at the federal level. I just hope that we continue to be lucky until we are prepared.

Justin Michlig from Central Maine Power has recently written to announce the restart of the study task force, expected for this month, September 2015.

Respectfully submitted,

The Honorable Andrea Boland
Former Maine State Representative
September 11, 2015

Pry's Postscript

Andrea Boland's concerns about Central Maine Power endlessly "studying" the EMP threat to the Maine power grid, and options for cost-effective protection, proved prescient. In 2015, after two years of study, Central Maine Power is still unwilling to protect the entire Maine electric grid from natural or manmade EMP: even though a cost-effective plan is now developed, that could be implemented immediately for $6 million dollars. This is less than what CMP wants to spend on a new billing system for ratepayers.

In 2014, Rep. Boland, due to term limits, lost her seat in the State House. She ran for State Senator, but lost by 13 votes.

In 2015, Senator David Miramant, guided by Andrea Boland, introduced LD-1363, a bill to require ISO New England and Central Maine Power to proceed to protect the Maine electric grid. LD-1363 would have succeeded, except the Energy, Utilities and Technology Commission had only 3 of the original members who supported Boland's original LD-131. Insufficient time was allowed, only one hearing, to educate the 9 new members of the EUT Committee on the EMP threat and solutions.

Nonetheless, LD-1363 passed the Maine House of Representatives by a substantial margin and failed to pass the Senate by just one vote.

If LD-1363 had passed, Maine would be the first state, or among the first states, to protect its electric grid from EMP. Critical to defeat of LD-1363 is a promise made by Central Maine Power to the Maine State Legislature that they are actively planning to protect the grid and will protect the grid when they are ready.

Thanks to the activism of Rep. Boland, Senator Miramant and the Maine State Legislature, Central Maine Power is taking some concrete steps to improve the resilience of parts of the Maine electric grid:

--Central Maine Power is installing two series capacitors to protect key parts of the Maine grid from natural EMP (GMD), including the 1,000 MW power line from New Brunswick, Canada, as part of the Maine Power Reliability Program, with completion expected in 2016.
--Installation of the series capacitors will enable and lead to updated modeling of the Maine transmission system, perhaps reducing the number of neutral blocking devices needed to protect all EHV transformers in the entire Maine grid from natural EMP.
--Central Maine Power is installing, by November 2015, monitors that can measure the effects of natural EMP on transformers, that can inform planning to protect the entire grid and operational procedures to save the grid in an emergency.
--Central Maine Power is developing options to utilize the Synchrophasor (a device for measuring electric waves impacting the grid) network of the Eastern Interconnection and ISO New England to monitor the Maine grid and help identify which specific EHV transformers need priority protection.
--By the second quarter of 2016, Central Maine Power may be prepared to install equipment to protect the grid, depending upon rulemaking by the U.S. Federal Energy Regulatory Commission on allowing cost recovery for such investments.

LD-131 and LD-1363 have, in two (2) years, moved the State of Maine from complete ignorance about EMP to the threshold of EMP preparedness. Maine is further ahead of the EMP threat than Washington, which--seven (7) years after receiving the EMP Commission recommendations--has still developed no adequate plan to protect the national electric grid from the EMP threat, that could kill 90 percent of the American people.

SUMMARY 1

This bill requires a person submitting a petition to the Public Utilities Commission for the purposes of receiving a certificate of public convenience and necessity for building a transmission line to include a description of design measures to be used that limit electromagnetic field levels and ensure the protection of the transmission and distribution system against damage from an electromagnetic pulse or geomagnetic storm. This bill also requires the commission to consider electromagnetic field levels, electromagnetic pulse protections and geomagnetic storm protections when determining the need for a transmission line.

This bill adds similar requirements for the deciding authority, when determining whether an energy infrastructure proposal is in the long-term interest of the State, to consider electromagnetic field levels and electromagnetic pulse and geomagnetic storm dangers. The bill directs the Public Utilities Commission, in consultation with the Department of Environmental Protection and within 6 months of the effective date of this Act, to adopt routine technical rules to identify effective design measures to limit electromagnetic field levels and ensure the protection of the transmission and distribution system against damage from an electromagnetic pulse or a geomagnetic storm.

Finally, the bill requires any transmission line currently under construction upon the effective date of the rules to incorporate design measures to limit electromagnetic field levels and ensure the protection of the transmission and distribution system against damage from an electromagnetic pulse or a geomagnetic storm.

LD-131 Main Text

Be it enacted by the People of the State of Maine as follows:

Sec. 1. 35-A MRSA §122, sub-§1, ¶A-1 is enacted to read:

A-1. "Electromagnetic pulse" means one or more pulses of electromagnetic energy 3 capable of disabling, disrupting or destroying a transmission and distribution system.

Sec. 2. 35-A MRSA §122, sub-§1, ¶C-1 is enacted to read:

C-1. "Geomagnetic storm" means a temporary disturbance of the Earth's magnetic field resulting from solar activity.

Sec. 3. 35-A MRSA §122, sub-§1-D, ¶B, as enacted by PL 2009, c. 655, Pt. A, §2, is amended to read:

B. The deciding authority shall determine whether an energy infrastructure proposal is in the long-term public interest of the State. In making that determination, the deciding authority shall, at a minimum, consider the extent to which the proposal:

(1) Materially enhances or does not harm transmission opportunities for energy generation within the State;

(2) Is reasonably likely to reduce electric rates or other relevant energy prices or costs for residents and businesses within the State relative to the expected value of those electric rates or other energy prices or costs but for the proposed energy infrastructure development;

(3) Increases long-term economic benefits for the State, including but not limited to direct financial benefits, employment opportunities and economic development;

(4) Ensures efficient use of the statutory corridor through collocation of energy infrastructure, collaboration between energy infrastructure developers and the preservation of options for future uses;

(5) Minimizes conflict with the public purposes for which the state-owned land or asset is owned and any management plans for the land or asset within the statutory corridor and, when necessary, mitigates unavoidable impacts;

(6) Limits and mitigates the effects of energy infrastructure on the landscape, including but not limited to using underground installation when economically and technically feasible;

(7) Increases the energy reliability, security and independence of the State; and

(8) Reduces the release of greenhouse gases.; and

(9) For an energy infrastructure proposal that is an electric transmission line, limits electromagnetic field levels and ensures the protection of the transmission and distribution system against damage from an electromagnetic pulse or a geomagnetic storm.

Sec. 4. 35-A MRSA §3131, sub-§1-B is enacted to read: Page 2 - **126LR0011(01)-1**

1-B. Electromagnetic pulse. "Electromagnetic pulse" means one or more pulses of electromagnetic energy capable of disabling, disrupting or destroying a transmission and distribution system.

Sec. 5. 35-A MRSA §3131, sub-§3-B is enacted to read:

3-B. Geomagnetic storm. "Geomagnetic storm" means a temporary disturbance of the Earth's magnetic field resulting from solar activity.

Sec. 6. 35-A MRSA §3132, sub-§2-C, as enacted by PL 2009, c. 309, §2, is amended to read:

2-C. Petition for approval of proposed transmission line. The petition for approval of the proposed transmission line must contain such information as the commission by rule prescribes, including, but not limited to:

A. A description of the effect of the proposed transmission line on public health and safety and scenic, historic, recreational and environmental values and of the proximity of the proposed transmission line to inhabited dwellings;

B. Justification for adoption of the route selected, including comparison with alternative routes that are environmentally, technically and economically practical; and

C. Results of an investigation of alternatives to construction of the proposed transmission line including energy conservation, distributed generation or load management.;

D. A description of the design measures to be used to protect the transmission and distribution system against damage from an electromagnetic pulse or a geomagnetic storm; and

E. A description of the design measures to be used to mitigate or minimize electromagnetic field levels of the transmission line.

Sec. 7. 35-A MRSA §3132, sub-§6, as repealed and replaced by PL 2011, c. 281, 26 §1, is amended to read:

6. Commission order; certificate of public convenience and necessity. In its order, the commission shall make specific findings with regard to the public need for the proposed transmission line. Except as provided in subsection 6-A for a high-impact electric transmission line, if the commission finds that a public need exists, it shall issue a certificate of public convenience and necessity for the transmission line. In determining public need, the commission shall, at a minimum, take into account economics, reliability, public health and safety, scenic, historic and recreational values, state renewable energy generation goals, the proximity of the proposed transmission line to inhabited dwellings, electromagnetic field levels, protections against damage from an electromagnetic pulse or geomagnetic storm and alternatives to construction of the transmission line, including energy conservation, distributed generation or load management. If the commission orders or allows the erection of the transmission line, the order is subject to all other provisions of law and the right of any other agency to approve the transmission line. The commission shall, as necessary and in accordance with subsections 7 and 8, consider the findings of the Department of Environmental Protection under Title 38, chapter 3, subchapter 1, article 6, with respect to the proposed transmission line and any modifications ordered by the Department of Environmental Protection to lessen the impact of the proposed transmission line on the environment. A person may submit a petition for and obtain approval of a proposed transmission line under this section before applying for approval under municipal ordinances adopted pursuant to Title 30-A, Part 2, Subpart 6-A; and Title 38, section 438-A and, except as provided in subsection 4, before identifying a specific route or route options for the proposed transmission line. Except as provided in subsection 4, the commission may not consider the petition insufficient for failure to provide identification of a route or route options for the proposed transmission line. The issuance of a certificate of public convenience and necessity establishes that, as of the date of issuance of the certificate, the decision by the person to erect or construct was prudent. At the time of its issuance of a certificate of public convenience and necessity, the commission shall send to each municipality through which a proposed corridor or corridors for a transmission line extends a separate notice that the issuance of the certificate does not override, supersede or otherwise affect municipal authority to regulate the siting of the proposed transmission line. The commission may deny a certificate of public convenience and necessity for a transmission line upon a finding that the transmission line is reasonably likely to adversely affect any transmission and distribution utility or its customers.

Sec. 8. 35-A MRSA §3132, sub-§§15 and 16 are enacted to read:

15. Rulemaking. The commission, in consultation with the Department of Environmental Protection, shall adopt rules to identify effective design measures for a transmission and distribution system to limit electromagnetic field levels and ensure the protection of the transmission and distribution system against damage from an electromagnetic pulse or a geomagnetic storm. The commission may include provisions in the rules that require a 3rd party to verify that the design measures are incorporated into the construction of a transmission line.

Rules adopted under this subsection are routine technical rules pursuant to Title 5, chapter 30 375, subchapter 2-A.

16. Penalties. The commission may impose penalties in accordance with section 32 1508-A if the design measures described under subsection 2-C are not incorporated into the construction of a transmission line.

Sec. 9. Implementation. The Public Utilities Commission shall adopt rules under the Maine Revised Statutes, Title 35-A, section 3132, subsection 15 within 6 months of the effective date of this Act. On the effective date of the adopted rules, notwithstanding any provision of law to the contrary, a person constructing a transmission line that has already been approved by the commission but has not yet been completed must incorporate design measures to protect the transmission and distribution system against damage from an electromagnetic pulse or a geomagnetic storm and mitigate or minimize the electromagnetic field levels of the transmission line.

STATE OF MAINE

**IN THE YEAR OF OUR LORD
TWO THOUSAND AND THIRTEEN**

H.P. 106-L.D. 131

Resolve, Directing the Public Utilities Commission To Examine Measures To Mitigate the Effects of Geomagnetic Disturbances and Electromagnetic Pulse on the State's Transmission System

Emergency preamble. Whereas, acts and resolves of the Legislature do not become effective until 90 days after adjournment unless enacted as emergencies, and

Whereas, the North American Electric Reliability Corporation has identified 2013 as a peak year of solar activity that could result in a geomagnetic disturbance, and

Whereas, the impact of a significant geomagnetic disturbance or electromagnetic pulse on the reliability of Maine's electric grid is unknown; and

Whereas, the Public Utilities Commission may be able to identify measures to protect Maine's electric grid through a focused examination; and

Whereas, in the judgment of the Legislature, these facts create an emergency within the meaning of the Constitution of Maine and require the following legislation as immediately necessary for the preservation of the public peace, health and safety; now, therefore, be it

Sec. 1. Examination of vulnerabilities and mitigation. Resolved: That the Public Utilities Commission shall examine the vulnerabilities of the State's transmission infrastructure to the potential negative impacts of a geomagnetic disturbance or electromagnetic pulse capable of disabling, disrupting or destroying a transmission and distribution system and identify potential mitigation measures. In its examination, the commission shall:

1. Identify the most vulnerable components of the State's transmission system;

2. Identify potential mitigation measures to decrease the negative impacts of a geomagnetic disturbance or electromagnetic pulse;

3. Estimate the costs of potential mitigation measures and develop options for low-cost, mid-cost, and high-cost measures;

4. Examine the positive and negative effects of adopting a policy to incorporate mitigation measures into the future construction of transmission lines and the positive and negative effects of retrofitting existing transmission lines;

5. Examine any potential effects of the State adopting a policy under subsection 4 on the regional transmission system;

6. Develop a time frame for the adoption of mitigation measures; and

7. Develop recommendations regarding the allocation of costs to mitigate the effects of geomagnetic disturbances or electromagnetic pulse on the State's transmission system and identify which costs, if any, should be the responsibility of shareholders or ratepayers; and be it further

Sec. 2. Monitor federal efforts regarding mitigation measures. Resolved:
That the Public Utilities Commission shall actively monitor the efforts by the Federal Energy Regulatory Commission, the North American Electric Reliability Corporation, ISO New England and other regional and federal organizations to develop reliability standards related to geomagnetic disturbances and electromagnetic pulse; and be it further

Sec. 3. Report. Resolved: That the Public Utilities Commission shall report the results of its examination required pursuant to section 1 and the progress of regional and national efforts to develop reliability standards under section 2 to the Joint Standing Committee on Energy, Utilities and Technology by January 20, 2014. The Joint Standing Committee on Energy, Utilities and Technology may submit a bill to the Second Regular Session of the 126th Legislature based on the report.

Emergency clause. In view of the emergency cited in the preamble, this legislation takes effect when approved.

REBUTTAL TO
PUBLIC UTILITIES COMMISSION REPORT
THAT RECOMMENDS DOING NOTHING
TO PROTECT
THE MAINE ELECTRIC GRID
FROM
ELECTROMAGNETIC PULSE (EMP)
AND OTHER THREATS

Dr. Peter Vincent Pry
Executive Director
Task Force on National and Homeland Security
December 10, 2013

The Public Utilities Commission (PUC) Report on protecting the Maine electric grid from natural and manmade EMP ignores the overwhelming preponderance of evidence, and the objective counsel of the Free World's foremost experts on EMP, who urge Maine to act now to protect its electric grid and the lives of its citizens from an EMP catastrophe. The PUC Report likewise ignores the sound judgment of the Maine Joint Energy Committee, the State House and Senate, whose Members voted unanimously or nearly unanimously to support Rep. Andrea Boland's Resolution for launching a State initiative to protect the Maine electric grid.

The Public Utilities Commission Report clearly is not fair and balanced, but slavishly seeks to advance the agenda of the electric power industry, ISO New England, and their national lobby the North American Electric Reliability Corporation (NERC). For five years, NERC has obstructed progress on protecting the national electric grid by buying influence with a few key members of the U.S. Congress. NERC and its allies in the electric power industry have successfully thwarted the will of the overwhelming majority in Congress who would support a GRID Act or SHIELD Act to protect the national electric grid--if the minions of NERC on key committees would allow these bills to come to the floor for a vote.

Now NERC and the electric power industry are determined to stop Maine from setting a good example for other States by launching an initiative requiring the protection of the Maine electric grid, as recommended in the Boland Resolution that passed the State legislature with near unanimity.

The Public Utilities Commission Report is little better than an act of ventriloquism by NERC and ISO New England. The Public Utilities Commission proves by publication of this Report that it is not truly an independent and objective actor, but a propagandist for ISO New England and the NERC.

The PUC Report does not deserve the dignity of a line-in line-out refutation since its authors have proven that they are indifferent to evidence and logic. **This rebuttal shall expose a few salient deficiencies as typical examples of why the PUC Report should not**

be trusted by the Maine Joint Energy Committee and State Legislature--who should ignore the PUC Report and act to protect the electric grid and people of Maine now.

Suppressing Public Commentary

The release of the Public Utilities Commission Report on the weekend of December 7, 2013, with a deadline for public commentary ending 11 days later on December 18, 2013, during the busy time just before the Christmas holidays, is transparently calculated to minimize opportunity for public scrutiny and comment.

Like a thief in the night, by allowing so little time to comment on their Report, the Public Utilities Commission hopes to steal from the People their opportunity to condemn the PUC Report and urge their State representatives to act now to protect both their electric grid and their lives.

Ironical and historically appropriate it is that the PUC Report became publicly available to critics over the weekend of December 7th--the anniversary of Pearl Harbor. The PUC Report is historically equivalent to the unwise counsel offered by those imprudent souls who, during the years before World War II, left the United States vulnerable to the surprise attack on Pearl Harbor on December 7th, 1941, and whose unpreparedness nearly enabled Imperial Japan and Nazi Germany to extinguish Freedom from the world.

Ambassador R. James Woolsey, former Director of the CIA, in his statement to the Public Utilities Commission warns that EMP is "the heavy artillery of cyber warfare" and urges the PUC to act now to protect the Maine electric grid--and thereby set a salutary example for the entire nation. The PUC Report chooses to ignore Ambassador Woolsey, and the testimony of many other senior statesmen and scientists of stellar reputation who have urged action now to protect the Maine grid.

Do Nothing PUC Report

Instead of heeding former CIA Director Woolsey, Ambassador Henry Cooper (former Director, Strategic Defense Initiative), Vice Admiral Robert Monroe (former Director, Defense Nuclear Agency), and many other senior statesmen and expert scientists--the PUC Report strongly suggests that Maine should do nothing, but wait and see if Washington and the NERC will act to protect the electric grid at the national level. The PUC Report concludes:

V. CONCLUSION

The material discussed in this report indicates that GIC, whether produced by GMD or EMP, presents a serious threat to the reliability of the bulk power system and thus to the ability of Maine's utilities to provide safe and reliable service. The comments also describe a variety of options for prevention and mitigation, some of which appear to be available at relatively modest costs. The comments also indicate, however, that federal and regional authorities with appropriate expertise and jurisdiction have been and are continuing to work to address the risks and consider the costs and benefits of mitigating the effects of GMD and EMP, and that there is a strong indication from those federal and regional authorities that coordination on a national and regional level in any prevention or mitigation efforts is vital due to the highly integrated nature of the bulk power system.

The last sentence above "...coordination on a national and regional level in any prevention or mitigation efforts is vital due to the highly integrated nature of the bulk power system" is nothing more than a talking point lifted directly from NERC lobbyists that is calculated to deter state and Federal authorities from doing anything to protect the grid from EMP. Since even the Federal Government, even if it had legal authority to protect the grid, cannot achieve coordination of EMP protection everywhere simultaneously "coordination on a national and regional level" becomes an excuse for doing nothing.

Arguing that everyone must be protected before anyone can be protected, or that everyone must agree that Maine can protect itself, is a formula for protecting no one.

Nor is it true that "federal and regional authorities with appropriate expertise and jurisdiction have been and are continuing to work to address the risks..." Copious evidence has been submitted to the Maine State Legislature and the Public Utilities Commission that ISO New England and NERC lack appropriate expertise on natural and nuclear EMP, and have been remiss in protecting Maine and the Nation from these catastrophic threats.

Indeed, testimony has been provided from independent observers who served on NERC's Geomagnetic Disturbance Task Force that NERC's work and published report is "junk science" that deliberately suppresses evidence, violates the rules of scientific inquiry and sound engineering practice. NERC continues to grossly underestimate the GMD threat and exaggerate the efficacy of "operational procedures" over technical hardening of the grid--the only realistic and workable solution.

The PUC Report makes much of the U.S. Federal Energy Commission (U.S. FERC) order to NERC to develop a plan to protect the national electric grid from geomagnetic disturbances (GMD or natural EMP). But the PUC Report makes no mention of the fact that the U.S. FERC order was imposed upon a resisting NERC, following a Technical Conference convened by U.S. FERC that demolished NERC's attempts to dismiss the threat from GMD.

The PUC Report Conclusion, quoted above, asserts that NERC and others are working to protect the national grid from both GMD and manmade EMP from nuclear and non-nuclear weapons. But this is untrue. NERC explicitly disavows any responsibility to protect the grid from manmade EMP, arguing that this is the job of the Department of Defense. Yet DOD has no jurisdiction or capability to protect the national grid from manmade EMP-- except by preventive war and missile defense, both highly unreliable solutions.

Even if NERC and ISO New England acted to protect the national electric grid from GMD tomorrow, grid vulnerability to nuclear EMP could still kill 9 of 10 Americans. Historically, NERC has failed to act expeditiously against any threat. After a falling tree branch caused the Great 2003 Northeast Blackout, NERC responded to U.S. FERC's order to develop an improved plan for "vegetation management" only after 10 years. After 5 years, NERC has still not developed a plan satisfactory to U.S. FERC to protect the national grid from cyber attacks.

If Maine waits for NERC and Washington to protect the national electric grid, Maine will wait forever, or until it is too late to save the people of Maine and lead the Nation to safety from an EMP catastrophe.

PUC Report Dishonest On EMP Preparedness Of NERC And Electric Utilities
The Public Utilities Commission Report "cherry picks" the evidence and propounds false arguments that the electric power industry, and their lobby the North American Electric Reliability Corporation (NERC), already have the EMP threat well in hand.

For example, the PUC Report quotes the National Oceanic Atmospheric Administration (NOAA) to credit the electric power industry with successfully using "operational procedures" to protect the electric grid from natural EMP generated by geomagnetic disturbances (GMD) caused by the Sun:

National Oceanic and Atmospheric Administration (NOAA) Technical Memorandum OAR SEC885 describes the performance of the United States based electric utilities during the 2003 Halloween Storm:

"Electrical companies took considerable efforts to prepare for and be aware of the storm onsets. Companies received the standard suite of geomagnetic storm watches, warnings and alerts, but SEC staff also supplemented standard support with several phone discussions. Preventive action helped to counter the GIC stresses that were observed. A representative from the North American Electric Reliability Council (NERC) commented: 'Although the bulk electric system was not significantly affected by the solar activity, some systems reported higher than normal GIC's that resulted in fluctuations in the output of some generating units, while the output of other units was reduced in response to the K-index forecast.' Responses to warnings included reducing system load, disconnecting system components, and postponing maintenance."

However, the National Oceanic Atmospheric Administration is not an agency having oversight authority or competence to assess the performance of the electric power industry or NERC. In fact, NOAA--whose expertise is monitoring solar storms and geomagnetic disturbances--has no independent means to objectively monitor and assess NERC and electric utility performance during the 2003 Halloween Storm, or during any other geomagnetic storm. The specific actions of the electric utilities, and the efficacy of such actions, are considered proprietary by NERC and the industry, are not a matter of public record, and typically are not known to NOAA or any other federal agency--including the U.S. Federal Energy Regulatory Commission.

In the quote above, NOAA is merely parroting what they were told by NERC about the electric power industry's allegedly exemplary performance during the 2003 Halloween Storm--and that this is so is self-evident within the quote itself, that cites NERC as the source of NOAA's opinion.

Thus, the PUC Report, either through ignorance or dishonesty, takes at face value NERC's assessment of its own performance during the 2003 Halloween Storm, and allows the electric power industry to grade itself. This point is crucial, as the PUC Report pretends that NERC and electric industry performance during the 2003 Halloween Storm is evidence that "operational procedures"--which NERC advocates instead of physically hardening the grid--are a realistic solution to the natural EMP threat from geomagnetic storms.

Nor does the PUC Report inform the reader that the National Oceanic and Atmospheric Administration is not an objective actor as regards the efficacy of "operational procedures" to protect the electric grid. NOAA's early warning to NERC and industry about solar flares and geo-storms is crucial to any success that might be realized by "operational procedures"--and is a chief justification for NOAA's budget. Indeed, NOAA and NASA both have billions of dollars at stake in satellites and programs to study space weather, in order to provide better early warning to NERC to protect the national electric grid by "operational procedures."

The bottom line is that there is no objective evidence the 2003 Halloween Storm posed a significant threat to the national electric grid, or that "operational procedures" contributed anything to protecting the grid. But the PUC Report tries hard to create the opposite impression.

So it is all the more shocking to find in the PUC Report that the very next paragraph treats the 1989 Hydro-Quebec Storm but briefly--and fails to draw the all too obvious conclusion that "operational procedures" do not work. The PUC Report admits that the 1989 Hydro-Quebec Storm was a disaster and caused significant damage to the grid, including the loss of an EHV transformer in the United States:

Another major GMD event in North America occurred in Quebec on March 13, 1989. This incident affected the Hydro Quebec (HQ) electric infrastructure and caused a widespread outage affecting nearly six million HQ customers for approximately nine hours. Additional damage was reported across North America, including damage to a 500 kV transformer at a nuclear facility in New Jersey. Other extra high voltage (EHV) electrical equipment in the United Kingdom was reportedly damaged as a result of the same solar storm.

One looks in vain for the PUC Report to do more than skim over the bare facts of the 1989 Hydro-Quebec Storm and draw a conclusion. **The conclusion reached by the Congressional EMP Commission, the Congressional Strategic Posture Commission, the National Academy of Sciences, the U.S. Department of Energy, and the U.S. Federal Energy Regulatory Commission is that "operational procedures" alone are insufficient to protect the grid. The 1989 Hydro-Quebec Storm proves that the grid must be hardened with some of the many technologies available.**

If the PUC Report was fair and balanced, and not shameless propaganda for the NERC viewpoint, it would say so too. Moreover, this would be a good place for an objective PUC Report to note that "operational procedures" are useless against nuclear and non-nuclear EMP attack, which would very likely occur with little or no warning.

The PUC Report, like the NERC, is so focused on natural EMP from geo-storms that its analysis frequently has amnesia about the manmade EMP threat. Yet manmade EMP is given equal weight to natural EMP in the Boland Resolution, which is supposed to be the subject of the PUC Report, not talking points provided by the NERC.

PUC Report Dishonest On The Necessity Of Federal Leadership
Perhaps the most egregious example of the PUC Report "cherry picking" the evidence to draw a false or misleading conclusion is its attempt to enlist the Congressional EMP Commission Report to counsel the State of Maine to do nothing to protect its electric grid, to "kick the can" upstairs to the Federal level. According to the PUC Report:

Report of the Commission to Assess the Threat to the United States from Electromagnetic Pulse, (EMP Report) April, 2008, at 45-46. The Report stresses the importance of a mitigation plan to be "jointly developed by the Federal Government and the electric power industry, instilled into systems operations, and practiced to maintain a ready capability to respond. It must also fully coordinated with interdependent infrastructures, owners and producers."

Moreover, the PUC Report quotes at length the Congressional EMP Commission Report to counsel the State of Maine that protecting the Maine electric grid is a Federal responsibility exclusively, belonging to the Department of Homeland Security:

The EMP Report concluded that the DHS has the responsibility and authority to coordinate responses to EMP attacks......"As a result of the formation of Department of Homeland Security (DHS) with its statutory charter for civilian matters, coupled with the nature of EMP derived from adversary activity, the Federal Government, acting through the Secretary of Homeland Security, has the responsibility and authority to assure the continuation of civilian U.S. society as it may be threatened through an EMP assault and other types of broad scale seriously damaging assaults on the electric power infrastructure and related systems.

It is vital that DHS, as early as practicable, make clear its authority and responsibility to respond to an EMP attack and delineate the responsibilities and functioning interfaces with all other governmental institutions with individual jurisdictions over the broad and diverse electric power system. This is necessary for private industry and individuals to act to carry out the necessary protections assigned to them and to sort out liability and funding responsibility. DHS particularly needs to interact with FERC, NERC, state regulatory bodies, other governmental institutions government facilities, such as independent power plants, to contribute their capability in a time of national need, yet not interfere with market creation and operation to the maximum extent practical. DHS, in carrying out its mission, must establish the methods and systems that allow it to know, on a continuous basis, the state of the infrastructure, its topology, and key elements. Testing standards and measurable improvement metrics should be defined as early as possible and kept up to date."

The PUC Report is grossly misleading in these citations of the EMP Commission Report, published 5 years ago   The EMP Commission was established to advise the Federal Government and the Congress on how to protect the Nation from EMP. So, of course, the recommendations of the EMP Commission in 2008 were aimed at the Federal Government and the Department of Homeland Security.

Unfortunately, after 2008 the EMP Commissioners, the Congress, and the Federal Government discovered that DHS and the U.S. FERC lack sufficient authority to implement the most important recommendations of the EMP Commission--because no one anticipated that the NERC would refuse to protect the national electric grid from EMP.

Congress has been trying to provide U.S. FERC with the necessary legal authority to compel NERC to protect the grid by the GRID Act and SHIELD Act. Lobbying by NERC has successfully thwarted these legislative initiatives for 5 years.

Today, the EMP Commissioners recognize that NERC has paralyzed progress on national EMP preparedness at the Federal level, and have wholeheartedly endorsed State initiatives to protect their grids. An entire book endorsed by the Congressional EMP Commission-- *Apocalypse Unknown: The Struggle To Protect America From An EMP Catastrophe*--was provided to the PUC informing them of EMP Commissioner support of State-led initiatives to protect their electric grids.

All of this history and the views of the EMP Commissioners supporting the Boland Resolution and urging Maine to protect its electric grid are ignored in the PUC Report.

Appended to the rebuttal of the PUC Report find a recent petition to the Maine State Legislature Joint Energy Committee supporting the Boland Resolution and urging Maine to proceed to harden its electric grid--regardless of objections by the PUC or NERC--signed by senior scientists and statesmen, including the foremost EMP experts in the Free World. First among these signatories is Dr. William R. Graham, Chairman of the Congressional EMP Commission.

Also conspicuous by its absence from the PUC Report is the number one recommendation of the EMP Commission Report, appearing immediately below the first paragraph quoted by the PUC Report, but apparently deliberately excluded by the PUC Report. **The primary EMP Commission Report recommendation for protecting the electric grid is: "1. Protect high-value assets through hardening." (p. 46).**

Also conspicuous by its absence from the PUC Report, located on the same page quoted from the EMP Commission Report, is the recommendation by the EMP Commission to protect the grid by creating EMP hardened "islands" especially in the Eastern Grid--which is exactly the objective of the Boland Resolution. The Boland Resolution would "island" the Maine grid to protect it from EMP, while still remaining connected to the regional grid, enjoying all the efficiencies and commercial advantages of such connectivity, without any of the vulnerabilities. This passage from the EMP Commission Report, ignored by the PUC Report, contradicts NERC assertions, prominently featured in the PUC Report, that EMP hardening the Maine grid would cause problems for Maine or neighboring States:

Separate the present interconnected systems particularly the Eastern Interconnection into several non-synchronous connected sub-regions or electrical islands. It is very important to protect the ability of the system to retain as much in operation as possible through reconfiguration particularly of the Eastern Connected System into a number of non-synchronous connected regions, so disruptions will not cascade beyond those EMP-disrupted areas. Basically, this means eliminating total NERC region service loss, while at the same time maintaining the present interconnection status and its inherent reliability and commercial elements. This is the most practical and easiest way to allow the system to break into islands of service and greatly enhance restoration timing...This is fiscally efficient and can leverage efforts to improve reliability and enhance security against the broad range of threats, not only EMP. It also can be beneficial to normal system reliability. (p. 46)

Note in the above quote from the EMP Commission Report, excluded from the PUC Report, that the 2008 EMP Commission Report endorses the Boland Resolution and hardening the Maine electric grid as "the most practical and easiest way to allow the system to break into islands of service and greatly enhance restoration timing."

Finally, one last example of the PUC Report's appalling misrepresentations is its lengthy quotation of Presidential Policy Directive 21 to imply that the State of Maine should do nothing to protect its grid, but "kick the can" upstairs to the Department of Homeland Security. Of course, the President expects DHS to take the lead on national cyber-security, and so PPD-21 is directed at DHS primarily. So Maine should do nothing to protect its grid from cyber and other threats unless specifically directed to do so by the President in a Presidential Policy Directive?

Conspicuous by its absence from the PUC Report is Presidential Policy Directive 8 titled *National Preparedness*. PPD-8 is the foundational presidential directive and provides context for understanding all subsequent presidential directives treating aspects of national preparedness, including PPD-21. The very first paragraph of PPD-8 *National Preparedness* calls upon "all levels of government, the private and nonprofit sectors, and individual citizens" to contribute to national preparedness:

This directive is aimed at strengthening the security and resilience of the United States through systematic preparation for the threats that pose the greatest risk to the security of the Nation, including acts of terrorism, cyber attacks, pandemics, and catastrophic natural disasters. Our national preparedness is the shared responsibility of all levels of government, the private and nonprofit sectors, and individual citizens. Everyone can contribute to safeguarding the Nation from harm.

PPD-8 is particularly concerned with protecting the critical infrastructures, especially the electric grid. **Why would the PUC Report exclude PPD-8, which is tantamount to a Presidential Directive calling upon the State of Maine to protect its electric grid?**

Conclusion

The PUC Report is erroneous and full of apparently deliberate misrepresentations of fact and evidence. Virtually every paragraph in the PUC Report designed to dissuade the State of Maine from protecting its electric grid and citizens, to instead wait for action from Washington, to instead trust NERC and the electric industry, can be deconstructed and exposed as poor reasoning or outright deception. **The few paragraphs critiqued here are representative of the PUC Report as a whole.**

The State of Maine and the Joint Energy Committee should ignore the PUC Report. Instead, heed the petition attached to this rebuttal from scientists and statesmen of historical reputation--all urging Maine to protect its electric grid now.

Attorney William Harris, a former senior manager of energy projects for the RAND Corporation and senior advisor to the Reagan Administration on national security issues, warns against waiting for Federal rescue of the Maine electric grid. Harris observes, "The Maine legislature needs to recognize that the states have opportunities to advance critical infrastructure reliability that is still lacking at the federal level." Harris:

...Federal efforts to provide cost-effective reliability standards are impaired by a bizarre regulatory system in which major electric utility firms, operating through NERC, have both the incentive and the opportunity to engage in risk-shifting to institutions in our society that lack the resources, the economies of scale, or the authority to implement sensible protections.

In contrast, the states have broad legal authority to utilize their police powers and their public utility statutes to set reliability standards, so long as these standards do not result in lesser reliability in other states. However, most of the state public utility commissions and state legislatures assume, incorrectly, that some combination of the Federal Energy Regulatory Commission and the Nuclear Regulatory Commission have the capacity to set needed standards. This assumption is incorrect....However, the present inability to develop a supporting federal & state regulatory system remains a barrier to protection of critical infrastructures. The Maine legislature needs to recognize that the states have opportunities to advance critical infrastructure reliability that is still lacking at the federal level.

Attached find a memo describing low-cost quick-fixes for the Maine electric grid that could be implemented immediately, and that would significantly improve grid resilience. Maine can and should do more than is described in the memo. **Prudence and wisdom dictates undertaking at least these modest measures for protecting the people of Maine and their electric grid from the existential threat that is EMP.**

Dr. Peter Vincent Pry is Executive Director of the Task Force on National and Homeland Security and the U.S. Nuclear Strategy Forum, both Congressional Advisory Boards, and served in the Congressional EMP Commission, the Congressional Strategic Posture Commission, the House Armed Services Committee, and the CIA.

V

VIRGINIA

State Senator Bryce Reeves

Summary

Senator Bryce Reeves introduced Senate Joint Resolution 61 "Directing the Joint Commission on Technology and Science to study strategies for preventing and mitigating potential damages caused by geomagnetic disturbances and electromagnetic pulses" in February 2014. All agencies of the Commonwealth of Virginia are to provide assistance to the Joint Commission upon request. The bill passed and has been signed into law by the Governor. By November 30, 2014, a report is to be delivered to the General Assembly making recommendations on how best to protect the Virginia electric grid and other critical infrastructures.

Senator Reeves' Narrative

I have a military background. Before being elected as a Senator in November 2011, I served as a Captain in the U.S. Army as an Airborne and Ranger qualified officer. I first heard about the threat from an electromagnetic pulse (EMP) at the U.S. Army War College, while attending a National Security Seminar. The course covered all of the weapons of mass destruction that terrorists could employ--nuclear, chemical biological.

There was a female professor named Dr. Biddle at the U.S. Army War College that taught this National Security Seminar that described how terrorists or a rogue state like Iran could use a nuclear EMP attack to plunge the entire nation into a protracted blackout. The consequences would be catastrophic for our society. Dr. Biddle made a big impression on me about this threat.

Subsequently, after my election to the Senate, my friend, Ambassador Henry Cooper (former Director of the Strategic Defense Initiative) and his son, Scott Cooper, both talked to me about protecting Virginia from a natural or nuclear EMP catastrophe.

In my role as a Virginia State Senator, I am still interested and have some responsibilities for homeland security and military affairs. For example, I am Co-Chair of the Military and Veterans Caucus. I am also involved in the Emergency Management and Assistance Compact (EMAC) that is an important part of Virginia's plan to protect and recover the State and its people from natural and manmade disasters.

The Virginia National Guard still has a long way to go to achieve EMP preparedness. The 116th Infantry Communications Unit has 3-4 mobile radio units that are EMP survivable. This is significant progress. Communications would be vital for recovery from an EMP, or any catastrophe.

Virginia plays an important role in the CAPITOL SHIELD exercise, that involves planning and training to protect the nation's capitol from foreign threats, including by evacuation to Northern Virginia. What happens if the nation's capitol in Washington, DC and Northern Virginia gets hit with an EMP? How are we to protect Northern Virginians and evacuate people from the capitol, perhaps 7 million people, in a protracted blackout?

Someone had to deal with this unaddressed threat. I decided to tackle EMP with my legislation.

Dominion Power, the main electric utility in Northern Virginia, has already done a lot to protect the grid from physical sabotage, like the sniper attacks that were made last year against transformers at the Metcalf substation outside San Jose, California. Dominion plans to spend millions to safeguard the Virginia electric grid against such threats.

My legislation to protect the Virginia electric grid from EMP is not intended to over-regulate Dominion Power or Appalachian Power or the other electric utilities. The plan is to work with the utilities. The plan is to bring in outside experts on EMP and grid hardening to help them, and not to second guess them.

The independent experts and the utilities should work together and row in the same direction--toward making the Virginia electric grid survivable through an EMP.

The Virginia EMP legislation is part of a bigger picture. Right now, the nation is waiting for Congress to act, to pass a bill to protect the national electric grid. But it isn't happening. The people of Virginia don't want to have to just hunker down in their houses waiting for Congress. The States can and should protect their people from EMP.

Hopefully, EMP protection initiatives at the State level will filter back up to the Federal level, and perhaps eventually result in some leadership from Washington on protecting the whole nation.

My strategy for passing the Virginia EMP bill was to build consensus and avoid partisan politics. Over the years, I have successfully passed 43 bills using this formula. Politics is like a mold in your shower--to be avoided.

Your job as a legislator is to work with your colleagues to address their concerns, to get the bill right, while not compromising away the purpose or effectiveness of the bill. Make sure the bill stays whole. Make sure the bill, once passed, will accomplish your intent.

Do not use the bill to grand stand or engage in partisan politics. My EMP bill is designed to find out the facts about Virginia's vulnerability to EMP. Where are the problems in the Virginia electric grid? What are the technical solutions and the range of options for fixing the problem? How much will it cost?

Anyone can understand these reasonable purposes. Working with my colleagues, educating them on the EMP threat and how my bill is designed to address the threat, helped build their confidence, win their trust, and persuaded them to support the bill.

I serve on the General Laws and Technology Committee, but not on the Finance Committee. The EMP bill had to go through the Finance Committee in order to pay for it. Several colleagues on the Finance Committee knew me and understood the importance of my bill because I went through the process described above to explain it to them and earn their trust.

Conservatives see EMP as a larger national security issue, and it is, and some use the threat to score partisan political points. My bill passed, in part, because I did not use the EMP issue for political grandstanding and partisan purposes.

I stuck to the data and the facts about the EMP threat and did not attempt to demonize anyone. I explained the threat in concrete terms that anyone can understand.

For example, earlier I had persuaded colleagues on the Finance Committee to appropriate money to prepare Virginia to cope with dangerous chemical spills that might occur from a train derailment. There was, in fact, a potentially dangerous situation with a train hauling chemical tanks cars through a minority neighborhood. That is a specific actionable item that everyone on the Finance Committee could understand.

So I explained the EMP threat in terms everyone could understand, as a specific actionable item, as an opportunity for the State of Virginia to do the right thing for its citizens.

The challenge for the policymaker is to make EMP real to his colleagues and to citizens. Everyone has experienced blackouts, so you can extrapolate from blackouts caused by snowstorms what an EMP catastrophe would be like. Most people remember Hurricane Katrina and the disastrous aftermath of New Orleans trying to live and slowly recover for weeks afterwards without electricity. This experience too can be equated to an EMP.

National Geographic made a docudrama, *American Blackout*, that realistically depicts the consequences of a nationwide blackout lasting ten days. This makes the idea of an EMP catastrophe more accessible and understandable to the average person.

People can also understand life insurance. They can understand, when the facts are explained to them in a reasonable way, that preparedness against an EMP catastrophe is like life insurance--it is just reasonable and prudent to be prepared.

This approach won broad support for my EMP bill. Senator Dave Marsten, my democrat colleague, supported the bill on the floor of the Assembly. It passed unanimously.

Pry's Postscript
Virginia is the first state in the nation to harden its electric grid from natural and manmade EMP. At the annual meeting of the Electric Infrastructure Security Council in Washington, DC, on July 21, 2015, Dominion Power, the chief electric utility for the state of Virginia, briefed the measures currently underway in Virginia to harden the Virginia electric grid from natural, nuclear, and non-nuclear EMP. The briefing provided technical detail on some of the measures being undertaken, including photographs of the work in progress, that included burying cables underground in trays protected from EMP, and the use of faraday cages to protect SCADAS, faraday screens to protect entire buildings. Dominion Power says it is also taking other measures that it will not publicly disclose for security reasons. Dominion Power acknowledges that they are EMP hardening the Virginia electric grid due to the legislation of Senator Bryce Reeves.

Thus, while Washington has passed no legislation to protect the national electric grid from EMP after seven (7) years of trying, Virginia's legislative initiative has commenced the EMP hardening of its state power grid in less than two (2) years.

2014 SESSION
INTRODUCED
14100988D
SENATE JOINT RESOLUTION NO. 61
Offered January 8, 2014
Prefiled January 7, 2014
Directing the Joint Commission on Technology and Science to study strategies for preventing and mitigating potential damages caused by geomagnetic disturbances and electromagnetic pulses.
Report.

Patron—Reeves

Referred to Committee on Rules

WHEREAS, geomagnetic disturbances and electromagnetic pulses have the capability of producing significant damage to the Commonwealth's infrastructure and electronic equipment; and

WHEREAS, the Commonwealth's vulnerability to such threats is increasing daily through heightened use of and dependence on electronic equipment; and

WHEREAS, the Joint Commission on Technology and Science may be able to identify measures to protect the Commonwealth's infrastructure through focused examination; now, therefore, be it

RESOLVED by the Senate, the House of Delegates concurring, That the Joint Commission on Technology and Science be directed to study strategies for preventing and mitigating potential damages caused by geomagnetic disturbances and electromagnetic pulses. In conducting its study, the Joint Commission on Technology and Science shall (i) study the nature and magnitude of potential threats to the Commonwealth caused by geomagnetic disturbances and electromagnetic pulses; (ii) examine the Commonwealth's vulnerabilities to the potential negative impacts of geomagnetic disturbances and electromagnetic pulses; (iii) identify strategies to prevent and mitigate the effects of geomagnetic disturbances and electromagnetic pulses on the Commonwealth's infrastructure; (iv) estimate the feasibility and costs of such preventative and mitigation measures; and (v) make recommendations regarding strategies the Commonwealth should employ to better protect itself from and mitigate damages caused by geomagnetic disturbances and electromagnetic pulses.

All agencies of the Commonwealth shall provide assistance to the Joint Commission on Technology and Science for this study, upon request.

The Joint Commission on Technology and Science shall complete its meetings by November 30, 2014, and the Chairman shall submit to the Division of Legislative Automated Systems an executive summary of its findings and recommendations no later than the first day of the 2015 Regular Session of the General Assembly. The executive summary shall state whether the Joint Commission on Technology and Science intends to submit to the General Assembly and the Governor a report of its findings and recommendations for publication as a House or Senate document. The executive summary and report shall be submitted as provided in the procedures of the Division of Legislative Automated Systems for the processing of legislative documents and reports and shall be posted on the General Assembly's website.

VI

ARIZONA

State Senator David Farnsworth

Summary
Senator David Farnsworth introduced Senate Bill 1476 "Electromagnetic Pulse Preparedness: Recommendations" on March 6, 2014. The bill passed the Arizona Senate 24-3 and Governor Jan Brewer signed it into law. SB-1476 requires Arizona's division of emergency management to develop preparedness recommendations for the general public on how to survive a natural or nuclear electromagnetic pulse catastrophe. Another bill is in preparation to protect the Arizona electric power grid.

Senator Farnsworth's Narrative
My first encounter with the idea of electromagnetic pulse (EMP) was in the science fiction novel *Time Storm 2012* by an author who happens to have the same last name as me, my sister, Juliann Farnsworth. This was later re-published as *Time Storm Shockwave*.

The novel made me more aware of and curious about EMP. I started paying more attention to news stories, magazine articles, and books about the real phenomenology and science of the EMP threat. I started storing this information and mulling it over in my mind.

On Saturday, April 16, 2005, U.S. Senator Jon Kyl (R-AZ) published an article in the Washington Post warning that natural EMP from the Sun or a nuclear EMP attack from terrorists or rogue states could blackout the national electric grid for a protracted period, causing millions of Americans to starve to death.

Senator Kyl is a highly credible source. He has long been a leader in the U.S. Senate and the nation on nuclear strategy and national security. His article had a huge impact on me. Kyl was warning that terrorists, armed with a single nuclear weapon, could destroy our entire nation with an EMP attack. This is an unprecedented existential threat to our nation.

When I first read Senator Kyl's article on EMP, I felt the chill of fear. And I am not a fearful person because I have prepared to care for my family in most emergencies. I moved my family to Snowflake, Arizona, in part because it is an area where we could better survive a national catastrophe.

I still have Senator Kyl's Washington Post article taped to the wall of my office.

I started asking myself, "As an Arizona State Senator, do I have a responsibility to do something about the EMP threat?"

A Duty To Protect
I am a member of the Church of the Latter Day Saints, a Mormon. Our religion teaches that someone who sees an imminent challenge oncoming, like recurrence of the Great Depression of the 1930s, has a responsibility to prepare. The Great Depression was a catastrophe for millions of people. Those who lived through it became what we would today call "survivalists."

The generation of the Great Depression tended to be better prepared for disaster than people today. For example, they would stockpile food, because hunger was commonplace during the Great Depression.

I personally have stockpiled enough wheat and other foodstuffs to last over 30 years.

I am 63 years old, and in the course of my life have seen many changes in our society. Our society has become increasingly dependent on technology and complex civilian critical infrastructures, to the point that most Americans cannot survive without them.

In America, our grocery stores always have an abundant supply of food. As a people, we are accustomed to that abundance. But I lived in Guatemala and El Salvador for two years, doing missionary work for the LDS Church. In those countries, their markets sometimes had no food or very little.

Once, during the 1960s, there was a blizzard in Arizona that caused a food shortage in grocery stores. There was no food in the stores. Trucks could not get in to resupply the markets.

Ezra Taft, President Eisenhower's Secretary of Agriculture, said that storing food and emergency preparedness is as vital today as it was in the time of Noah.

Senator Kyl's 2005 article in the Washington Post indicates that the preparedness of individuals, families and communities to survive through a catastrophe remains as important as ever, perhaps even more important because of the looming EMP threat. In the aftermath of an EMP catastrophe, Senator Kyl writes, "Those who survive would be transported back to the United States of the 1880s."

By that Kyl means that EMP would wipe-out modern technology and collapse the modern critical infrastructures--communications, transportation, business and finance, food and water--that Americans depend upon to survive. The technological level of our society would return to the horse and buggy days.

But it would be worse than that.

If we lost all electricity, we would be worse off than in the 1880s--because there are no 19th century critical infrastructures anymore. There are no horse and buggies. There are no coal-fired trains or railroads capable of running without electricity. There are no means of growing, transporting, and distributing food to feed our population without electricity.

Moreover, an EMP would occur in a flash, at the speed of light. Suddenly, millions of Americans would find themselves stranded, cut off from their families, with no phone, no car. How can I contact my wife and kids? How do I get home to be with them? Walk 35 miles?

I personally am prepared, am self-sufficient, and don't fear life. But most Americans are utterly dependent on modern technology. I would survive. But many Americans would not.

Our nation has been visited by catastrophic food shortages before. Our generation did not experience the Great Depression. However, our parents did, and we learned their stories.

Now we face something far worse than the Great Depression--an EMP catastrophe. Sitting in the chamber of the Arizona Senate, I decided that I did have a responsibility to prepare the people of my State to survive.

Prepare People First

I pondered deeply on what to do. I thought about trying to protect the electric grid to survive an EMP. But I concluded that the politics of trying to achieve grid protection would be uncertain of success and would probably take a long time to accomplish, if politically possible at all.

Why did I not start by trying to protect the electric grid from EMP, as they are trying to do at the federal level in Washington, D.C.?

I noted that in the U.S. Congress, Rep. Trent Franks, who is from Arizona, has been trying to pass a bill called the SHIELD Act, that would protect the national electric grid from EMP. Lobbyists from the electric power industry have prevented passage of the SHIELD Act for years.

Arizona is probably even more susceptible to outside influence and lobbying than the U.S. Congress. Since Arizona became a State in 1912, much of Arizona's land, including portions crossed by the electric grid, has been given away to the federal government and is under federal jurisdiction. So Arizona may not have jurisdiction over parts of its own electric grid.

Moreover, the Arizona Constitution is easily changed by moneyed interests who want to block legislation or to mandate spending tax dollars on pet projects. Any citizen can bring forward an initiative to change the Arizona Constitution.

These factors would make passing legislation to protect the Arizona electric grid, and financing that project, an extremely difficult challenge.

And we may not have a long time to prepare for an EMP catastrophe. The Sun could hurl at us a geomagnetic super-storm, like the 1859 Carrington Event, tomorrow. Tomorrow, terrorists or an unpredictable rogue state like North Korea could make an EMP attack.

I decided that, as an Arizona State Senator, my first and highest priority should be to advance EMP preparedness among the people of my State by educating them about the threat and enabling them to grow and store their own food supply, so that they would not starve to death.

My strategy for preparing Arizona for a catastrophic EMP event, instead of focusing on big government and the big utilities, focuses on the people of Arizona first. People have more common sense than government. My first priority is to give the people a chance to prepare themselves for an EMP by being able to feed their families.

The Home Grown Freedom Act SB-1151

Shortly after becoming a Senator, an acquaintance of mine, Galen Luth, explained that the people of Arizona were being prevented from raising food on their own property by the law. I discovered that there are many illegal "backyard farms" in Arizona. Never before had I heard that term--"backyard farm"--and did not know that this lifestyle, traditional since pioneer days, was now illegal.

Government and Home Owner Association restrictions on backyard farming are an impediment to EMP preparedness by the people. People have been farming their backyards since before there was a State of Arizona in order to survive.

Galen gave me a tour of an illegal backyard farm, located in Chandler, Arizona. The owner's name is Donna. She has a lovely, immaculate home. Donna's farming includes raising goats, rabbits, and chickens. Her neighbors do not mind and did not report Donna's illegal activity.

All laws are not sacred. Lawbreaking may be justified because a law is bad and should be changed. Backyard farming is illegal because of deed restrictions imposed by Home Owner's Association regulations.

Over the years regulations and deed restrictions have become increasingly onerous impositions on owner's property rights. People can be fined because of the color of their house or because their grass is too tall. In one case, a person was fined $25 dollars because a tomato plant grew six inches taller than their wall.

I told Galen Luth that we had to organize the backyard farmers so they could become a political force to defend their interests. Galen started on FaceBook a new organization--Backyard Farmers United--that started with 100 members. Now it has over 1,000 members.

Donna and Galen started holding small meetings of backyard farmers. I would meet with groups of 17 people at one meeting, 47 people at another.

I tried to begin legalizing backyard farming with a bill--the Home Grown Freedom Act--that included permitting the raising of backyard poultry. I knew this would make me the object of political ridicule, and it did. A local radio station, 550 AM, delights in lampooning Arizona politicians, and lost no time in re-naming the Home Grown Freedom Act as the "Chicken Bill" accompanied with clucking and cackling sound effects.

To increase the chance for passage of the Home Grown Freedom Act, I divided it into two bills. One bill would lift restrictions imposed on backyard farming by the Home Owners Association. The other bill would reduce restrictions imposed by municipalities.

I thought dividing into two bills would increase the chances that one would pass. The lobby for the Home Owners Association is very powerful. I hoped their opposition to backyard farming might be lessened if one bill did not target their regulatory power.

In the end, I did not even introduce the bill that tried to override opposition to backyard farming by the Home Owners Association. Their lobby proved to be just too powerful.

The other version of the Home Grown Freedom Act passed the Senate with near unanimity--only one vote opposed. Unfortunately, in the House, the League of Cities lobbied against the bill, because it would stop municipalities from outlawing backyard farming. This carried Democrats in the House away from the bill, despite overwhelming support by Democrats in the Senate.

So the Home Grown Freedom Act failed to pass, leaving the people of Arizona more vulnerable to an EMP catastrophe.

The EMP Preparedness Act SB-1476

My bill Electromagnetic Pulse Preparedness: Recommendations (SB-1476) passed the Arizona Senate by near unanimity (24-3) and passed the House. It was signed by Governor Jan Brewer, and is now the law.

The Arizona Capitol Times lampooned me for the EMP bill with a cartoon. I had the cartoon turned into a poster.

I regard this bill as a version of the Home Grown Freedom Act as both bills have as their purpose saving the lives of the people by empowering them to prepare for an EMP catastrophe. The EMP Preparedness Act educates the people about the threat and warns them to prepare by being able to feed themselves and be self-sufficient in other ways.

Realistically, I do not think the U.S. Department of Homeland Security or the U.S. Federal Emergency Management Agency are prepared or have the resources to rescue the American people from a major EMP event. Even if the U.S. Congress eventually passes the SHIELD Act, I doubt the electric utilities will act in time to protect themselves and the people from the catastrophic consequences of an EMP.

Our first responsibility must be to warn the people, to give them the information they need to prepare to save themselves.

This is the purpose of the EMP Preparedness Act. The Act requires Arizona's Department of Emergency and Military Affairs (DEMA) to educate the people about the EMP threat, including by posting information on their website, and to make recommendations on how to prepare to survive. For example, DEMA has to inform individuals and families how to stockpile food and water, and how to meet their other survival needs, like having a medical kit and knowing how to use it.

The first obligation of government is to tell the truth to the people, and not pretend that the government is prepared to save them from an EMP.

One important factor accounting for my success in passing the EMP Preparedness Act deserves mention here. On arriving in the Senate, I tried hard to get to know personally every member of the Arizona Senate and House.

I purchased a book with biographies on all the Senators and Representatives. I tried to meet with them all face-to-face. Meetings with every one of them were scheduled, sometimes at 15-minute intervals, for five days a week.

There are 30 Senators and 60 House members, or 90 in all. I did not succeed in meeting all of them, but did become acquainted with probably about 70. The House members were not accustomed to Senators like myself reaching out to meet them, as the Senate in Arizona, like in the U.S. Capitol, has a reputation for being elitist.

Not very long after introducing the EMP Preparedness Act, I had at least a dozen co-sponsors. Getting to know my colleagues personally, and personally meeting with them to discuss the EMP bill, definitely helped.

Lori Frantzve and Larry Guinta played an important role in passage of the EMP bill. Lori is President and CEO of Az-Tech International, a firm that designs micro-grids that are survivable against EMP, and has done EMP work for the U.S. Department of Energy. Larry is her lieutenant.

Lori and Larry had a short video describing an EMP event and its catastrophic consequences for national survival. We had a breakfast for the legislators to see the video and be briefed on the EMP threat and on my bill.

The EMP video was dramatic and made a striking impression. One of the attendees said, "Any American who sees that video clip will want to support your bill." Among the attendees who supported my bill was the President of the Senate. Indeed, everyone who came to the breakfast and saw the video ended up voting for the EMP bill.

Lori and Larry and their educational video were probably the decisive factor in passing the EMP Preparedness Act.

Tactically, having a working breakfast or a working lunch is a great way to educate legislators on EMP, or on any issue. People outside the legislature do not understand that their Senators and Representatives really are very hard working. They do not have a lot of time to spare, so you often have the best chance to get on their schedule for breakfast or lunch. Even then, it is advisable to frequently remind them and their schedulers to keep their breakfast or lunch appointment.

Roadblock

One significant roadblock to the EMP Preparedness Act was Rep. Bob Robson, Chairman of the Rules Committee, who sat on the bill, and would not let it come up for a vote in the House. But Galen Luth and I rallied the backyard farmers to press Rep. Robson to allow a vote on the EMP bill.

Congressman Trent Franks called Robson and helped break lose the bill, which passed the House.

After the EMP preparedness bill passed the Senate and House, I thought Governor Jan Brewer would veto it. The Department of Emergency and Military Affairs officially opposed the bill. They thought the bill preempted their authority and compelled them to do something they did not want to do.

Although they would not admit it, DEMA probably did not want to implicitly acknowledge that they are unprepared to rescue the people of Arizona from an EMP.

I personally met with DEMA to ask them not to oppose the bill, and to explain its necessity. Again, Galen Luth and the backyard farmers came to the rescue. They called and wrote Governor Brewer, asking her to sign the bill.

Again, Congressman Trent Franks came to the rescue too. He asked Governor Brewer to sign the bill. And she did.

Lesson Learned

I learned some lessons from working on the EMP Preparedness Act and achieving its passage that may be useful to legislators in other states.

I tried to meet with every Senator and House member to ask if they had any questions or concerns, and if they would support the bill? That personal effort, and the personal relationship forged by a face-to-face meeting, I think was very significant in winning broad support for the EMP Preparedness Act. .

As I said earlier, the educational video on EMP was probably the decisive factor in the bill passing through the Senate and House. If I did it all over again, I would start promoting the bill to my colleagues as early as possible. I would have had working breakfasts earlier to show the EMP video to as many legislators as possible.

I also would have met with DEMA earlier to educate them on the necessity of the EMP bill. I should have shown them the EMP video early-on, and had them read Senator Jon Kyl's article warning about the EMP threat.

I would strongly advise legislators in other States trying to pass a bill to protect their people from EMP--keep your bill simple. My EMP Preparedness Act is very short and simple deliberately.

Legislators will not pass a bill that they do not understand. The longer and more complex the bill, the less likely it will pass.

My philosophy is to make progress in baby steps. For example, in the 1990s, Arizona outlawed anyone from buying and selling more than 3 cars yearly without a dealer's license, whereas previously the law allowed selling up to 6 cars yearly without a dealer's license.

So in 2014, I successfully passed a bill to go back to allowing the sale of up to 6 cars yearly without a license. The auto dealers decided not to oppose this modest bill, because they have bigger fish to fry. But this small change in the law represents a big rollback of government over-regulation, and a significant restoration of property rights to the people.

As to the next step toward greater EMP preparedness in Arizona, right now I have no definite plans. Lori and Larry, who were so helpful in passing the EMP bill, think we should next try to protect the Arizona electric grid. They have great hopes that Senator Don Shooter, Chairman of the Appropriations Committee in the Arizona legislature, will provide funding to protect the State grid from EMP.

But I am skeptical. Next year may be too early for such an ambitious project, with all the attendant political impediments that I described earlier. We need to build more support and build a consensus in Arizona for protecting the electric grid. I am a big believer in masterminding problems.

We need to get Congressman Franks and other experts in a meeting to work out a master plan for protecting Arizona from EMP.

I am an optimist by nature. But I am not optimistic that we can prepare sufficiently to save everyone's life from an EMP catastrophe. If all of us put forth a monumental effort, we can save many, many lives.

I am not optimistic that the government will act, or act in time, to save the people from the EMP threat. For example, DEMA's response to my legislation was disappointing. DEMA is supposed to have the lead in protecting the people of Arizona--and they did not even want to tell the truth to the people about EMP. And at the federal level in Washington, the President has not acted. Nor has the U.S. Congress acted.

The people themselves have become too dependent on government. Too many have their hands out for government largess. Too many have a false consciousness that government will always be there to take care of them and to save them from anything.

However, the numbers of "preppers" and "survivalists" are growing by leaps and bounds. There is hope that the old fashioned virtues of self-reliance and rugged individualism may once again become normative. Historically, Americans have been a resilient people.

The only way to get government to act as it must to prepare for the EMP threat is through individual awareness. When enough people know about the EMP threat, there will be a critical mass to move the politicians to action. In the meantime, preparedness of individuals and families must come first.

Every person that we warn is potentially a person that we save.

Lori Frantzve and Larry Guinta's Narrative

LORI: I worked for General Electric for 17 years in the 1970s, under Jack Walsh, doing educational and technical marketing. GE sent me into mines to figure out how to provide them with lighting systems that would not fail in that challenging environment. I worked with jet engine engineers and learned how to tear down and reassemble aircraft engines.

EMP first came to my attention in the 1980s, when I was working for GE. There I learned that EMP could cause an airplane to crash. Later, I learned a lot more about EMP when I did contract work for the U.S. Government on protecting the 13 critical infrastructures.

I left GE because they would not let women sell aircraft engines.

I worked in Europe for six years in the telecommunications industry on cybersecurity.

In 2003, I founded AZ-Tech, and am today the President of this firm. Larry and I and our colleagues at AZ-Tech do counterterrorism assessments and evaluate the vulnerability of critical infrastructures to various hazards.

In 2011, AZ-Tech developed for the U.S. Department of Energy an Electrical Emergency Plan that became the "poster-child plan" for protecting and recovering electric power systems. Later, we worked for the State of Maine, through the Governor's Office, on their Emergency Preparedness and Energy Assurance Plan.

We are excited about a new microgrid technology developed by AZ-Tech that we think is a partial answer to the EMP threat.

LARRY: I have a BA degree in Industrial Technology and Mechanical Engineering. My focus has been on designing and building and automated engineering.

I worked on medical technology, and led a team of 12 people. One problem was working on specialized control systems that had to continue operating in hazardous environments. I also worked for McDonnell Douglas in technical sales.

Lori and I teamed together in 1994 to develop the Scientific Assessment Technology, which we patented. This is the first methodology to use algorithms to calculate risks from any threat using automated software.

In 2003, we started doing assessments for the Department of Defense on critical infrastructure protection. DOD asked us to look at the threat to critical infrastructures from EMP.

I first heard about EMP during the 1980s, and didn't know much. But I learned a lot more from the DOD project. From our 2004 Defense Department project, we learned that people might know how to spell EMP, but nothing else.

Our nation is not at all prepared for an EMP event.

LORI and LARRY: Congressman Trent Franks, who is the national leader on EMP preparedness and is from Arizona, is a frequent visitor to AZ-Tech. Rep. Franks has toured our facility in Scottsdale and is familiar with our work. As an electrical engineer himself, Rep. Franks is particularly impressed with our Genesis microgrid project as a means of restoring electric power to critical nodes after an EMP event.

Helping Senator Farnsworth

We received a call from Rep. Franks telling us that Arizona State Senator David Farnsworth needed our help to advance his bill to educate and protect the people of Arizona from an EMP catastrophe.

Our first meeting with Senator Farnsworth was on February 21, 2014. We met in our Scottsdale facility, which has a big screen projector and excellent audio-visual equipment for briefings. The facility has a big room, a high-tech auditorium, that we use for training and exercises, simulating crises. It looks like North American Aerospace Defense (NORAD) headquarters.

Also present was Wendy Smith Reeves from Arizona's Department of Emergency and Military Affairs (DEMA). Senator Farnsworth hoped DEMA would support his bill.

We showed them the excellent National Geographic documentary "Electronic Armageddon" which National Geographic describes as "a briefing for Presidents" on the threat from natural and nuclear EMP. It is really excellent. The documentary, about 45 minutes long without commercials, is a first rate tutorial on the science of EMP and the catastrophic impact on the electric grid and other critical infrastructures--all explained in layman's terms and with graphics and imagery that anyone can understand.

Senator Farnsworth challenged us to build a 5-minute video on EMP to educate the Arizona State Legislature. We did. Not only did we successfully edit down "Electronic Armageddon" to 5 minutes, but we improved upon it with a second short video made by borrowing the best bits and pieces from other documentaries and interviews on EMP.

EMP for Breakfast

Our original plan was to bring every member of the Arizona Senate and House here, to our Scottsdale facility, to see our video briefings on EMP. But that proved impractical.

Instead, we moved our operation to the Capitol. Senator Farnsworth arranged a room and advertised weekly breakfasts for all Senators, Representatives and their staffs to see the videos.

We first showed the videos at the first breakfast on February 28, 2014. We ran both videos repeatedly at each breakfast, the room being open to all comers from 8:00-10:30 AM. We continued the EMP breakfasts for two months, trying to reach every member.

We ourselves did not offer a formal briefing at the breakfasts, but let the videos do the talking. The videos are like getting a short tutorial on EMP taught by our nation's top experts, like Dr. William Graham, Chairman of the EMP Commission, and Dr. Peter Vincent Pry. Dr. Pry also works with Congressman Franks and both are very supportive of efforts to protect the States from EMP, as in Arizona.

At the video breakfasts, we were there as subject matter experts to answer questions.

Results

The videos clearly made a huge impression. We got a lot of questions, mostly about practical personal matters, like: "Will I lose my cell phone? Will my car start? Will a cell phone survive if wrapped in aluminum foil? Will unplugging appliances save them?"

Young staffers in particular were alarmed that their cell phones would not work.

Others were quicker on the uptake, quicker to realize the implications of an EMP catastrophe: "I didn't realize airplanes could fall from the sky! How do first responders respond to a crashed airplane, rescue survivors, fight fires, when nothing works? Oh my God, I hadn't thought of that! This thing could kill me!"

Everyone--you could see it in their faces and hear it in the tone of their voices--even if it was not reflected in their questions, was grappling with the dawning realization that EMP is a game changer. For the first time everyone was realizing a protracted blackout lasting weeks, months, or years could happen--and would change everything.

They were learning about a new version of the Apocalypse that they had never seen before. Several State Representatives commented that EMP does not care about your political party--for everyone it would be a bipartisan catastrophe.

Senator Don Shooter, Chairman of the Appropriations Committee, after watching the videos dragged us out into the hall and started quizzing us about how to protect the State of Arizona. Senator Shooter, perhaps the most powerful member of the Arizona Senate, then and now thinks the Farnsworth bill does not go far enough.

Much to his credit, at that very moment, Senator Shooter started planning to do more, to protect the Arizona electric grid and other critical infrastructures from EMP.

Everyone who attended the breakfasts and saw the videos voted for Senator Farnsworth's EMP bill, SB-1476. On April 16, 2014, the bill passed almost unanimously, with just one abstention. Less than ten days later, on April 25 2014, Governor Jan Brewer signed SB-1476 into law.

*****

Senate Bill 1476 "Electromagnetic Pulse Preparedness: Recommendations"

SB 1476

Be it enacted by the Legislature of the State of Arizona:
Section 1. Title 26, chapter 2, article 1, Arizona Revised Statutes,
is amended by adding section 26-305.03, to read:
26-305.03. Electromagnetic pulse preparedness recommendations;
posting

THE DIVISION SHALL DEVELOP PREPAREDNESS RECOMMENDATIONS FOR THE PUBLIC REGARDING THE TYPE AND QUANTITY OF SUPPLIES, INCLUDING FOOD, WATER AND MEDICAL SUPPLIES, THAT EACH PERSON IN THIS STATE SHOULD POSSESS IN PREPARATION FOR AN ELECTROMAGNETIC PULSE THAT MIGHT OCCUR OVER THE UNITED STATES. THE DIVISION SHALL POST THE PREPAREDNESS RECOMMENDATIONS ON ITS WEBSITE.

VII

FLORIDA

State Representative Michelle Rehwinkel Vasilinda

Summary

Representative Michelle Rehwinkel Vasilinda in 2014 introduced several innovative initiatives to advance EMP preparedness in Florida.

Most promising is a petition to Florida's Governor Rick Scott to invoke his emergency powers to direct the utilities and relevant State agencies to protect the Florida electric power grid (petition appended to this chapter). This is a new pathway toward national EMP preparedness, as all State governors have authority under their emergency powers and responsibility for homeland security to undertake extraordinary measures to protect the people.

Chapter IX includes a generic Executive Order that could be issued by any governor to protect the electric power grid in their State.

Representative Rehwinkel Vasilinda also proposed a directive to the Florida congressional delegation to proactively support efforts at the federal level in Washington to protect the national electric grid, including by urging action by the White House and U.S. Department of Homeland Security (bill appended to this chapter).

Representative Rehwinkel Vasilinda also innovated another new way to advance EMP preparedness--by amending the charter of the Florida Division of Emergency Management to protect and recover Florida from an EMP catastrophe (bill appended to this chapter). Although this would not directly protect the Florida grid, it would mobilize the considerable resources of State emergency planners and providers, including police and fire departments and hospitals, to be prepared for an EMP.

Since EMP preparedness would be greatly facilitated by an electric grid resistant to EMP effects, the bill would have the practical effect of enlisting emergency planners and first responders on the side of EMP protection for the grid. Every State has an emergency management agency or agencies that would benefit greatly from legislation for EMP preparedness.

Representative Rehwinkel Vasilinda

During the summer of 2013, Florida State Representative Michelle Rehwinkel Vasilinda was among those at the meeting of the National Conference of State Legislatures in Atlanta, Georgia who attended briefings on the EMP threat. Briefings on EMP and solutions were given by a panel comprising Maine State Representative Andrea Boland; Dr. George Baker of the Task Force on National and Homeland Security, who also served on the Congressional EMP Commission; and Dr. Peter Vincent Pry, Executive Director of the Task Force on National and Homeland Security who served on the EMP Commission.

Rep. Boland appealed to legislators from other States to protect their electric grids and people from EMP, as her State of Maine is in the process of doing--the first State in the Union to do so--because of legislation she sponsored. Rep. Boland and the experts on her panel explained to the National Conference of State Legislatures that it is technically and legally possible to "island" the electric grid within a State, to protect its vital components like EHV transformers and generators, and to "harden" the grid against EMP on a cost-effective basis.

EMP protection of a State grid would not interfere with the normal day-to-day operations of electric power transmission. Blocking devices, surge arrestors, faraday cages and other technologies for protecting the grid are passive defenses. They would block EMP from entering the electric system or from damaging crucial components. But EMP protection would in no way interfere with or make less efficient normal electric transmission-- including the import or export of electric power from neighboring States.

EMP protection of the electric grid would also mitigate all other threats, including cyber attack, sabotage, and severe weather.

Rep. Rehwinkel Vasilinda and Dr. Pry talked at length in a private conversation about how "islanding" the electric grid within a State would also benefit neighboring States. If one State within a larger regional electric grid survives an EMP or other disaster, it would become significantly easier to "bring the lights back on" in neighboring States that are in blackout. A "Black Start"--trying to recover an electric grid in complete blackout--would be the most difficult challenge, has never been planned for or exercised on a national scale, and may not even be possible.

A Leader at the NCSL

At a second EMP briefing for the National Conference of State Legislatures, given that evening, Rep. Michelle Rehwinkel Vasilinda publicly endorsed the recommendations of the panel, agreeing with the experts that natural and nuclear EMP constituted an existential threat to the United States. She pledged that she would introduce legislation to protect the electric grid in the State of Florida.

She proved better than her word.

In 2014 State Rep. Michelle Rehwinkel Vasilinda proposed several initiatives to protect the nation and the State of Florida from an EMP catastrophe, more than any other State Legislator. Moreover, her initiatives are uniquely bold and ingenious, pioneering new pathways to achieve EMP preparedness that could serve as models for other States. Unfortunately, none of these initiatives were allowed a hearing or a vote.

Characteristic of Rep. Rehwinkel Vasilinda's legislative initiatives is that they seek "the biggest bang for the buck" by using relatively modest legislative vehicles, that should be easy to pass, that would greatly increase EMP preparedness if enacted.

The EMP "Memorial"

Her first EMP legislative initiative attempted to advance national EMP preparedness through a "Memorial" proposed to the Local and Federal Affairs Committee, Florida House of Representatives. A Memorial in the Florida House is similar to a "Sense of the Congress" in the U.S. Congress in lacking the binding authority of law, but nonetheless being the official view of the Florida State Legislature, just as a Sense of Congress is the official view of the U.S. Congress.

Rep. Rehwinkel Vasilinda's EMP Memorial would have sent a loud and clear message from the State of Florida to the President, the Department of Homeland Security, the U.S.

Congress, and the Florida congressional delegation to protect the nation from an EMP catastrophe. Her entire Memorial is shown later in this chapter, but the heart is reproduced below:

NOW, THEREFORE,
Be It Resolved by the Legislature of the State of Florida:
That the United States Congress is urged to direct the Secretary of the United States
Department of Homeland Security to request needed resources to:
(1) Protect and recover from the impacts of serious electromagnetic pulse threats and
geomagnetic storms in the United States; and
(2) Assure Congress and the American people that plans, resources, and implementing
structures are in place to accomplish these objectives, specifically with respect to the
electromagnetic pulse threat and the threat of geomagnetic storms.
BE IT FURTHER RESOLVED that copies of this memorial be dispatched to the President
of the United States, to the Secretary of the United States Department of Homeland
Security, to the President of the United States Senate, to the Speaker of the United States
House of Representatives, and to each member of the Florida delegation to the United
States Congress.

Amending the FDEM Charter

Next, Rep. Rehwinkel Vasilinda proposed an amendment to law describing the duties of the Florida Division of Emergency Management (FDEM) that would have made mandatory that FDEM educate and prepare the people of Florida for an EMP catastrophe and "convene an annual conference to assess and promote the State's preparedness against electromagnetic pulse attacks and geomagnetic storm events."

Thus, her amendment to the Florida Division of Emergency Management would in a few paragraphs legally require the State of Florida to protect itself and its citizens from an EMP event, and to continually improve EMP preparedness plans. Her entire amendment is shown later in this chapter, but the most important provision, making mandatory that the Florida Division of Emergency Management prepare for an EMP event, is below:

Section 10. Electromagnetic pulse attacks and geomagnetic storm events.—
(1)(a) The Legislature finds that it is in the public interest to include defense against
electromagnetic pulse attacks and geomagnetic storm events in its preparedness planning
because such attacks and events lie within the full range of risks, threats, and hazards
confronting the state and are areas of vital concern with regard to the state's energy policy
and emergency and disaster preparedness.

Part of the genius of Rep. Rehwinkel Vasilinda's legislative strategy is that, typically, it is much easier to amend existing legislation, in this case the legislative charter of the Florida Division of Emergency Management, than to pass an entirely new stand-alone bill with the objective of protecting Florida from EMP. Such a bill of necessity would probably be very large and complicated and much less likely to pass than a simple amendment.

Further, her amendment, by requiring the Florida Division of Emergency Management to hold an annual conference on EMP, would both ensure that FDEM develops expertise on EMP and do so in a way attractive to the Agency. Most government agencies welcome the opportunity to hold conferences. So this provision gave FDEM an incentive to support the amendment.

The "Memorial" and FDEM Amendment Fail

Unfortunately, neither the Memorial or the amendment were given a formal hearing or a vote.

Both were "a bridge too far" for a Florida House that was largely ignorant of the EMP threat. Aside from one or two briefings to one committee, most Florida legislators had no acquaintance with EMP and received no opportunity to vote on the Memorial and the amendment.

Rep. Rehwinkel Vasilinda carried on the crusade for EMP preparedness in the State of Florida largely alone. The national EMP preparedness movement, such as it is, let her down. There were too few experts and not enough resources to adequately support all the several States with EMP initiatives during the same legislative season.

If, for example, the Task Force on National and Homeland Security was able to provide the same kind of support to Rep. Rehwinkel Vasilinda in Florida that was provided to Rep. Andrea Boland in Maine, at least one and perhaps both of the Florida EMP initiatives probably would have passed.

Despite these disappointments, Rep. Rehwinkel Vasilinda tried again with another new idea.

EMP Executive Order

At her request, Dr. Peter Vincent Pry, Executive Director of the Task Force on National and Homeland Security, drafted a petition to Florida Governor Rick Scott. The petition asked Governor Scott to use his emergency powers to order Florida utilities and regulatory agencies to protect the Florida electric grid from an EMP catastrophe.

The petition notes that looming threats from nuclear terrorism and from an inevitable geomagnetic super-storm constitute an emergency warranting that Governor Scott issue an executive order to protect the Florida grid and Floridians from an EMP event. The petition is signed by prominent scientific and national security experts. Among the signatories: Dr. William Graham (President Reagan's Science Advisor, Administrator of NASA, and Chairman of the Congressional EMP Commission); Ambassador R. James Woolsey (former Director of Central Intelligence); Ambassador Henry Cooper (former Director of the Strategic Defense Initiative); Vice Admiral Robert Monroe (former Director of the U.S. Defense Nuclear Agency) and others, led by Rep. Michelle Rehwinkel Vasilinda herself, who has a good working relationship with Governor Scott.

The full petition is reproduced later in this chapter.

Perhaps "the third time is the charm." Governor Scott responded positively to the petition. The Governor ordered the Director of the Florida Division of Emergency Management, Bryan Koon, to meet with Rep. Rehwinkel Vasilinda to discuss the EMP threat. Books by the Task Force on National and Homeland Security, providing in depth analysis of the EMP threat and options for protecting electric grids and other critical infrastructures, were provided to the Governor and the Florida Division of Emergency Management.

On July 22, 2014, Rep. Rehwinkel Vasilinda brought Dr. Pry into a teleconference with Director Koon and his staff to discuss in greater technical detail the EMP threat and how to protect Florida. Director Koon agreed to recommend to Governor Scott the formation of a

Florida EMP Task Force--comprising the utilities, regulatory agencies, and independent experts--to assess the vulnerability of the Florida electric grid and propose cost-effective options for its protection.

This is the first time that a State has attempted to advance EMP preparedness through the executive authority of the Governor--and the results so far appear very promising. This strategy, pioneered by Rep. Rehwinkel Vasilinda in Florida, is appropriate to the emergency represented by the existential threat that is EMP. Bypassing the long and cumbersome legislative process, Governors may by their emergency powers be able to achieve EMP protection much faster.

Pry's Postscript

On April 13, 2015, the Florida State Legislature convened the first hearing before the newly established Cyber and EMP Legislative Working Group--the brainchild of Rep. Rehwinkel Vasilinda supported by Governor Scott. Testifying before the Working Group were Bryan Koon (Director of the Florida Division of Emergency Management), Ambassador R. James Woolsey (former Director of Central Intelligence), Frank Gaffney (President of the Center for Security Policy), Dr. Alberto Ramirez Orquin (President of Resilient Grids), and Dr. Peter Vincent Pry (Executive Director of the Task Force on National and Homeland Security). The event received heavy media attention in the State of Florida.

The purpose of the Cyber and EMP Legislative Working Group is to investigate and assess cost-effective options for protecting the Florida electric grid from Cyber and EMP threats for action by the legislature or the governor.

EMP PREPAREDNESS PETITION TO GOVERNOR SCOTT

The Honorable Rick Scott
Governor of Florida
The Capitol
400 South Monroe Street
Tallahassee, Florida 32399-0001

Dear Governor Scott:

We the undersigned entreat you to use your emergency powers to require all regulated utility companies in Florida (including but not limited to Florida Power & Light and Progress Energy), as well as all non-regulated utility companies and electric cooperatives, to implement protections that would safeguard Florida's electric grid from the catastrophic consequences of cyber attacks, physical sabotage, and natural or manmade electromagnetic pulse (EMP) that could plunge the State of Florida into a protracted blackout potentially lasting weeks or months.
All of these threats are a clear and present danger to the State of Florida that warrants an emergency response.

Every day, electric utilities and other critical infrastructures nationwide are barraged with hundreds of computer viruses and hacking attempts to breach their security. The U.S. Department of Homeland Security warns that, sooner or later, one of these cyber attacks will succeed in causing a state-wide or even a nation-wide blackout--unless the electric grid is protected.

On April 16, 2013, saboteurs using AK-47s, the favorite assault rifle of terrorists and rogue states, attacked the Metcalf transformer substation near San Jose, California, in what the U.S. Navy SEALS described as a highly professional military operation. The attack nearly caused a protracted blackout of the Silicon Valley, and could have triggered cascading grid failures that would have left much of the west coast in the dark.

Jon Wellinghoff, former Chairman of the U.S. Federal Energy Regulatory Commission (FERC), and other experts describe Metcalf as a terrorist attack--and as a probable dry run for a larger and more ambitious attack on the national electric grid. According to a study by the U.S. FERC, Metcalf style sabotage of just nine key transformer substations could blackout the national grid for months.

The most serious threat is electromagnetic pulse or EMP, that can be likened to a super-energetic radio wave that can disrupt and destroy electronics and potentially cause a protracted blackout across the entire continental United States lasting months or years.

Catastrophic natural EMP can be caused by the sun, by a solar flare that generates a rare geomagnetic super-storm, like the 1859 Carrington Event or the 1921 Railroad Storm. The National Academy of Sciences estimates that, if the 1921 Railroad Storm recurred today, given the current unpreparedness of the grid, a nationwide blackout would result lasting 4-10 years. The Congressional EMP Commission estimates that, if the 1859 Carrington Event (ten times more powerful than the Railroad Storm) recurred today, electric grids would collapse worldwide and the lives of billions would be at risk.

Most scientists assess the world is overdue for the recurrence of another Carrington Event. The National Intelligence Council, that speaks for the entire U.S. intelligence community, in its unclassified National Intelligence Estimate *Global Trends 2030* warns that, by or before 2030, recurrence of a Carrington-class geomagnetic super-storm is one of only eight "Black Swan" events that could change the course of global civilization.

Nuclear EMP attack--the detonation of a nuclear weapon lofted by balloon or missile over the United States to high-altitude (30-300 kilometers)--could cause even deeper and longer lasting damage to the electric grid than natural EMP from a Carrington Event.

The Congressional EMP Commission found that Iran wants the bomb so that it can make a nuclear EMP attack that would eliminate the United States as an actor from the world stage. Iranian open source military writings describe making an EMP attack on the United States. Iran has conducted missile exercises practicing the high-altitude detonation of a weapon consistent with EMP attack-- including launching a missile from a freighter, so an EMP attack could be launched from near the U.S. coast, executed anonymously to escape retaliation.

Beginning last February, the Iranian Revolutionary Guard Navy has commenced patrols of the U.S. Atlantic seaboard. Of particular interest to Floridians, these vessels could enter the Gulf of Mexico, where they might launch ballistic missiles against which we are currently undefended, to create an EMP over the entire continental U.S. And Iran is working with Venezuela which also could pose a threat to the south.

The Congressional EMP Commission also found that North Korea, China, and Russia all currently have contingency plans and the capability to make a nuclear EMP attack against the United States. Indeed, during the April 16, 2013, attack on the Metcalf transformers in California--which occurred amidst threats from North Korea to make a nuclear missile strike on the United States--North Korea's KSM-3 satellite was over the Washington, D.C.-New York City corridor, at the optimum altitude and location for an EMP attack that would black out the Eastern Grid, that generates 75 percent of electricity in the United States.

The Congressional EMP Commission, former CIA Director R. James Woolsey in congressional testimony, and the U.S. Army War College study *In The Dark,* all warn that an all-out Cyber Warfare Operation by Iran, North Korea, China, or Russia would not be limited to computer viruses and hacking--but would include Metcalf style sabotage and nuclear EMP attack. Their military doctrines for Cyber Warfare advocate a combined arms offensive utilizing computer bugs, physical sabotage, and EMP.

Therefore, the electric grid must be protected against all of these threats. **Protecting against the worst case threat--nuclear EMP attack--will mitigate all lesser threats, and will also improve grid resilience against more pedestrian hazards, such as tropical storms and hurricanes.**

Unfortunately, the Federal Government in Washington is so broken that lobbying by the electric power industry has prevented the passage of bills, such as the GRID Act and SHIELD Act, designed to protect the national electric grid, despite these bills enjoying broad bipartisan support.

States such as Maine, Virginia, and Arizona have successfully passed legislative initiatives to protect their State electric grids from EMP and other threats. Although most States are part of a larger regional grid, it is technically possible to "island" a State electric grid by using surge arrestors, blocking devices and other technologies to passively protect the grid. Such technical hardening does not interfere with the normal operations of the grid, but will protect the grid from an EMP or other threats when needed.

Governor Scott, please use your emergency powers under statute 252.44 (appended) to order all of Florida's utility companies and electric cooperatives, along with the relevant state agencies, to implement protections of the Florida grid against nuclear EMP attack and the other threats described here. Since the North American Electric Reliability Corporation (NERC) has been a major obstacle to advancing grid security, we ask that these protections be implemented in consultation with independent experts--such as the Task Force on National and Homeland Security and the EMP Coalition, who will provide their services pro bono.

For your further information, enclosed you will find a DVD that has a tutorial on the EMP threat and includes studies by two Congressional Commissions--the EMP Commission and the Strategic Posture Commission--and several other major U.S. Government studies, all warning that the electric grid must be protected to avoid catastrophic consequences. Also enclosed find a book, *Apocalypse Unknown: The Struggle To Protect America From An Electromagnetic Pulse Catastrophe,* that describes the sad history and current status of failed efforts to protect the grid in Washington, the role of NERC in thwarting these efforts, and several cost-effective plans for protecting electric grids.

Governor Scott, the Congressional EMP Commission warns that, if the grid is not protected, within one year of an EMP event that causes a protracted nationwide blackout, up to 9 of 10 Americans could perish from starvation, disease, and societal collapse.

Yet there is no excuse for the Florida grid to be vulnerable to EMP. The Congressional EMP Commission made recommendations for protecting the electric grid at reasonable cost using proven technologies.

Moreover, EMP preparedness would likely be an economic boon to Florida. International businesses and many departments and agencies of the U.S. government will want to re-locate in Florida when it can offer energy security and critical infrastructure resiliency almost unique in the United States and the world.

Cyber and EMP preparedness are the defense industries of the future. The technical expertise and knowledge that will be acquired by Florida firms in the process of protecting the grid is a highly valuable commodity that will be marketable to other states and nations.

Very Respectfully,

State Representative Michelle Rehwinkel Vasilinda (HD 9) has introduced a Memorial in the Florida House of Representatives urging the Florida congressional delegation to support the SHIELD Act and the Critical Infrastructure Protection Act and to demarche the White House and the Department of Homeland Security on grid protection.

Dr. William R. Graham was President Reagan's Science Advisor, Administrator of NASA, Chairman of the Congressional EMP Commission, and on the defense science team that first discovered EMP in the 1962 STARFISH nuclear test.

R. James Woolsey was Director of Central Intelligence and the CIA, Ambassador and Delegate to U.S.-Soviet nuclear and conventional treaty negotiations, and Under Secretary of the Navy.

Ambassador Henry Cooper is Chairman of High Frontier, was Director of the Strategic Defense Initiative, Assistant Director of the U.S. Arms Control and Disarmament Agency, and Ambassador to U.S.-Soviet space treaty negotiations.

VADM Robert Monroe was Director of the U.S. Defense Nuclear Agency, responsible for protecting U.S. military systems from EMP and other nuclear effects, Director of Navy Systems Analysis, and commanded the U.S. Atlantic Fleet.

Fritz Ermarth served as Special Assistant to President Ronald Reagan, Chairman of the National Intelligence Council that drafts National Intelligence, and is among the strategic thinkers who guided the U.S. to victory over the USSR in the Cold War.

Jack Caravelli served in the White House, National Security Council, advising President William Clinton on nonproliferation in Russia and the Middle East, was a Deputy Secretary of Energy working on nuclear nonproliferation, and served in the CIA.

Fred Celec was Assistant to the Secretary of Defense for Nuclear, Chemical, and Biological Defense Programs under both the Bush and Obama administrations.

Dr. William Radasky is President of Metatech, holds the Lord Kelvin Medal for Electromagnetic Protection Standards, is Chairman of SC 77C (EMP and EM protection) for the International Electrotechnical Commission, and has EMP hardened power grids.

Dr. George Baker is a Professor at James Madison University, was Principal Scientist for EMP at the Defense Nuclear Agency, a Director of Research at the Defense Threat Reduction Agency, and served on the Congressional EMP Commission.

Bronius Cikotas was the Principal Scientist for EMP at the U.S. Defense Information Systems Agency, "Father" of the Ground Wave Emergency Network for U.S. strategic nuclear forces survivable communications.

John Kappenman is President of Storm Analysis Consultants, the nation's foremost expert on the effects of geomagnetic storms on power grids.

David Trachtenberg served President George W. Bush as a Principal Deputy Assistant Secretary of Defense, in the Congressional EMP Commission, on the House Armed Services Committee, and as Vice President for Homeland Security at National Security Research.

Brigadier General (USA retired) Ken Chrosniak is on the faculty of the U.S. Army War College, worked for the Joint Chiefs of Staff, won the Bronze Star and Combat Action Badge in Iraq, and is a volunteer firefighter.

Professor Cynthia E. Ayers is a 40 year veteran of the National Security Agency, an expert on cyber security and counterterrorism, a Professor for 8 years at the U.S. Army War College, and serves on the Task Force on National and Homeland.

Frank Gaffney is Founder of Secure the Grid, an alliance of groups to protect the national power grid, is President and CEO of the Center for Security Policy, served President Reagan as an Assistant Secretary of Defense, and is one of the nation's foremost national security experts.

Dr. Peter Vincent Pry is Executive Director of the Task Force on National and Homeland Security, served on the Congressional EMP Commission, the Congressional Strategic Posture Commission, the House Armed Services Committee, and the CIA.

FLORIDA HOUSE OF REPRESENTATIVES

House Memorial
A memorial to the Congress of the United States, urging Congress to direct the Secretary of the Department of Homeland Security to request needed resources to protect and recover from the impacts of serious electromagnetic pulse threats and geomagnetic storms.

WHEREAS, geomagnetic storms are natural phenomena involving disturbances in the earth's geomagnetic field caused by solar activity, and

WHEREAS, disruptions of electrical power caused by geomagnetic storms, such as the collapse of Quebec Hydro grid during the geomagnetic storm of 1989, have occurred many times in the past, and

WHEREAS, the Congressionally mandated Commission to Assess the Threat to the United States from Electromagnetic Pulse Attack found, in its report delivered July 2004, that an enemy using a low-yield nuclear weapon detonated at a high altitude above the United States could make an electromagnetic pulse attack against the United States, and that an electromagnetic pulse attack has the potential to place our society at risk and to defeat our military forces, and

WHEREAS, Congress has commissioned other numerous hearings and reports on this issue, including, the House National Security Committee hearing on the EMP Threat, 1997; the House Military Research and Development Subcommittee hearing on the threat to the United States of potential EMP attacks, 1999; the creation of the Commission to Assess the Threat to the United States from Electromagnetic Pulse Attack, 2001; the congressional commission report, "Critical National Infrastructures," 2008; the United States Navy Naval Sea Systems Command EMP program, 2010; the North American Electric Reliability Corporation/Department of Energy report, "High-Impact, Low-Frequency Event Risk to the North American Bulk Power System," 2010; and the Department of Homeland Security testimony to a House Committee on Homeland Security, "The Electromagnetic Pulse (EMP) Threat: Examining the Consequences," 2012, and

WHEREAS, in April 2013, an electrical substation in San Jose, California, was attacked with gunfire, leaving transformers disabled for nearly four weeks in an apparent attempt to disrupt power to Silicon Valley, raising questions about the vulnerability of power grids across the United States,

NOW, THEREFORE,
Be It Resolved by the Legislature of the State of Florida:

That the United States Congress is urged to direct the Secretary of the United States Department of Homeland Security to request needed resources to:
(1) Protect and recover from the impacts of serious electromagnetic pulse threats and geomagnetic storms in the United States; and
(2) Assure Congress and the American people that plans, resources, and implementing structures are in place to accomplish these objectives, specifically with respect to the electromagnetic pulse threat and the threat of geomagnetic storms.

BE IT FURTHER RESOLVED that copies of this memorial be dispatched to the President of the United States, to the Secretary of the United States Department of Homeland Security, to the President of the United States Senate, to the Speaker of the United States House of Representatives, and to each member of the Florida delegation to the United States Congress.

Amendment No. 070707
Approved For Filing: 4/23/2014 1:46:12 PM Page 1 of 3

CHAMBER ACTION
Senate House

Representative Rehwinkel Vasilinda offered the following:

Amendment (with title amendment)
Between lines 353 and 354, insert:

Section 10. Electromagnetic pulse attacks and geomagnetic storm events.—
(1)(a) The Legislature finds that it is in the public interest to include defense against electromagnetic pulse attacks and geomagnetic storm events in its preparedness planning because such attacks and events lie within the full range of risks, threats, and hazards confronting the state and are areas of vital concern with regard to the state's energy policy and emergency and disaster preparedness.
(b) The Legislature finds that it is in the public interest to educate Floridians about the threat of electromagnetic pulse attacks because such attacks could cause massive loss of electric power and disruption to telecommunications and other vital services, including health, safety, food, and transportation services, which depend on reliable electric power.
(c) The Legislature further finds that it is in the public interest to encourage municipalities and private industry to educate themselves on the consequences of electromagnetic pulse attacks and geomagnetic storms, to examine critical vulnerabilities in their infrastructures, and to prepare for massive disruptions that could be caused by electromagnetic pulse attacks and geomagnetic storms.
(2) The Office of Energy within the Department of Agriculture and Consumer Services, in coordination with other relevant agencies and stakeholders identified by the department, shall develop preparedness recommendations for the public regarding the type and quantity of supplies, including food, water, and medical supplies, that each person in the state should possess in preparation for an electromagnetic pulse attack or geomagnetic storm event. The preparedness recommendations shall be posted on the Division of Emergency Management's website. The division, in coordination with the department, shall convene an annual conference to assess and promote the state's preparedness against electromagnetic pulse attacks and geomagnetic storm events.
Between lines 34 and 35, insert:
providing legislative findings with regard to preparedness against electromagnetic pulse attacks and geomagnetic storm events; directing the Office of Energy within the department, in coordination with other relevant agencies and stakeholders, to develop preparedness recommendations for the public; requiring that such recommendations be posted on the Division of Emergency Management's website; directing the division, in coordination with the department, to convene an annual conference to assess and promote the state's preparedness against electromagnetic pulse attacks and geomagnetic storm events;

VIII

OKLAHOMA

State Senator Ralph Shortey
and
Michael Hoehn

Summary

State Senator Ralph Shortey and public advocate Michael Hoehn partnered to introduce a bill to the Oklahoma State Legislature requiring a public referendum on protecting the Oklahoma electric grid from EMP. The bill is appended to this chapter.

Their innovative legislation, the first of its kind, would put the average voter in the driver's seat with a "Yes" or "No" vote to protect the Oklahoma grid, to be paid for with a rate increase. The vote would also trigger a directive to the Oklahoma utilities to protect their electric grid assets to standards set by independent experts, including the Department of Defense EMP hardening standard used for military forces. This would prevent the utilities from "low balling" the threat and inventing other excuses to do nothing.

The idea of a public referendum is very promising as recent polling indicates there is broad and growing awareness among the American people about the EMP threat, as well as sharply increased concern about national security. Grassroots support for EMP preparedness through a popular referendum could achieve rapid progress by bulldozing lobbyists and their political allies out of the way.

Unfortunately, the people of Oklahoma never got to vote on EMP preparedness. Lobbying by the utilities and the North American Electric Reliability Corporation defeated Senator Shortey's bill for a popular referendum. Appended to this chapter is an example of the disinformation used by lobbyists to defeat the bill.

Nonetheless, the bill and lessons learned by Senator Shortey and Michael Hoehn, light the way forward for other States. And Shortey and Hoehn will try again to protect Oklahoma from a catastrophic blackout

Senator Shortey and Michael Hoehn's Narrative

Our goal in Oklahoma is to pass legislation requiring public utilities to harden their transformers and install shunts on the power lines coming into their plants. In order to circumvent the opposition we have seen previously from the utilities and the regulators, part of our legislation was to put a State Question on the ballot this year (2014) to let the voters decide whether they want to pay a one-time charge for this initiative in order to protect their families from an EMP event.

With the structure we already have in place, the organization upon which we can call and the groundwork that has already been laid, Oklahoma is uniquely situated to enact a legislative model to serve as an example for other States. We have a Counterterrorism Caucus in the Oklahoma legislature that is willing to take the lead and several of the Counterterrorism Caucus leaders have been briefed on the EMP threat and our legislative solution.

In addition, we have several grass roots organizations with which we can work to help us publicize the issues. Further, we have been in contact with Governor Mary Fallin's office and have found some members of her cabinet with whom we can work.

In short, we have the basic pieces in place to move forward immediately. Unfortunately, our first attempt to pass an EMP initiative to protect the electric grid in Oklahoma failed.

Educating Oklahoma on EMP

We briefed key leaders in the Oklahoma legislature about the threat of EMP and on our plan to address the problem. Mike Hoehn spent considerable time working with our Counterterrorism Caucus and community leaders pitching and refining our plan based on their feedback and input.

Moreover, at least one national security expert came from Washington, D.C. to Oklahoma to give several briefings on EMP, both public and private. Frank Gaffney, President of the Washington-based Center for Security Policy, personally laid out the nature and extent of the EMP threat. He made a big impression.

We held a planning session with legislative and community leaders, members of the Governor's cabinet, regulators and representatives of the public utilities. Our goal was to get everyone around a conference table for a briefing about the threat and a discussion with leading scientists and national security experts about some of the issues involved in addressing the EMP threat.

For the planning session, we had everyone from Oklahoma around a table in a room. We brought in the experts, who were mostly located in Washington, D.C., by Skype to brief us by videoconference and teleconference.

Among the experts was Ambassador R. James Woolsey, former Director of the CIA; Frank Gaffney; Thomas Popik of the Foundation for Resilient Societies and also a member of the Task Force on National and Homeland Security; Dr. George Baker of the Task Force who also served on the Congressional EMP Commission; and Dr. Peter Vincent Pry, Executive Director of the Task Force on National and Homeland Security who served on the EMP Commission.

The planning session went very well. The experts established that EMP is a clear and present danger, and that cost-effective protection of the Oklahoma electric grid is realistic and necessary. Although the public utilities and regulators may not have wanted to do anything, they raised no objections and offered no good arguments for inaction. We gave them an opportunity to disagree with the experts, to prove them wrong, but the utilities and regulators remained silent.

Senate Bill 2016

We filed Senate Bill 2016, a bill for a popular referendum on protecting the Oklahoma electric grid from EMP, on December 20, 2013.

Senator Ralph Shortey, the sponsor of SB 2016, briefed the bill in all its particulars to the Senate Republican Caucus. He thought he had enough votes to pass the bill. And SB 2016 did pass both the Senate and House energy committees, which is excellent. This usually means a bill will pass the full Senate and House.

Surprisingly, when Senator Shortey brought SB 2016 to the Senate floor, it was defeated on the first vote.

Senator Shortey later brought SB 2016 up again on a Motion to Reconsider. Before the vote, the Senate broke for dinner. Our polling of the members indicated we had more than enough votes before dinner.

However, after the Senate returned from dinner to vote--SB 2016 lost again.

Lessons Learned

Later, we learned that the public utilities lobbied against SB 2016, raising two false arguments, one of which defeated the bill.

The first argument was that EMP protection of the grid is not necessary because the threat is unlikely and the utilities are already prepared for anything. The legislators, on the whole, did not buy this argument.

The second argument by the lobbyists was that the cost of EMP protection would be outrageously high, unaffordable for Oklahoma. Their argument was weak. But we are not EMP experts and could not credibly respond to their technical arguments with hard and fast answers.

None of our EMP experts was personally present in Oklahoma to be on hand to defend SB 2016. They were all in Washington, D.C. or elsewhere, not even in the same time zone as Oklahoma. This proved a fatal flaw in our plans for SB 2016.

We lost round one on SB 2016, but we are not defeated. The Senators want more information, more definitive answers, regarding the costs of EMP protection. Consequently, we are going to do a Joint Senate-House Interim Study before the next session.

That is where we are now in Oklahoma.

Adam Smith said that the first responsibility of a sovereign is to protect its citizens. But our federal government has failed us. Our best hope is to go to the States and empower them to protect their people.

The plan we propose is the best. Our plan is clear, realistic and achievable. Most importantly, our plan relies upon the voters. We can bypass the bureaucrats and the public utilities. If the federal government will not protect Oklahoma, we will go directly to, "We the people."

What we do in Oklahoma can serve as a template for the rest of the country. That is our rally cry. In a very real sense, Oklahoma can lead the way for the rest of the nation to survive and recover from an EMP catastrophe.

OKLAHOMA BILL FOR POPULAR REFERENDUM ON EMP PROTECTION

STATE OF OKLAHOMA

2nd Session of the 54th Legislature (2014)

COMMITTEE SUBSTITUTE
FOR
SENATE BILL NO. 2016   By: Shortey

COMMITTEE SUBSTITUTE

An Act relating to electromagnetic shield protection; requiring electric providers to install certain technology on critical infrastructure and facilities by certain date; requiring the Southwest Power Pool to identify critical equipment; requiring certain design standards; authorizing recovery of certain costs within certain time period; providing for codification; providing ballot title; and directing filing.

BE IT ENACTED BY THE PEOPLE OF THE STATE OF OKLAHOMA:

SECTION 1. Pursuant to Section 3 of Article V of the Oklahoma Constitution, there is hereby ordered the following legislative referendum which shall be filed with the Secretary of State and addressed to the Governor of the state, who shall submit the same to the people for their approval or rejection at the next General Election.

SECTION 2.   NEW LAW   A new section of law to be codified in the Oklahoma Statutes as Section 158 of Title 17, unless there is created a duplication in numbering, reads as follows:

A. All electric service providers operating electric generation and transmission facilities in this state shall, by January 1, 2017, have installed and operational electromagnetic shield protection technology on electric infrastructure and facilities identified as critical for such protection by the Southwest Power Pool Regional Transmission Organization.

B. The electric service providers shall utilize electromagnetic shield protection technology which shall at a minimum meet the engineering design guidelines for protecting critical communications and data centers as outlined in Department of Defense MIL-STD-188-125-1 or a successor standard adopted by the United States Department of Defense.

C. All electric utility providers are authorized to implement a rate increase to recover the cost of installing such equipment. Public utility providers regulated by the Corporation Commission shall be granted a customer rate increase necessary to recoup the costs associated with implementing the equipment, as required by subsection A of this section, within five (5) years. Municipalities and self-governing electric cooperatives are authorized to implement a customer charge in an amount deemed necessary to implement the requirements of this section.

SECTION 3. The Ballot Title for the proposed act shall be in the following form:

BALLOT TITLE

Legislative Referendum No. _____   State Question No. _____

THE GIST OF THE PROPOSITION IS AS FOLLOWS:
This measure requires electric transmission operators in this state to install certain electromagnetic shield protection on critical equipment by January 1, 2017. There shall be a rate increase to recover costs of installing this equipment.

SHALL THE PROPOSAL BE APPROVED?
FOR THE PROPOSAL — YES   _____
AGAINST THE PROPOSAL — NO   _____

SECTION 4. The President Pro Tempore of the Senate shall, immediately after the passage of this order for legislative referendum, prepare and file in accordance with Section 3 of Article V of the Oklahoma Constitution, one copy of this order for legislative referendum, including the Ballot Title set forth in SECTION 3, with the Secretary of State and one copy with the Attorney General.

54-2-3232   MJM   11/20/2015 9:17:44 AM

Geomagnetic Disturbances and their Impact on the Electric Grid

Types of GMD Disturbance
GMDs come primarily from two sources:

- Geomagnetic disturbances (GMD) occur when solar storms on the sun's surface send electrically charged particles toward earth, where they interact with the earth's magnetic field. If the intensity and duration of a disturbance is sufficient, these abnormal electric currents may reduce system voltage and in the worst case cause a widespread power outage. Solar storms typically occur in 11-year cycles. Solar Cycle 24 began in 2008 and the solar storm frequency during this cycle peaked in 2013. During more than a century of operation, American Electric Power's (AEP) system has experienced numerous geomagnetic disturbances. In that time some temporary effects have been observed, but there has been no lasting damage or consequences. AEP is less susceptible than utilities closer to the earth's magnetic poles or in areas with more rocky soils. (www.AEP.com)

- A nuclear weapon detonated in or above the earth's atmosphere can create an electromagnetic pulse (EMP), a high-density electrical field. An EMP acts like a stroke of lightning but is stronger, faster, and shorter. An EMP can seriously damage electronic devices connected to power structures or antennas. This includes communication systems, computers, electrical appliances, and automobile or aircraft ignition systems. The damage could range from a minor interruption to actual burnout of components. Most electronic equipment within 1,000 miles of a high-altitude nuclear detonation could be affected. Battery-powered radios with short antennas generally would not be affected. Although an EMP is unlikely to harm most people, it could harm those with pacemakers or other implanted electronic devices. (www.DHS.gov)

Federal activity
Several federal initiatives already are underway to protect against GMDs, whether natural or manufactured.

- The North American Electric Reliability Corporation (NERC)--responsible for all electric reliability via the Energy Policy Act of 2005, is establishing reliability standards for GMD events and today's electric utilities are expected to live up to them. Two sets of standards are underway. The first was approved by NERC in November and is awaiting FERC approval. The second set is still in the formation process. Although the first set has little/no cost associated, the second set will be costly. Estimates of the investment needed are difficult until the standards are finalized.

- The FERC has a proposed rulemaking currently out for public comment with a rule expected soon.

Costs
State-specific regulations requiring electric utilities to meet additional preparation requirements will exacerbate costs for the disaster preparation already required. For

instance, Public Service Oklahoma's Total Electric Plant value is $4.21 billion (PSO FERC Form 1 Filing, 2012, p. 110). AEP Oklahoma Transmission Co. Inc.'s total plant for the same time is $170 million (AEP Oklahoma Transmission FERC Form 1 Filing, 2012, p. 110).

To replicate this entire investment to create redundant resources as a safeguard against the threat of a terrorist nuclear attack in Oklahoma likely falls far short of the prudent expenditures test for the Oklahoma Corporation Commission. The investment sought in legislation would multiply consumers' electric bills many times over, to serve as insurance against a single threat.

GENERIC EMP BILL AND EXECUTIVE ORDER

Legislative versus Executive Strategy

Appended to this chapter is a generic bill to protect a State electric grid from electromagnetic pulse (EMP) that could be introduced into the legislature of any State. Appended also is a generic Executive Order that could be issued by any Governor to protect the electric grid of his State.

Legislative versus executive strategies for achieving protection of a State electric grid have different advantages and disadvantages. Typically, passing a bill through a State Legislature will take longer and be more complex than an Executive Order issued by the Governor.

However, the so-called disadvantages of the legislative process can also be viewed as advantages.

The legislative process is lengthy in part because it requires educating relevant committees, the State House, the State Senate, the Governor and the public on the necessity of protecting the electric grid. As the process moves forward, crucial questions get answered in whole or in part, such as: Is there a threat? What is the risk? What are the technical solutions? How much will they cost?

As the bill graduates from committee, to State House, to State Senate, to Governor, it must past new scrutiny from a different set of actors with different interests and different constituencies. If the bill survives, the net result is building support for protection of the electric grid by political consensus.

Through this process of discovery and consensus building, the legislative strategy offers the opportunity to educate policymakers and a public that may have been ignorant or deeply skeptical of the EMP threat. Consensus building for passage of a bill may take longer than executive action--but the legislative strategy promises to mobilize much broader and deeper and longer-lasting support.

Of course, the legislative strategy, in addition to being slower, is also less certain of success than the executive strategy.

Governors have broad authority to provide for the homeland security of their State and can invoke their emergency powers to swiftly address threats to the public safety. Security of the State electric grid is fundamental to homeland security and public safety and is within the power of the Governor to regulate through various relevant departments and agencies, including the public utilities commission.

The generic bill and Executive Order appended to this chapter may be sufficient to achieve EMP protection for a State electric grid just by filling in the blanks. They are certainly sufficient to serve as a starting point for crafting a bill or Executive Order custom-made for a particular State.

GENERIC EMP BILL

A BILL TO PROTECT THE ELECTRICAL TRANSMISSION GRID SYSTEM WITHIN THE STATE OF _____

SECTION 1. <u>LEGISLATIVE INTENT.</u> The Legislature finds and declares as follows:

(a) The maintenance of _____'s (State) electrical transmission grid system is critical to ensure the health and safety of the People of this State.

(b) It is recognized that such electrical transmission grid system within the State of _____ is part of a regional system that is governed and administered by the _____(Regional Electric Reliability Organization).

(c) It is further recognized that such regional system is vulnerable to natural and nuclear electromagnetic pulse (EMP) and other man-made and natural acts that could disrupt service from said system for a period of time that could pose significant risk to the national security of the region and the Nation.

(d) It is thus incumbent upon the People of _____, to take measures through its elected leadership to protect the portion of the electrical transmission grid system located within this State to the greatest extent possible.

(e) It is further recognized that such protection cannot be implemented without the support and cooperation of _____'s electric utility organizations, regulatory authorities and security agencies.

(f) It is the intent of the Legislature that such cooperation be conducted in such a manner so as to preserve the confidential nature of certain elements of the grid system but also to ensure that the system is satisfactorily protected.

SECTION 2. It is hereby directed as follows:

(a) All electrical utilities in this State, both publicly and privately owned shall develop and implement a plan to address the vulnerability of the electrical transmission grid system within their boundaries to natural and nuclear EMP and other man-made or natural acts that could pose a threat to local, state or national security. The plan shall uniformly be called "THE PLAN OF THE (NAME OF ELECTRIC UTILITY) TO PROTECT THE ELECTRICAL TRANSMISSION GRID SYSTEM WITHIN ITS BOUNDARIES FROM MAN-MADE OR NATURAL ACTS OF DISRUPTION" (referred to in this Act as "The Plan").

(b) The Plan shall include:
    1. A description of the electrical grid system within its jurisdictional boundaries;
    2. An analysis of potential man-made and natural short, medium and long-term threats to the system;
    3. The utility's plan for addressing such threats including the anticipated costs of implementing such measures;
    4. The time-table for implementation based upon a prioritization of vulnerabilities and mitigation measures;
    5. The plan to ensure minimum 72 hour back-up electrical supply for critical community infrastructure.

(c) The Plan shall be reviewed by independent EMP experts and the Plan and expert review submitted to both the State's Adjutant General and Director of Emergency Services no later than _____. The State's Adjutant General and the Director of Emergency Services shall review the Plan and jointly submit a report to the Governor with their comments and recommendations no later than _____. The Governor shall then approve, conditionally approve or disapprove the Plan.

(d) The Plans prepared by the utilities as well as the report prepared by the State Adjutant General and Director of Emergency Services shall be deemed to be Classified and protected by applicable regulations from public disclosure.

(e) The costs borne by the utilities in both the development and implementation of the above-referenced plan shall be deemed to be a recoverable cost item to be paid by the consumer as determined by the _____ Public Utility Commission.

(f) The State's Adjutant General and Director of Emergency Services shall develop their own action plans consistent with the Plan as approved or conditionally approved by the Governor.

(g) The State's Adjutant General and Director of Emergency Services shall coordinate with their counterparts in the states comprising the regional grid system as well as with the Federal Energy Regulatory Commission to assist in the development of a regional response to regional grid vulnerabilities.

GENERIC EXECUTIVE ORDER

EXECUTIVE ORDER

EXECUTIVE DEPARTMENT

STATE OF _____

EXECUTIVE ORDER NO._____

by the

GOVERNOR OF THE STATE OF _____

WHEREAS, the reliable operation of [STATE]'s electrical transmission grid system is critical to ensure the health and safety of the People of the _____; and

WHEREAS, it is recognized that such electrical grid system within the State of _____ is part of a regional system that is governed and administered by the _____ (Regional Electric Reliability Organization); and

WHEREAS, it is further recognized however that such regional grid system is dangerously vulnerable to natural and nuclear electromagnetic pulse (EMP) and other man-made and natural acts that could disrupt service for a period of time that could pose significant risk to the security of the People of _____ as well as to the security of our Nation; and

WHEREAS, such vulnerability constitutes an extant energy emergency; and

WHEREAS, it is thus incumbent upon this Office to take measures through the Executive Department to protect the portion of the transmission grid system located within the State of _____ to the greatest extent possible;

NOW THEREFORE, I_____, Governor of the State of _____, hereby do declare that an energy emergency exists within the State of _____. I do hereby further declare that such energy emergency is based upon the existing vulnerability of the electrical transmission grid located within the State of _____ to natural and nuclear EMP and other man-made and natural acts that could disrupt service for a period of time that could pose significant risk to the security of People of this State.

IT IS FURTHER DECLARED AND ORDERED that no later than _____, all investor owned and public utilities shall file a secure, confidential report to the Adjutant General and the Director of Emergency Services that shall identify grid vulnerabilities and their individual plans to address such vulnerabilities, which plans shall be reviewed by independent EMP experts; and

IT IS FURTHER DECLARED AND ORDERED that no later than (60 days from the above date) the Adjutant General and the Director of Emergency Services shall submit a combined secure and confidential report to the Office of the Governor summarizing the above-referenced reports and plans and setting forth their specific recommendations for securing the transmission grid system located within _____.

IT IS FINALLY DECLARED that the actions set forth in this Order are authorized by Article __, Section _____ of the Constitution of the State of _____; and further specifically authorized by _____.

                                  IN WITNESS WHEREOF I have hereunto set my hand and caused the Great Seal of the State of

_____

to be affixed this __day of ____, 2014.

_____

Governor of _____

X

DO NOT WAIT FOR WASHINGTON

Summary

Governors and State Legislatures launching initiatives to protect their State electric grids from natural electromagnetic pulse, termed Geo-Magnetic Disturbance (GMD) by the electric power industry, will almost certainly be told by the utilities and the North American Electric Reliability Corporation (NERC) that action by the States to protect their grids is unnecessary. NERC will point to its Geo-Magnetic Disturbance Standard--proposed by NERC and swiftly approved by the U.S. Federal Energy Regulatory Commission (FERC) in 2014--as proof that Washington is acting to protect the national electric grid from geomagnetic storms, including super-storms like the Carrington Event.

Industry will reassure the States, as they have attempted to do in Maine, Virginia, Arizona, Oklahoma and elsewhere, that they can just sit back and relax and trust NERC to protect the electric grid.

Yet NERC's grossly deficient GMD Standard for protecting the national electric grid from geomagnetic storms, approved by the U.S. FERC--despite being obviously inadequate-- proves that the States cannot trust the bureaucrats in Washington and the electric power industry to protect the grid. Few arguments are better than NERC's own hollow GMD Standard for geomagnetic storms to prove that the States should not wait for Washington, but should act now to protect their grids and the lives of their peoples.

Regulatory Malfeasance

As noted repeatedly elsewhere in this book, Washington's process for regulating the electric power industry has never worked well, in fact has always been broken. The electric power industry is the only civilian critical infrastructure that is allowed to regulate itself.

The North American Electric Reliability Corporation is the industry's former trade association, which continues to act as an industry lobby. NERC is not a U.S. government agency. It does not represent the interests of the people. NERC in its charter answers to its "stakeholders"--the electric utilities that pay for NERC, including NERC's highly salaried executives and staff.

The U.S. Federal Energy Regulatory Commission, the U.S. government agency that is supposed to partner with NERC in protecting the national electric grid, has publicly testified before Congress that U.S. FERC lacks regulatory power to compel NERC and the electric power industry to protect the grid from natural and nuclear EMP and other threats.

Consider the contrast in regulatory authority between the U.S. Federal Energy Regulatory Commission and, as examples, the U.S. Federal Aviation Administration (FAA), the U.S. Department of Transportation (DOT), or the U.S. Food and Drug Administration (FDA):

--FAA has regulatory power to compel the airlines industry to ground aircraft considered unsafe, to change aircraft operating procedures considered unsafe, and to make repairs or improvements to aircraft in order to protect the lives of airline passengers.
--DOT has regulatory power to compel the automobile industry to install on cars safety glass, seatbelts, and airbags in order to protect the lives of the driving public.

--FDA has power to regulate the quality of food and drugs, and can ban under criminal penalty the sale of products deemed by the FDA to be unsafe to the public.

Unlike the FAA, DOT, FDA or any other U.S. government regulatory agency, the Federal Energy Regulatory Commission does not have legal authority to compel the industry it is supposed to regulate to act in the public interest. For example, U.S. FERC lacks legal power to direct NERC and the electric utilities to install blocking devices, surge arrestors, faraday cages or other protective devices to save the grid, and the lives of millions of Americans, from a natural or nuclear EMP catastrophe. Or so the FERC has testified to the Congress.

Congress has responded to this dilemma by introducing bipartisan bills, the SHIELD Act and the GRID Act, to empower U.S. FERC to protect the grid from an EMP catastrophe. Lobbying by NERC has stalled both bills for years.

Currently, U.S. FERC only has the power to ask NERC to propose a standard to protect the grid. NERC standards are approved, or rejected, by the electric power industry.

Historically, NERC typically takes years to develop standards to protect the grid that will pass industry approval. For example, NERC took a decade to propose a "vegetation management" standard to protect the grid from tree branches in 2012. This after ruminating for ten years over the tree branch induced Great Northeast Blackout of 2003, that plunged 40-50 million Americans into the dark.

Once NERC proposes a standard to U.S. FERC, FERC cannot modify the standard, but must accept or reject the proposed standard. If U.S. FERC rejects the proposed standard, NERC gets to go back to the drawing board, and the process starts all over again.

The NERC-FERC arrangement is a formula for thwarting effective U..S. government regulation of the electric power industry. Fortunately, Governors, State Legislatures and their Public Utility Commissions have legal power to compel utilities to protect the grid from natural and nuclear EMP and other threats.

Critics argue that the U.S. Federal Energy Regulatory Commission is corrupt--because of a too cozy relationship with NERC and a rotating door between FERC and the electric power industry--and cannot be trusted to secure the grid, even if given legal powers to do so. U.S. FERC's approval of NERC's hollow standard for geomagnetic storms appears proof positive that Washington is too corrupt to be trusted.

NERC's Hollow GMD Protection Standard

Observers serving on NERC's Geo-Magnetic Disturbance Task Force, that developed the NERC standard for grid protection against geomagnetic storms, have denounced the NERC GMD Standard and published papers exposing, not merely that the Standard is inadequate, but that it is hollow, a pretended or fake Standard. These experts opposed to the NERC GMD Standard include the foremost authorities on geomagnetic storms and electric grid vulnerability in the Free World. See:

--John G. Kappenman and Dr. William A. Radasky, *Examination of NERC GMD Standards and Validation of Ground Models and Geo-Electric Fields Proposed in this NERC GMD Standard*, Storm Analysis Consultants and Metatech Corporation, July 30, 2014 (Executive Summary appended to this chapter).

--EIS Council Comments on Benchmark GMD Event for NERC GMD Task Force Consideration, Electric Infrastructure Security Council, May 21, 2014.
--Thomas Popik and William Harris for The Foundation for Resilient Societies, *Reliability Standard for Geomagnetic Disturbance Operations*, Docket No. RM14-1-000, critiques submitted to U.S. FERC on March 24, July 21, and August 18, 2014.

Kappenman and Radasky, who served on the Congressional EMP Commission and are among the world's foremost scientific and technical experts on geomagnetic storms and grid vulnerability, warn that NERC's GMD Standard consistently underestimates the threat from geo-storms: "When comparing...actual geo-electric fields with NERC model derived geo-electric fields, the comparisons show a systematic under-prediction in all cases of the geo-electric field by the NERC model."

The Foundation for Resilient Societies, that includes on its Board of Advisors a brain trust of world class scientific experts--including Dr. William Graham who served as President Reagan's Science Advisor, director of NASA, and Chairman of the Congressional EMP Commission--concludes from their participation on the NERC GMD Task Force that NERC "cooked the books" to produce a hollow GMD Standard:

The electric utility industry clearly recognized in this instance how to design a so-called "reliability standard" that, though foreseeably ineffective in a severe solar storm, would avert financial liability to the electric utility industry even while civil society and its courts might collapse from longer-term outages. In this instance and others, a key feature of the NERC standard-setting process was to progressively water down requirements until the proposed standard obviously benefitted the ballot participants and therefore could pass. In the process, any remaining public benefit was diluted beyond perceptibility...

The several Foundation critiques identify numerous profound and obvious holes in what it describes as NERC's "hollow" GMD Standard, and rightly castigates U.S. FERC for approving what is, in reality, a paper mache GMD Standard that would not protect the grid from a geomagnetic super-storm:

--"FERC erred by approving a standard that exempts transmission networks with no transformers with a high side (wye-grounded) voltage at or above 200 kV when actual data and lessons learned from past operating incidents show significant adverse impacts of solar storms on equipment operating below 200 kV."
--"The exclusion of networks operating at 200kV and below is inconsistent with the prior bright-line definition of the Bulk Electric System" as defined by U.S. FERC."
--"FERC erred by approving a standard that does not require instrumentation of electric utility networks during solar storm conditions when installation of GIC [Ground Induced Current--Pry] monitors would be cost-effective and in the public interest."
--"FERC erred by approving a standard that does not require utilities to perform the most rudimentary planning for solar storms, i.e., mathematical comparison of megawatt capacity of assets at risk during solar storms to power reserves."
--"FERC erred by concluding that sixteen Reliability Coordinators could directly communicate with up to 1,500 Transmission and Generator Operators during severe GMD events with a warning time of as little as 15 minutes and that Balancing Authorities and Generator Operators should not take action on their own because of possible lack of GIC data."

--"FERC erred by assuming that there would be reliable and prompt two-way communications between Reliability Coordinators and Generator Operators immediately before and during severe solar storms."

The Foundation is also critical of U.S. FERC for approving a NERC GMD Standard that lacks transparency and accountability. The utilities are allowed to assess their own vulnerability to geomagnetic storms, to devise their own preparations, to invest as much or as little as they like in those preparations, and all without public scrutiny or review of utility plans by independent experts!

Dr. William Radasky, who holds the Lord Kelvin Medal for setting standards for protecting European electronics from natural and nuclear EMP, and John Kappenman, who helped design the ACE satellite upon which industry relies for early warning of geomagnetic storms, conclude that the NERC GMD Standard so badly underestimates the threat that "its resulting directives are not valid and need to be corrected." Kappenman and Radasky:

These enormous model errors also call into question many of the foundation findings of the NERC GMD draft standard. The flawed geo-electric field model was used to develop the peak geo-electric field levels of the Benchmark model proposed in the standard. Since this model understates the actual geo-electric field intensity for small storms by a factor of 2 to 5, it would also understate the maximum geo-electric field by similar or perhaps even larger levels. Therefore, the flaw is entirely integrated into the NERC Draft Standard and its resulting directives are not valid and need to be corrected.

The excellent Kappenman-Radasky critique of the NERC GMD Standard represents the consensus view of all the independent observers who participated in the NERC GMD Task Force, including the author. Appended to this chapter is the Executive Summary of their critique, which warns NERC and U.S. FERC that, "Nature cannot be fooled!"

Perhaps most revelatory of U.S. FERC's untrustworthiness, by approving the NERC GMD Standard that grossly underestimates the threat from geo-storms--U.S. FERC abandoned its own much more realistic estimate of the geo-storm threat. It is incomprehensible why U.S. FERC would ignore the findings of its own excellent interagency study, one of the most in depth and meticulous studies of the EMP threat ever performed, that was coordinated with Oak Ridge National Laboratory, the Department of Defense, and the White House.

U.S. FERC's preference for NERC's "junk science" over U.S. FERC's own excellent scientific assessment of the geo-storm threat can only be explained as incompetence or corruption or both.

The bottom line is that the States cannot trust NERC and U.S. FERC to protect the national electric grid from natural EMP. They probably cannot trust NERC and the U.S. FERC to protect the grid from anything.

States should protect their own electric grids, and their people who depend upon the grid for survival, from the worst threat--nuclear EMP attack--so they will be ready for everything.

More Washington Dysfunction

The White House has not helped matters by issuing a draft *National Space Weather Strategy* (The White House, National Science and Technology Council, April 2015) for protecting the national grid from natural EMP--but that trusts NERC and the electric utilities to set the standards. This grave error alone guarantees that the National Space Weather Strategy will be a placebo, not worth the paper it is written on, as a defense against a natural EMP catastrophe.

As demonstrated above, NERC and the electric power industry cannot be trusted to set standards, or to make and implement realistic recommendations, to protect the nation from a geomagnetic super-storm or from manmade EMP.

The testimony of Ambassador R. James Woolsey, former Director of Central Intelligence, to the Senate Homeland Security Committee ("Heading Toward An EMP Catastrophe" July 22, 2015) on Washington dysfunction toward the EMP threat bears repeating here as reasons the States should not wait for Washington to act:

--"Nor has the White House or the U.S. FERC challenged NERC's assertion that it has no responsibility to protect the electric grid from nuclear EMP or Radio-Frequency Weapons."

--"Nor has the White House or the U.S. FERC done anything to prevent NERC and the utilities from misinforming policymakers and the public about the EMP threat and their lack of preparedness to survive and recover from an EMP catastrophe."

--"Consequently, policymakers in the States who are alarmed by the lack of progress in Washington on EMP preparedness, find themselves seriously disadvantaged in efforts to protect their State electric grids by the utilities and their well-funded lobbyists who falsely claim Washington and the utilities are making great progress partnering on the EMP problem. So far in 2015, State initiatives to protect their electric grids have been defeated by industry lobbyists in Maine, Colorado, and Texas."

--"Texas State Senator Bob Hall, a former USAF Colonel and himself an EMP expert, characterizes as "equivalent to treason" the behavior of the electric utilities and their lobbyists:"

As a Texas State Senator who tried in the 2015 legislative session to get a bill passed to harden the Texas grid against an EMP attack or nature's GMD, I learned first hand the strong control the electric power company lobby has on elected officials. We did manage to get a weak bill passed in the Senate but the power companies had it killed in the House. A very deceitful document which was carefully designed to mislead legislators was provided by the power company lobbyist to legislators at a critical moment in the process. The document was not just misleading, it actually contained false statements. The EMP/GMD threat is real and it is not "if" but WHEN it will happen. The responsibility for the catastrophic destruction and wide spread death of Americans which will occur will be on the hands of the executives of the power companies because they know what needs to be done and are refusing to do it. In my opinion power company executives, by refusing to work with the legislature to protect the electrical grid infrastructure are committing an egregious act that is equivalent to treason. I know and understand what I am saying. As a young US Air Force Captain, with a degree in electrical engineering from The Citadel, I was the project officer who lead the Air Force/contractor team which designed, developed and installed the modification to "harden" the Minuteman Strategic missile to protect it from an EMP attack. The American people must demand that the power company executives that are hiding the truth stop deceiving the people and immediately begin protecting our electrical grid so that life as we know it today will not end when the terrorist EMP attack comes.

--"Ironically, while electric power lobbyists are fighting against EMP protection in Washington, Texas, Maine, Colorado and elsewhere, the Iranian news agency MEHR reported on June 13, 2015, that Iran is violating international sanctions and going full bore to protect itself from a nuclear EMP attack:"

Iranian researchers...have built an Electromagnetic Pulse (EMP) filter that protects country's vital organizations against cyber attack. Director of Kosar Information and Communication Technology Institute Saeid Rahimi told MNA correspondent that the EMP (Electromagnetic Pulse) filter is one of the country's boycotted products and until now procuring it required considerable costs and various strategies. "But recently Kosar ICT...has managed to domestically manufacture the EMP filter for the very first time in this country," said Rahimi. Noting that the domestic EMP filter has been approved by security authorities, Rahimi added "the EMP filter protects sensitive devices and organizations against electromagnetic pulse and electromagnetic terrorism." He also said the domestic EMP filter has been implemented in a number of vital centers in Iran. (MEHR News Agency, "Iran Builds EMP Filter For 1st Time" June 13, 2015)

While Washington dithers, Iran is beating the United States to achieving national EMP preparedness. Why is Iran undertaking such preparations? Who do they suspect may wish to make--or retaliate for--a nuclear EMP attack?

Since leadership is not, and may never, come from Washington, the States must fill the void and act now to protect the American people from an EMP catastrophe.

Examination of NERC GMD Standards and Validation of Ground Models and Geo-Electric Fields Proposed in this NERC GMD Standard

A White Paper by:
John G. Kappenman, Storm Analysis Consultants
and
Dr. Willam A. Radasky, Metatech Corporation
July 30, 2014

Executive Summary

The analysis of the US electric power grid vulnerability to geomagnetic storms was originally conducted as part of the work performed by Metatech Corporation for the Congressional Appointed US EMP Commission, which started their investigations in late 2001. In subsequent work performed for the US Federal Energy Regulatory Commission, a detailed report was released in 2010 of the findings. In October 2012, the FERC ordered the US electric power industry via their standards development organization NERC to develop new standards addressing the impacts of a geomagnetic disturbance to the electric power grid. NERC has now developed a draft standard and has provided limited details on the technical justifications for these standards in a recent NERC White Paper.

The most important purpose of design standards is to protect society from the consequences of impacts to vulnerable and critical systems important to society. To perform this function the standards must accurately describe the environment. Such environment design standards are used in all aspects of society to protect against severe excursions of nature that could impact vulnerable systems: floods, hurricanes, fire codes, etc., are relevant examples. In this case, an accurate characterization of the extremes of the geomagnetic storm environment needs to be provided so that power system vulnerabilities against these environments can be accurately assessed. A level that is arbitrarily too low would not allow proper assessment of vulnerability and ultimately would lead to inadequate safeguards that could pose broad consequences to society.

However from our initial reviews of the NERC Draft Standard, the concern was that the levels suggested by NERC were unusually low compared to both recorded disturbances as well as from prior studies. Therefore this white paper will provide a more rigorous review of the NERC benchmark levels. NERC had noted that model validations were not undertaken because direct measurements of geo-electric fields had not been routinely performed anyway in the US. In contrast, Metatech had performed extensive geo-electric field measurement campaigns over decades for storms in Northern Minnesota and had developed validated models for many locations across the US in the course of prior investigations of US power grid vulnerability. Further, various independent observers to the NERC GMD tasks force meetings had urged NERC to collect decades of GIC observations performed by EPRI and independently by power companies as these data could be readily converted to geo-electric fields via simple techniques to provide the basis for validation studies across the US. None of these actions were taken by the NERC GMD Task Force.

It needs to be pointed out that GIC measurements are important witnesses and their evidence is not being considered by the NERC GMD Task Force in the development of these standards. GIC observations provide direct evidence of all of the uncertain and variable parameters including the deep Earth ground response to the driving geomagnetic disturbance environment. Because the GIC measurement is also obtained from the power grid itself, it incorporates all of the meso-scale coupling of the disturbance environments to the assets themselves and the overlying circuit topology that needs to be assessed. Separate discreet measurements of geo-electric fields are usually done over short baseline asset arrays which may not accurately characterize the real meso-scale interdependencies that need to be understood. The only challenge is to interpret what the GIC measurement is attempting to tell us, and fortunately this can be readily revealed with only a rudimentary understanding of Ohm's Law, geometry and circuit analysis methods, a tool set that are common electrical engineering techniques. Essentially the problem reduces to: *"if we know the I (or GIC) and we know the R and topology of the circuit, then Ohm's law tells us what the V or geo-electric field was that created that GIC"*. Further since we know the resistance and locations of power system assets with high accuracy, we can also derive the geo-electric field with equally high certainty. These techniques allow superior characterization of deep Earth ground response and can be done immediately across much of the US if GIC measurements were made available. Further these deep Earth ground responses are based upon geological processes and do not change rapidly over time. Therefore even measurements from one storm event can characterize a region. Hence this is a powerful tool for improving the accuracy of models and allows for the development of accurate forward looking standards that are needed to evaluate to high storm intensity levels that have not been measured or yet experienced on present day power grids. Unfortunately this tool has not been utilized by any of the participants in the NERC Standard development process.

It has been noted that the NERC GMD Task Force has adopted geo-electric field modeling techniques that have been previously developed at FMI and are now utilized at NRCan. The same FMI techniques were also integrated into the NASA-CCMC modeling environments and that as development and testing of US physiographic regional ground models were developed, efforts were also undertaken by the USGS and the NOAA SWPC to make sure their geo-electric field models were fully harmonized and able to produce uniform results. However, it appears that none of these organizations really did any analysis to determine if the results being produced were at all accurate in the first place. For example when recently inquired, NRCan indicated they will perhaps begin capturing geo-electric field measurements later this year to validate the base NERC Shield region ground model, a model which provides a conversion for all other ground models. In looking at prior publications of the geo-electric field model carried out in other world locations, it was apparent that the model was greatly and uniformly under-predicting for intense portions of the storms, which are the most important parameters that need to be accurately understood.

In order to examine this more fully, this white paper will provide the results of our recent independent assessment of the NERC geo-electric field and ground models and the draft standard that flows from this foundation. Our findings can be concisely summarized as follows:

-- Using the very limited but publicly available GIC measurements, it can be shown how important geo-electric fields over meso-scale regions can be characterized and that these measurements can be accurately assessed using the certainty of Ohm's Law. This provides a very strict constraint on what the minimum geo-electric field levels are during a storm event.

--When comparing these actual geo-electric fields with NERC model derived geo-electric fields, the comparisons show a systematic under-prediction in all cases of the geo-electric field by the NERC model. In the cases examined, the under prediction is particularly a problem for the rapid rates of change of the geomagnetic field (the most important portions of the storm events) and produce errors that range from factor of ~2 to over factor of ~5 understatement of intensity by the NERC models compared to actual geo-electric field measurements. These are enormous errors and are not at all suitable to attempt to embed into Federally-approved design standards.

--These enormous model errors also call into question many of the foundation findings of the NERC GMD draft standard. The flawed geo-electric field model was used to develop the peak geo-electric field levels of the Benchmark model proposed in the standard. Since this model understates the actual geo-electric field intensity for small storms by a factor of 2 to 5, it would also understate the maximum geo-electric field by similar or perhaps even larger levels. Therefore this flaw is entirely integrated into the NERC Draft Standard and its resulting directives are not valid and need to be corrected.

The findings here are also not simply a matter of whether the NERC model agrees with the results of the Metatech model. Rather the important issue is the degree that the NERC model disagrees with actual geo-electric field measurements from actual storm events. These actual measurements are also confirmed within very strict tolerances via Ohm's Law, a fundamental law of nature. The results that the NERC model has provided are not reliable, and efforts by NERC to convince otherwise and that utilization of GIC data cannot be done are simply misplaced. Actual data provides an ultimate check on unverified models and can be more effectively utilized to guide standard development than models because as Richard Feynman once noted; "Nature cannot be fooled"!

XI

THE CRITICAL INFRASTRUCTURE PROTECTION ACT

Congress Wants the States to Protect Their Grids

Four days before Halloween, on the Sunday morning that was October 27, 2013, the Knights Templars drug cartel used bombs and small arms to blackout Mexico's Michoacan state, terrorizing 420,000 people. Nearly a half million men, women and children suddenly found themselves cut off from civilization, at the mercy of the merciless. The Knights went into towns and villages and publicly executed leaders opposed to the drug trade, killing the bravest and the best.

By coincidence, that evening in the United States, the National Geographic aired its television docudrama "American Blackout"--a realistic portrayal of the chaos and anarchy that would ensue if terrorists blacked out the U.S. electric grid. Electric utilities and the NERC, apparently unaware that life had already anticipated art in Mexico, criticized National Geographic for exaggerating the threat and unnecessarily alarming the public.

Such denial behavior by the electric power industry proves the constitutional wisdom of the Founding Fathers in entrusting most societal functions to the individual and the private sector--except that "the common defense" must be the responsibility of government.

Three days after the airing of "American Blackout" and after the real life Michoacan terror blackout, on October 30, 2013, Congressman Trent Franks (R-AZ) introduced before the House Homeland Security Committee the Critical Infrastructure Protection Act (CIPA, H.R. 3410). CIPA is designed to prepare and recover the United States from an EMP catastrophe, and so thwart a real life "American Blackout" from happening.

The Critical Infrastructure Protection Act enjoys the support of Congressman Michael McCaul, Chairman of the House Homeland Security Committee. CIPA passed the House unanimously and went to the Senate on December 2, 2014. But the Senate failed to act--despite a promise by then Senate Majority Leader Harry Reid to do so--and H.R. 3410 died at the end of the 113th Congress.

However, the Critical Infrastructure Protection Act was reintroduced as H.R. 1073 in the new 114th Congress, still enjoying broad bipartisan support in both houses. Senator Ron Johnson, Chairman of the Senate Homeland Security and Governmental Affairs Committee, introduced a similar bill (S 1846). CIPA, reincarnated as H.R. 1073, again passed the House unanimously on November 16, 2015.

As of this writing on November 20, 2015, the Critical Infrastructure Protection Act awaits action in the Senate.

The Critical Infrastructure Protection Act is deliberately crafted to avoid the jurisdiction of the House Energy and Commerce Committee and the Senate Energy and Natural Resources Committee, where influence by the North American Electric Reliability Corporation is strongest. Lobbying by NERC and the electric power industry in these committees has successfully impeded passage of the SHIELD Act and GRID Act, bills that would protect the national power grid from natural and nuclear electromagnetic pulse.

The heart of the Critical Infrastructure Protection Act is a provision that directs the Department of Homeland Security to establish a new National Planning Scenario based on a natural or nuclear EMP event, and to educate and assist all levels of government--including the States--to prepare to survive and recover from an EMP event. National Planning Scenarios are the basis for all Federal, State, and local emergency planning, training, and resource allocation. Obviously, protection of electric grids is indispensable to survival and recovery from an EMP.

Thus, CIPA is both an invitation and an appeal by the Congress to the States to take the initiative in protecting their electric grids.

States should not wait for passage of the Critical Infrastructure Protection Act before moving to protect their electric grids. Washington is so broken that even super-majorities in support of a bill are often not sufficient to overcome clever lobbying and the congressional committee system--that enables a single member of the House or Senate to block a bill from coming to a vote.

For example, in 2010 the GRID Act passed the House unanimously. NERC lobbied a single member of the Senate Energy and Natural Resources Committee to keep a hold on the bill, preventing GRID from coming to a vote before the Senate, until it died in committee.

The will of the Congress to protect our nation from an EMP catastrophe is manifest in the establishment of the Congressional EMP Commission, the Congressional Strategic Posture Commission (which also urged protection of the electric grid from EMP), the Congressional EMP Caucus, unanimous House passage of the GRID Act, broad bipartisan support for the SHIELD Act (which has been blocked from a vote in committee), numerous hearings supporting protection of the grid from EMP, and now passage through the House of the Critical Infrastructure Protection Act--twice unanimously.

Appended is expert testimony supporting the Critical Infrastructure Protection Act and the full text of the bill. Significantly, no experts testified against CIPA.

The Critical Infrastructure Protection Act is like a signal flare in the night, another warning from Congress to the American people.

Time for the States to follow the examples of Maine, Virginia, Arizona, Florida, and Oklahoma. Time for the States to succeed where Washington has failed. Time for Governors and State Legislatures to swiftly lead the nation to safety from an EMP apocalypse from the Sun or from the New Barbarians. Time to prevent, figuratively and literally, a blackout of civilization, that could cancel Mankind's monumental progress in science, industry, and human rights made since the Age of Enlightenment--by the advent of a New Dark Age.

DR. PETER VINCENT PRY
TESTIMONY BEFORE THE
SUBCOMMITTEE ON CYBERSECURITY,
INFRASTRUCTURE PROTECTION AND SECURITY TECHNOLOGIES
HOUSE COMMITTEE ON HOMELAND SECURITY
"ELECTROMAGNETIC PULSE: THREAT TO CRITICAL INFRASTRUCTURE"
May 8, 2014

Thank you for this opportunity to testify at your hearing on the threat posed by electromagnetic pulse (EMP) to critical infrastructure.

Natural EMP from a geomagnetic super-storm, like the1859 Carrington Event or 1921 Railroad Storm, and nuclear EMP attack from terrorists or rogue states, as practiced by North Korea during the nuclear crisis of 2013, are both existential threats that could kill 9 of 10 Americans through starvation, disease, and societal collapse.

A natural EMP catastrophe or nuclear EMP attack could blackout the national electric grid for months or years and collapse all the other critical infrastructures--communications, transportation, banking and finance, food and water--necessary to sustain modern society and the lives of 310 million Americans.

Passage of the SHIELD Act to protect the national electric grid is urgently necessary. In 2010, after the House unanimously passed the GRID Act, if one Senator had not put a hold on the bill, today in 2014 the nation would already be protected, since it would take about 3.5 years to harden the grid.

Passage of the Critical Infrastructure Protection Act (CIPA) to create a new National Planning Scenario focused on EMP is urgently necessary. As the National Planning Scenarios are the basis for all federal, state and local emergency planning, training, and resource allocation, an EMP National Planning Scenario would immediately and significantly improve national preparedness for an EMP catastrophe.

The single most important thing Congress could do to protect the American people from EMP, and from all other threats to critical infrastructures, is pass the Critical Infrastructure Protection Act, which bill is or soon will be before this Committee for consideration.

Thousands of emergency planners and first responders at the federal, state, and local level want to protect our nation and their States and communities from the EMP threat. But they are seriously hindered and even prohibited from doing so because the EMP threat is not among the 15 canonical National Planning Scenarios utilized by the Department of Homeland Security.

Passage of the Critical Infrastructure Protection Act would immediately mobilize thousands of emergency planners and first responders at all levels of government, and educate millions of others, about the EMP threat and how to prepare for it.

Passage of the Critical Infrastructure Protection Act would immediately help States that are frustrated with lack of action on EMP in Washington, and are trying to launch initiatives protecting their electrical grids from EMP, as is being attempted now in Maine, Virginia, Oklahoma, and Florida.

Passage of the Critical Infrastructure Protection Act would educate all States about the EMP threat and help them protect their critical infrastructures.

For example, projects in New York and Massachusetts to harden their State grids against severe weather caused by climate change should include protection against an EMP event, which is the worst threat to the grid. If the grid is protected against EMP, it will mitigate all lesser threats, including cyber attack, sabotage, and severe weather.

Given the amounts of money being spent in New York and Massachusetts on grid hardening against severe weather, significant EMP protection can probably be accomplished now within their current budgets. But the cost of EMP protection will increase significantly if they delay and attempt remediation later.

EMP is a clear and present danger. A Carrington-class coronal mass ejection narrowly missed the Earth in July 2012. Last April, during the nuclear crisis with North Korea over Kim Jong-Un's threatened nuclear strikes against the United States, Pyongyang apparently practiced an EMP attack with its KSM-3 satellite, that passed over the U.S. heartland and over the Washington, D.C.-New York City corridor. Iran, estimated to be within two months of nuclear weapons by the Administration, has a demonstrated capability to launch an EMP attack from a vessel at sea. The Iranian Revolutionary Guard Navy commenced patrols off the East Coast of the United States in February.

Thank you for your attention to EMP, which is the least understood but gravest threat to our society. This concludes my remarks.

TESTIMONY OF DR. MICHAEL J. FRANKEL
HOUSE HOMELAND SECURITY COMMITTEE
HEARING
SUB-COMMITTEE ON CYBER SECURITY, INFRASTRUCTURE PROTECTION, AND SECURITY TECHNOLOGIES, HOUSE CANNON OFFICE BUILDING, ROOM 311, MAY 8, 2014

Mr. Chairman and Honorable Members of the Committee, thank you for the opportunity to testify today about an important but relatively neglected vulnerability that affects the resilience of all of our nation's critical infrastructures. My name is Mike Frankel. I'm a theoretical physicist by trade and presently a member of the senior scientific staff at Penn State University's Applied Research Laboratory. I've spent a career in government service developing technical and scientific expertise on the effects of nuclear weapons, managing WMD programs, and performing scientific research in a variety of national security positions with the Navy, the old Defense Nuclear Agency, and the Office of the Secretary of Defense. I appear before you today pursuant my service as the Executive Director of the EMP Commission during its entire span of activity, commencing with authorization if the Floyd D. Spence National Defense Authorization Act of 2001 and culminating with delivery of its final, classified, assessment to the Congress in 2009 The conclusions of the Commission were documented in a series of five volumes, three of them classified, and in particular the Commission's perspectives related to infrastructure protection were documented in an unclassified volume *"Critical National Infrastructures"*, released in November of 2008. What I'd like to do is expand on some of the Commission's conclusions in light of recent developments since submitting our final report. I should also like to emphasize a new topic that was not referenced in that final report, and that is the nexus between the cyber security threat and EMP.

One of the major insights of the EMP Commission was to highlight the unique danger to the electric grid caused by simultaneous failures induced by the large number of components that fall within an EMP's damaging footprint on the ground. As first reported in the journal Foreign Affairs and picked up a month later by the Wall Street Journal, on the night of April 16, 2013, a locked PG&E substation was infiltrated and a number of high voltage transformers attacked by still unidentified individuals firing rifles. Damaged transformers went off line but the SCADA controls automatically re-routed the electrical distribution along alternate paths. In this case, standard engineering practice which designs around the possibility of single point failure, kicked in just as it should. and little effect was noticed by the general population. However, it took nearly a full month to repair the damaged transformers and return them to service. An important analytic contribution of the Commission was to highlight the possibility of highly multiple numbers of component failures, as might be expected within the wide area encompassed by an EMP event footprint. No one designed against such a possibility and it was the Commission's conclusion, based on its own analyses and on a close collaboration with power industry engineers, that such a scenario would inevitably lead to very wide spread, and very long term collapse of the nation's electric grid, with potentially devastating economic and ultimately physical and health consequences. The PG&E incident should remind us that the Commission's analytic insight extends far beyond EMP. While in this case only a single substation was attacked, had there been a coordinated physical attack against many simultaneous targets, or for that matter by localized EMP sources such as readily available HPM/RF sources, it seems inevitable that electric service to much larger fraction of the population would have been compromised and for an indefinitely prolonged period. And of course, the same result could be achieved by simultaneous cyber-attack, with much reduced physical exposure by the perpetrators. So there's a real vulnerability there that needs to be addressed.

I should also like to turn some attention to the generally unremarked overlap between electromagnetic vulnerability of the type described by the EMP Commission and the more general issue of cyber vulnerability. While not often considered in tandem, it is more correct to consider EMP vulnerabilities as one end of a continuous spectrum of cyber threats to our electronic based infrastructures. They share both an overlap in the effects produced – the failure of electronic systems to perform their function and possibly incurring actual physical damage – as well as their mode of inflicting damage. They both reach out through the connecting electronic distribution systems, and impress unwanted voltages and currents on the connecting wires. In the usual cyber case, those unwanted currents contain information – usually in the form of malicious code – that instructs the system to perform actions unwanted and unanticipated by its owner. In the EMP case, the impressed signal does not contain coded information. It is merely a dump of random noise which may flip bit states, or damage components, and also ensures the system will not behave in the way the owner expects. This electronic noise dump may thus be thought of as a "stupid cyber". When addressing the vulnerability of our infrastructures to the cyber threat, it is important that we not neglect the EMP end of the cyber threat spectrum. And there is another important overlap with the cyber threat. With the grid on the cusp of technological change in the evolution to the "smart grid", the proliferation of sensors and controls which will manage the new grid architecture must be protected against cyber at the same time they must be protected against EMP. Cyber and EMP threats have the unique capability to precipitate highly multiple failures of these many new control systems over a widely distributed geographical area, and such simultaneous failures, as previously discussed, are likely to signal a wider and more long lasting catastrophe.

Another important legacy of the EMP Commission was to first highlight the danger to our electric grid due to solar storms, which may impress large - and effectively DC -currents on the long runs of conducting cable that make up the distribution system. While this phenomenon has long been known, and protected against, by engineering practices in the power industry, the extreme 100-year storm first analyzed by the Commission is now widely recognized to represent a major danger to our national electrical system for which adequate protective measures have not been taken and whose consequences – the likely collapse of much of the national grid, possibly for a greatly extended period, may rightly be termed catastrophic. At this point, the only scientific controversy attending the likelihood of our system being subject to a so-called super solar storm, is related to the time-constant. But these events have already occurred within the last century or so, they will occur again. We should be ready.

The most important legacy of the EMP Commission however, was in the recommendations which were provided that would, if acted upon, protect key assets of both the civilian and military infrastructures, And it is here that I should like to point to an important divergence in the government's response. The (classified) recommendations that were provided to the Department of Defense were formally considered, in the large main concurred with, and then acted upon. The Secretary of Defense issued a classified action plan, out-year funding was POM'd in the FYDP, an office and an official of responsibility were appointed, a standing Defense Science Board committee was stood up, an active research program is maintained, and survivability and certification instructions were issued by both DOD and by USSTRATCOM. Today, while vigilant oversight continues to be warranted, an EMP awareness pervades our acquisition system and operational doctrine. The response on the civilian side of the equation was not so rosy. The final report of EMP Commission contained seventy five recommendations to improve the survivability, operability, resilience, and recovery of all the critical infrastructures, and in particular of the most key of all, the electrical grid. Most of these recommendations were pointed towards the Department of Homeland Security. While there have been some conversations, it has been hard to detect much of an active resonance at all issuing from the Department. They have not, as far as I know, even designated EMP as a one of their ten of fifteen disaster scenarios for advanced planning circumstances. And this at a time when they do include a low altitude nuclear disaster -certainly disastrous but not one that would produce wide ranging EMP.

In the end, it is hard to deal with seventy five recommendations, all at once. But the solution is not to ignore all of them. If there is only a single essentially a no-cost step I would leave this Committee with, it would be to task the Department of Homeland Security with responding to the still languishing recommendations of the EMP Commission. The Department of Defense did issue a response, as mandated by the legislation which originally created that Commission. But no such mandatory response was levied at the time on the Department of Homeland Security, which did not even exist when the Commission legislation was passed as part of the National Defense Authorization Act of 2001. The DHS should be required to explain which recommendations they concur with and/or with which they non-concur, and why. They should be asked to prioritize amongst the seventy five and come back with implementation recommendations, or explain why they think it is unnecessary. And finally, I would also urge the Committee to support passage of the Critical Infrastructure Protection Act.

I wish to thank the Committee for this opportunity to present my views of this most important issue.

TESTIMONY OF CHRIS BECK
VICE PRESIDENT FOR POLICY AND STRATEGIC INITIATIVES, ELECTRIC INFRASTRUCTURE SECURITY COUNCIL
FOR THE
SUBCOMMITTEE ON CYBERSECURITY, INFRASTRUCTURE PROTECTION, AND SCIENCE AND TECHNOLOGY
May 8, 2014

Introduction

Good afternoon Chairman Meehan, Ranking Member Clarke, and Members of the Subcommittee. Thank you for holding this hearing on one of the most significant threats to our National and Homeland Security. As many of you know, before I joined EIS Council, I worked for this committee, focusing on Critical Infrastructure Protection and Science and Technology issues. It was through that work that I first became aware of the threats facing our critical electric infrastructures, and I found the issue to be so important that I felt compelled to focus on it exclusively.

The Electric Infrastructure Security Council's mission is to work in partnership with government and corporate stakeholders to host national and international education, planning and communication initiatives to help improve infrastructure protection against electromagnetic threats (e-threats) and other hazards. E-threats include naturally occurring geomagnetic disturbances (GMD), high-altitude electromagnetic pulses (HEMP) from nuclear weapons, and non-nuclear EMP from intentional electromagnetic interference (IEMI) devices – the focus of today's hearing.

EMP - Defining the Issue

The Problem: Developed nations are vulnerable to serious national power grid disruption from e-threats, both natural and malicious.

The Severity: The impact can range from a broad regional blackout with serious economic consequences to, in the worst case, a catastrophe that would threaten societal continuity. With even the most benign scenarios projecting high societal costs, the Committee is correct to focus on this as an issue deserving serious attention.

The Timing: For severe space weather, the most recent events occurred roughly 90 and 150 years ago, but the timing of the next such occurrence, as with all extreme natural disasters, is unknown. Either local (non-nuclear) or sub-continental (nuclear) EMP could occur at any time, encouraged by ongoing vulnerability, and triggered by changing geopolitical realities.

Key Questions

1. What should our national strategy be? At top level, there are two alternative paths:

a. Hope for the best: Accept the status quo.

i. For severe space weather, this means hoping the most optimistic projections will turn out to be correct, and the impact will not be catastrophic.

ii. EMP has been called, "The most powerful asymmetric weapon in history." This approach means hoping no terrorist organization or rogue state will ever take advantage of the power of such devastating weapons.

b. The other alternative:

Encourage cost-effective resilience, restoration and response planning.

2. If we respond, what is the path?
How should we address interconnect-wide interdependence, and how should we proceed with implementation?

3. If we respond, who should be involved?
Who should take responsibility to define the path, and implement it? How should the balance between public mandates and private, corporate initiative be determined?

4. How broad should our response be?
Should both GMD and EMP be included?

Consensus Recommendations

1. Hope vs Preparation: Choosing a strategy.
 A common theme of all the many government reports studying these risks, also reflected in the deliberations of the Electric Infrastructure Security Summits over the last several years, is that the risks associated with severe e-threats are serious. It is hard to find anyone who would assert that, in today's world, "hoping for the best" is a good strategy for GMD, EMP or IEMI.

2. What is the path?
Our national power grid is organic in design, but administratively complex. This means approaches are needed that address both of these factors.

--Organization and coordination: Given the grid's organic design, the consensus of government studies is that coordinated planning and standards will be important. Finding the best possible balance between broadly accepted, pro-active corporate coordination and government action will be important to assure fast, effective progress in achieving an e-threat resilient grid.

--Technical: A key point, not always recognized, is there is no need to "gold plate" the system.

For Severe Space Weather, there is already growing discussion of a range of strategies, and none of the approaches under active discussion – from planning measures to comprehensive automated hardware protection – appear high in cost, relative to existing logistics budgets and investment models.

For EMP, protection planning can focus – not on hardening every component in the power grid – but on protection of a fraction of grid facilities and hardware. In other words, enough resilience investment, and associated restoration planning, to protect enough generation resources and critical loads to allow for both effective restoration and for prioritized support to critical users and installations.

3. Who should be involved?
Given the likelihood of a large regional power outage after a natural or malicious e-threat, power companies will need to be operating in an environment of extensive response and recovery support from federal and state government authorities, as well as community-response NGOs. Thus, the evolution of planning to address these concerns should include the broadest possible involvement of all of these stakeholders, each contributing in its own domain of authority and expertise.

4. How broad should our scope be?

For all the E-threats under consideration here, efforts at protection, if they are to be effective, must primarily be focused where the impact will occur – in the power grid. For severe space weather, there is clearly no other alternative. For malicious threats, EMP and IEMI, U.S. and allied government security officials and experts at the highest levels agree that neither deterrence nor active military measures can alone guarantee the security of our homeland against a determined aggressor prepared to use such weapons.

In conclusion, I should note that there appear to be no significant technical or financial barriers to mitigating this threat. The technologies and operational procedures needed are well understood, and the cost – based on both government estimates and recent corporate experience – is reasonable. One of the primary needs is for education to increase awareness and therefore willingness to address the problem, and for coordination to address the administrative complexity of our nation's power grid.

This summary of consensus-based themes and recommendations reflects, I believe, not only the conclusions of the many major government studies of these issues, but also the deliberations of the past four international Electric Infrastructure Security Summits, with participation by the highest levels of many departments and agencies of the U.S. and allied governments, and of a broad range of scientists and domain experts working in this field
I would welcome the opportunity to discuss any of these points in greater detail.

This concludes my prepared testimony, and I would be happy to answer any questions.

SUMMARY
CRITICAL INFRASTRUCTURE PROTECTION ACT
H.R. 3410 - H.R. 1073

Critical Infrastructure Protection Act or CIPA - Amends the Homeland Security Act of 2002 to require the Assistant Secretary of the National Protection and Programs Directorate to: (1) include in national planning scenarios the threat of electromagnetic pulse (EMP) events; and (2) conduct a campaign to proactively educate owners and operators of critical infrastructure, emergency planners, and emergency responders at all levels of government of the threat of EMP events.

Directs the Under Secretary for Science and Technology to conduct research and development to mitigate the consequences of EMP events, including: (1) an objective scientific analysis of the risks to critical infrastructures from a range of EMP events; (2) determination of the critical national security assets and vital civic utilities and infrastructures that are at risk from EMP events; (3) an evaluation of emergency planning and response technologies that would address the findings and recommendations of experts, including those of the Commission to Assess the Threat to the United States from Electromagnetic Pulse Attack; (4) an analysis of available technology options to improve the resiliency of critical infrastructure to EMP; and (5) the restoration and recovery capabilities of critical infrastructure under differing levels of damage and disruption from various EMP events.

Includes among the responsibilities of the Secretary of Homeland Security (DHS) relating to intelligence and analysis and infrastructure protection to prepare and submit to specified congressional committees: (1) a comprehensive plan to protect and prepare the critical infrastructure of the American homeland against EMP events, including from acts of terrorism; and (2) biennial updates of such plan.

H.R. 3410 passed the House unanimously and went to the Senate on December 2, 2014--but the Senate failed to act upon the bill, where it died at the end of the 113th Congress. However, H.R. 3410 was reintroduced in the new 114th Congress as H.R. 1073 and passed the House, again unanimously, on Monday, November 16, 2015. As of this writing on November 20, 2015, the bill awaits action by the Senate.

H. R. 3410

To amend the Homeland Security Act of 2002 to secure critical infrastructure against electromagnetic pulses, and for other purposes.

IN THE HOUSE OF REPRESENTATIVES
OCTOBER 30, 2013

Mr. FRANKS of Arizona (for himself and Mr. SESSIONS) introduced the following bill; which was referred to the Committee on Homeland Security

A BILL

To amend the Homeland Security Act of 2002 to secure critical infrastructure against electromagnetic pulses, and for other purposes.

Be it enacted by the Senate and House of Representatives of the United States of America in Congress assembled,

SECTION 1. SHORT TITLE.

This Act may be cited as the ''Critical Infrastructure Protection Act'' or ''CIPA''.

SEC. 2. EMP PLANNING, RESEARCH AND DEVELOPMENT, AND PROTECTION AND PREPAREDNESS.

(a) IN GENERAL.—The Homeland Security Act of 2002 (6 U.S.C. 121) is amended—

(1) in section 2 (6 U.S.C. 101), by inserting after paragraph (6) the following:

''(6a) EMP.—The term 'EMP' means—''(A) an electromagnetic pulse caused by intentional means, including acts of terrorism; and ''(B) an electromagnetic pulse caused by solar storms or other naturally occurring phenomena.'';

(2) in title V (6 U.S.C. 311 et seq.), by adding at the end the following:

''SEC. 526. NATIONAL PLANNING SCENARIOS AND EDUCATION.

''The Secretary, acting through the Assistant Secretary of the National Protection and Programs Directorate, shall—

''(1) include in national planning scenarios the threat of EMP events; and

''(2) conduct a campaign to proactively educate owners and operators of critical infrastructure, emergency planners, and emergency responders at all levels of government of the threat of EMP events.'';

(3) in title III (6 U.S.C. 181 et seq.), by adding at the end of the following:

''SEC. 318. EMP RESEARCH AND DEVELOPMENT.

''(a) IN GENERAL.—In furtherance of domestic preparedness and response, the Secretary, acting through the Under Secretary for Science and Technology, and in consultation with other relevant agencies and departments of the Federal Government and relevant owners and operators of critical infrastructure, shall conduct research and development to mitigate the consequences of EMP events.

''(b) SCOPE.—The scope of the research and development under subsection (a) shall include the following:

''(1) An objective scientific analysis of the risks to critical infrastructures from a range of EMP events.

''(2) Determination of the critical national security assets and vital civic utilities and infrastructures that are at risk from EMP events.

"(3) An evaluation of emergency planning and response technologies that would address the findings and recommendations of experts, including those of the Commission to Assess the Threat to the United States from Electromagnetic Pulse Attack.

"(4) An analysis of technology options that are available to improve the resiliency of critical infrastructure to EMP.

"(5) The restoration and recovery capabilities of critical infrastructure under differing levels of damage and disruption from various EMP events."; and

(4) in section 201(d) (6 U.S.C. 121(d)), by adding at the end the following:

"(26)(A) Prepare and submit to the Committee on Homeland Security of the House of Representatives and the Committee on Homeland Security and Governmental Affairs of the Senate—

"(i) a comprehensive plan to protect and prepare the critical infrastructure of the American homeland against EMP events, including from acts of terrorism; and

"(ii) biennial updates of such plan.

"(B) The comprehensive plan shall—

"(i) be based on findings of the research and development conducted under section 318;

"(ii) be developed in consultation with the relevant Federal sector-specific agencies (as defined under Homeland Security Presidential Directive–7) for critical infrastructures;

"(iii) be developed in consultation with the relevant sector coordinating councils for critical infrastructures; and

"(iv) include a classified annex.".

(b) CLERICAL AMENDMENTS.—The table of contents in section 1(b) of such Act is amended—

(1) by adding at the end of the items relating to title V the following:

"Sec. 526. National planning scenarios and education."; and

(2) by adding at the end of the items relating to title III the following:

"Sec. 318. EMP research and development.".

(c) DEADLINE FOR INITIAL PLAN.—The Secretary of Homeland Security shall submit the comprehensive plan required under the amendment made by subsection (a)(4) by not later than one year after the date of the enactment of this Act.

(d) REPORT.—The Secretary shall submit a report to Congress by not later than 180 days after the date of the enactment of this Act describing the progress made in, and an estimated date by which the Department of Homeland Security will have completed—

(1) including EMP (as defined in the amendment made by subsection (a)(1)) threats in national planning scenarios;

(2) research and development described in the amendment made by subsection (a)(3);

(3) development of the comprehensive plan required under the amendment made by subsection (a)(4); and

(4) beginning a campaign to proactively educate emergency planners and emergency responders at all levels of government regarding the threat of EMP events.

XII

NUCLEAR POWER AS A MAJOR RESOURCE TO PREVENT LONG TERM OUTAGE (LTO) OF THE NATION'S POWER GRID

Dr. George H. Baker
Professor Emeritus, James Madison University
Foundation for Resilient Societies

Summary

State and federal governments or private utilities--whoever takes the lead in protecting power grids from natural and manmade electromagnetic pulse (EMP) and other threats--should give highest priority to protecting nuclear power reactors. Unprotected nuclear reactors pose one of the greatest hazards during a long term power outage from the meltdown of fuel rods and the release of radioactivity that can contaminate vast territories similar to events at Fukushima Daiichi. Most of the over 100 nuclear power reactors in the U.S. are in the eastern half, where resides most of the population. If protected, nuclear reactors can make a significant contribution to recovery from a protracted blackout. South Carolina, which has new nuclear reactors under construction, could be a good place to start incorporating EMP and other protection into nuclear reactor designs.

Long Term Outages (LTOs)

The President's National Security Telecommunications Advisory Committee (NSTAC) met during the period of the Congressional EMP Commission to consider catastrophes involving the interruption of electricity for months to years over large geographic regions. The NSTAC referred to such contingencies as "long term outages" or LTOs. The LTO phenomenon involves interruption of electricity for a period long enough, and within a large enough geographic region, to hamper providing electric power even by alternative means. Such an outage has not occurred in North America.[1] The present chapter discusses possible new roles for nuclear power plants vis-à-vis LTO contingencies. It will become clear that nuclear plants offer some major advantages over other sources of electric power in averting such catastrophes.

The NSTAC LTO scenario anticipated the conclusions of the EMP Commission and the significant issues that continue to emerge concerning the fragility of the electric power grid confirmed by recent physical and cyber attacks on the grid and statements by the administrators of the Federal Energy Regulatory Commission and the National Security Agency. LTOs may be precipitated by one or a combination of initiators including severe weather, coordinated physical and/or cyber attacks, solar superstorms, and EMP from high altitude nuclear bursts. A major concern is the general lack of awareness and preparedness of civil authorities, industry, and the American citizenry vis-à-vis these threats.

The consequences of LTO contingencies are existential. It is significant that the NSTAC recognized the interdependency between not only the electric power grid and telecommunications networks, but infrastructures in general. Loss of electric power will affect every other critical infrastructure. In the absence of planning, the critical infrastructures necessary for emergency response, water, food, transportation, financial transactions, medical services, and governance will collapse. Double jeopardy applies since

---

[1] *NSTAC Report* to *the President on Telecommunications and Electric Power Interdependencies: The Implications of Long-Term Outages,* December 19, 2006

debilitation of these infrastructures causes not only immediate losses but also greatly complicates and impedes the recovery processes.

Black Start

Prevention of LTOs--and ensuring recovery should prevention fail--place a premium on survivable electric power generation to sustain emergency life-support services, and reconstitute local, state and national infrastructures. An important first step in reconstituting infrastructure services is to "black start" the electric power grid, i.e. restart the grid from a complete blackout initial condition. Because it takes electricity to make electricity, it will be important to ensure that a selected complement of electric power generation plants will survive and, preferably, be able to "operate through" the events causing the blackout, be they natural or malicious. Most regional electric system operators have specially-designated "black start" plants to be used during blackout contingencies. Black start plants should be highest priority for protection against the list of LTO initiators.

The fundamental difference between a "normal" black start of the electric power grid and a black start in an LTO scenario is the large size of the affected area. As a result, other critical infrastructures that would normally be available to support the black start effort will not be available. During previous blackout events caused by ice storms, hurricanes and moderate solar storms, neighboring utilities have retained grid functionality post-event. During an LTO event, it is likely that neighboring power grids will also be mostly (if not completely) dysfunctional, precluding assistance from the "edges" of the affected area. The lack of electricity available to black start the power grid is a major challenge that must be overcome to minimize the collateral damage from a geomagnetic storm or EMP event.

Presently, no national plan exists to black start the composite grid in a potential LTO contingency. Up-front planning between industry and Government on cross-sector, situational-analysis data structures and tools will be needed to foster a common operating picture. Access to and sustainment of adequate fuel supplies will be critical in the event of an LTO. National planning must include cross-sector black start procedures for situations as severe as an LTO. Black start planning has occurred in some regions. But the transition from local to regional to national management of an LTO has not been defined and nor have the attending governance issues. It is encouraging that national-level LTO exercises have, beginning in 2011, been initiated by the National Defense University, the Johns Hopkins Applied Physics Laboratory, and the FBI's Infragard EMP Special Interest Group. It will be important that LTO contingencies be incorporated into future federal, state, and local government exercises.

Black start planning and exercises are important because there is a premium on rapidly restarting the grid – before generation plant machinery cools if possible. It is known that power outages result in social unrest within days. In addition, as outages persist, cascading failures multiply. Other infrastructures will suffer outages with varying delays due to the dark electric power grid. For example, initially water supplies will be available from water towers and holding tanks; however within a few days, should the outage continue, water supplies will be depleted. The same is true for fuel supplies. Backup generators at telecommunications and Internet exchange carrier centers, medical centers, government centers and nuclear power plants will deplete their fuel supplies within days to weeks.

The black start task will truly be a race against the clock. With each passing hour, the grid will degrade further and the effects of the loss of other infrastructures, affected by power outages, will continue to grow. Rapid black start is also important to avoid lockup of plant spinning machinery including turbines, motors and generators. Breakers and equipment at substations are notoriously difficult to restart in cold weather. Generation plants cool rapidly during cold weather, complicating the restart process. Decisions made early in the event will affect the success or failure of the black start.

Hydro and coal plants have been primary black start power sources. The best plants for blackstarting the grid are hydroelectric generation plants because they do not depend on fuel reserves and it is straightforward to keep hydro turbines spinning. Also, coal-fired generation plants usually have a 90-day supply of coal on hand.[2]

A new trend is to use gas plants as primary black start[3] but during LTO contingencies gas pipelines are likely to be nonfunctional. This is because gas pipelines require pumping stations to pressurize the contents in order to create flow. These pumps operate by either electricity or natural gas; increasingly, electrical pumps are replacing gas-powered pumps.[4] Unless all the gas pipeline pumping stations from source to destination are powered by gas, which is unlikely, fuel will not move once the electricity goes out. Without electricity to power these pumps, only a few hours of gas will be available until the pressure of the gas lines drops below the threshold required to maintain flow. The primary concern is the inability to restart gas-fired power generation plants. These plants will not be able to be brought back online until electricity is restored to gas pumping stations.[5] If all stations from source to destination are powered by natural gas, the system is likely to function, provided SCADA systems do not interrupt operations.

Wide-area communications to coordinate with neighboring grid operators and generation station operators may be a problem, especially following EMP/GMD events. Due to grid collapse it is likely that SCADA systems will be unable to provide central operators an accurate view of the current state of the grid. These systems may be completely nonfunctional or send out inaccurate reports.

Nuclear Reactor Vulnerabilities

Notwithstanding nuclear plants U235 fuel multi-year longevity offers major advantages over other plants in potential LTO contingencies, present nuclear power plant configurations do not allow for an "operate through" capability. The current policy is to shut down nuclear plants during grid collapse situations. The reason is the potential for reactor cores to overheat leading to the possibility of Fukushima-type catastrophes. Factors contributing to overheating conditions include:

    1) Loss of the grid load on the nuclear plant generators necessitating the shut-down of the generator steam turbines which in turn curtails coolant flow within plants.

    2) Drop in grid voltage levels and AC frequency fluctuation during blackouts can cause coolant pumps and other plant safety equipment to malfunction.

The combined reactor shutdown and blackout of off-site power jeopardizes the continued coolant flow to the reactor core because of the inadequate long-term on-site backup power capacity and fuel reserves. Nuclear power plants now depend on the delivery of fuel for

[2] CENTRA Technology Group. *Geomagnetic Storms.* Washington, D.C.: Office of Risk Management and Analysis, U.S. Department of Homeland Security, 2011, p. 29.

[3] Black Start, Blackout, and Diesels: Some Clarity, Yes Vermont Yankee, Blot Site, 13 August 2012

[4] Association of Oil Pipe Lines. *About Pipelines.* n.d. http://www.aopl.org/aboutPipelines/ (accessed March 3, 2012).

[5] Natural Gas Supply Association. *The Transportation of Natural Gas.* n.d. http://www.naturalgas.org/naturalgas/transport.asp (accessed March 2, 2012).

backup generators to cool reactor cores should the grid fail. In the event of a prolonged power outage, government agencies have promised around-the-clock deliveries of diesel fuel for nuclear power plants.[6] However, this fuel would likely not be available during a severe EMP or GMD event due to electric fuel pump failure.

Nuclear power plants typically only have one week of fuel available on-site. Once this fuel is depleted, if additional fuel cannot be delivered, the pumps supplying water for cooling will fail. This situation would be similar to what occurred during the catastrophic failure of the Fukushima Daiichi nuclear reactors. The tsunami did not directly cause the meltdown; rather, it was the loss of offsite electricity and damage to backup generators that prevented the reactor cooling pumps from operating. Nuclear fuel rods have a zirconium cladding which, when super-heated and exposed to air, burns like magnesium. When burning cladding is exposed to water, the reaction produces explosive hydrogen gas, responsible for blowing the roofs off the reactor containment structures at Fukushima. Thermal shock causes the fuel rods to rupture releasing highly radioactive material.

The storage pools containing spent fuel rods are also of concern and more dangerous than the reactors themselves. Typically spent fuel rods remain in cooling pools from 3 to 5 years, after which they can be moved to air-cooled storage. Should coolant pumps fail due to the loss of electricity, the "boil-down time" for these containment pools is between 4 and 22 days. At most storage sites the spent fuel rod pools contain larger quantities of radioactive material than the active reactors. Overheating of this material, through processes similar to reactor fuel rod ignition and thermal shock, results in the release of highly radioactive material into the environment. Because the spent fuel storage pools are typically on or near the nuclear plant sites, sustaining nuclear plant reactor operation to provide onsite electricity will eliminate the need for shipping power from offsite locations to run the spent fuel storage coolant pumps. A major reason for sustaining nuclear reactor operation in a potential LTO situation is that, should nuclear plants be shut down automatically or intentionally, it is not possible to restart them. The large amounts of off-site power required for restart would not be available in a wide-area blackout. For pressurized water reactors, the amount of off-site restart power runs into the tens of megawatts.

As we consider the engineering challenge of designing or retrofitting nuclear power plants with the ability to "operate through" grid blackouts, it is important to understand why plants presently need to be shut down during blackout contingencies. Most of the large electric loads inside nuclear plants are rotating machinery such as electric motors on pumps, compressors, valves, and fans. Such loads are largely associated with the essential plant cooling systems. Since motors are driving fixed mechanical loads they must draw a fixed amount of power from the power line. Since power is the product of current and voltage, when the voltage drops, the motors will draw a larger amount of current to maintain necessary torque. Rising current with motors can result in overheating and short circuits. In addition, as the grid collapses, its 60 Hz operating frequency also decreases. This forces reactor coolant pumps to rotate at lower rpm, slowing the movement of water through the reactor, leading to elevated fuel temperatures.[7]

---

[6] Natural Gas Supply Association. *The Transportation of Natural Gas.* n.d. http://www.naturalgas.org/naturalgas/transport.asp, p. 11.
[7] Wheeler, John. This Week in Nuclear, 18 April 2011.

Nuclear plant generators are controlled so that their output matches the voltage and frequency of the larger grid. Plants are designed to sense changes in grid voltage and frequency. If grid parameter values deviate outside set operating limits, safety systems are designed to trigger automatic plant shut down. Designing or reconfiguring a nuclear plant to be able to operate through a loss of off-site power will be challenging especially with respect to the reactor safety systems.

In addition to assuring sustainment of the electrical power to the equipment inside the plant in the event of the loss of off-site power (LOOP), another engineering challenge is enabling mechanical and control systems to withstand what can be a near-instantaneous drop in generator load. Immediately prior to a blackout the reactor will be producing 100% power. If the grid collapses quickly, the next instant the load could consist only of on-site loads. By their nature, nuclear reactors behave best when loads change slowly. Immediately after the loss of grid load, reactor power will be much greater than the load and the energy normally delivered to the grid will be confined within the reactor, generating excess internal heat. This excess heat is dissipated in the water within the reactor coolant system, causing it to expand and possibly burst pipes and pressure vessels.[8]

Protecting Nuclear Reactors

A first solution to building plants that can operate through a grid collapse is to increase the capacity of the reactor coolant system. To safely respond to a rapid loss of grid load requires a reactor coolant system with a large surge volume to accommodate expanding water plus an expanded heat removal system to quickly transfer excess heat energy. Although these capabilities can be included in reactor designs, up until now they have been considered too costly given the low incidence of blackouts involving the complete loss of grid load. Also, past blackouts have been quite limited in geographic area and duration. New information on the risks of wide area, long duration LTO contingencies provides cause to reconsider the cost-benefits of building an "operate through" capability into selected nuclear power plants.

A second engineering approach to meet the engineering challenge of operating through large area, long duration blackouts would be to provide controllable load banks to compensate for loss of grid load and thus keep the load on plant generators constant. A heuristic diagram of this scheme appears in Figure 1.

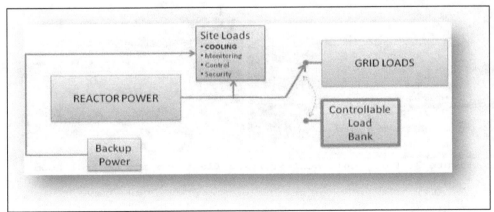

Figure 1. Nuclear Power Plant Protection using Load Bank

During a grid collapse situation, this concept would isolate plant generators from the grid to avoid the effects of voltage sag and AC frequency drop on coolant pump motors and other

---

[8] Ibid.

safety equipment. A fail-over load bank would prevent major load swings on generators enabling turbines to continue spinning. The load bank should be designed to enable load balancing in partial blackout situations where portions of the grid load remain intact. A controllable, surrogate load bank will require some real estate and must be designed to match changes in reactive power characteristics. A three megawatt, air-cooled, high voltage load bank is pictured in Figure 2. Load banks can be constructed in systems of multiple units paralleled to achieve the desired plant load value.

Figure 2. 3MW HV Air-Cooled Load Bank Unit[9]

A second alternative technique would be to allow the nuclear power plant to initially shut-down, isolate it from the grid, but provide the on-site back-up generator capacity necessary to restart the plant quickly. The Perry, Ohio nuclear plant (Figure 3) was designed in this manner for black start contingencies. The plant's ability to restart itself in short order makes it available to assist in black starting the rest of the grid. Perry uses a GE BWR/6 design boiling water reactor that requires less power to restart than pressurized water reactors. Thus the required on-site backup generation capacity is lower. However, GE BWR/6 reactors are scarce – there are only four in the United States. GE has designed an "Enhanced Safety BWR" but none have been built. The GE BWR/6 and the Enhanced Safety BWR designs should be evaluated for their potential to avert LTOs. Note that this option may also require load banks for contingencies where no grid load survives, i.e. the entire grid is dark due to electric transmission system damage from physical attack or EMP/GMD effects.

Figure 3. Perry Ohio Nuclear Power Plant and its Control Room[10]

A third technique for actualizing operate-through nuclear plants is to use small modular reactor (SMR) designs. New SMR designs eliminate reactor coolant pumps and the need for large bore piping, avoiding large-break loss of coolant accidents (LOCA). An example

[9] Ref. http://www.simplexdirect.com/Product.aspx?ProdID=12
[10] Ref. http://www.wksu.org/news/story/35836

design is shown in Figure 4. The NuScale module includes a reactor vessel, steam generators, pressurizer and containment in an integral package. Each module produces 50 megawatts and is factory built. NPMs can be incrementally added to match load growth – up to 12 modules to achieve a 600 megawatt output capacity. The small size of modules facilitates transport and installation as single units. Each module has its own skid-mounted steam turbine-generator and condenser. Plants can safely self-cool indefinitely with no operator action, no AC or DC power, and no additional water.[11]

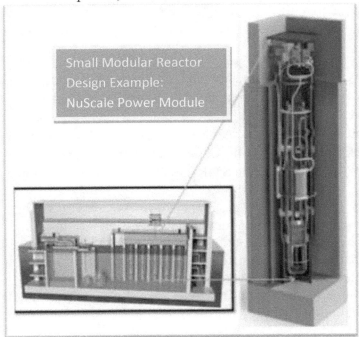

Figure 4. Small Modular Reactor Design[12]

South Carolina is in a unique position to develop improved nuclear plant designs since the first U.S. nuclear plants in 30 years are being built there at the Summer Nuclear Power Station (Figure 5). Because 60% of South Carolina's electric power is supplied by nuclear power plants, it would benefit greatly from plants engineered to operate through or recover quickly during large-scale blackouts. Although the plant contracts have been awarded, it is not too late to consider implementation enhancements to improve plant ability to operate through or rapidly recover from wide-area blackouts.

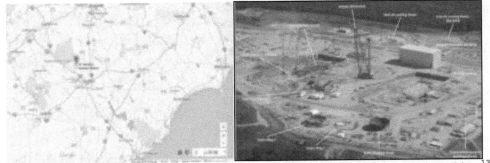

Figure 5. New SC Nuclear Power Plant Location and Construction Site[13]

---

[11] Surina and McGough, The NuScale Value Proposition, unpublished briefing, February 18, 2015.

[12] Ibid.
[13] Ref. http://enformable.com/wp-content/uploads/2014/03/VC-Summer-nuclear-power-plant.jpg

In summary, enabling nuclear power plants to sustain operations offers major advantages in recovery from large scale blackouts and hence averts long term outages (LTOs) that could otherwise last months or years. Their large power output (unlike most hydro plants), years of latent endurance of nuclear fuel (unlike coal and natural gas plants), and their inability to restart in the absence of off-site power during wide-area blackouts, argue for their inclusion as primary black start assets. Present nuclear power plant designs are not commensurate with this function due to safety concerns. There are several options for sustaining nuclear power during blackouts, involving challenging, but known and surmountable engineering solutions:

- Augmentation of existing nuclear plant cooling systems and capacities.
- Equipping existing nuclear plants with controllable load banks to compensate for lost grid load.
- Augmentation of existing nuclear station on-site generators to allow for rapid restart.
- Use of black start ready boiling water reactors in new installations.
- Use of small modular reactor (SMR) designs in new installations.

At least one U.S. nuclear plant at Perry Ohio is already designed for black start contingencies. Another encouraging development is the recent designation of SMRs as clean energy sources. It is noteworthy that South Carolina is in a unique position to address the engineering challenges posed here in its development of the first new U.S. nuclear plants in thirty years. The state would greatly benefit from taking steps to assure that nuclear plants continue to operate during large area blackouts since nuclear power provides 60% of its electrical energy.

XIII

AN IMMEDIATE PLAN TO
DEFEND THE U.S. AGAINST NUCLEAR EMP ATTACK

Ambassador Henry F. Cooper

Summary
Considered below are: the nature of the electromagnetic pulse (EMP) threat posed by several ballistic missile attack scenarios; near term ways to defend against such scenarios by missile defenses; and a possible diplomatic adjunct to assure the effectiveness of some of these defenses.[14] Even a layered missile defense will not be perfect, so the electric power grid should be hardened as a top national priority.

Nature Of The New Nuclear EMP Threat
During the Cold War, U.S. strategic planners assumed that any Soviet attack would begin with high-altitude nuclear detonations over the United States to generate EMP and disrupt or destroy strategic mission critical communications and other electronic systems.[15] Our strategic forces and supporting command, control and communication systems were hardened so that the National Command Authority could direct, and our strategic forces could execute, a devastating retaliatory strike. This "assured destruction" strategy was intended to deter any attack; so, our critical civil infrastructure was not protected.

While our current strategic force planning still includes such "nuclear deterrence" plans, the range of international adversaries and threat scenarios has expanded since the end of the Cold War. In addition to states with large nuclear arsenals such as Russia and China, the United States is now threatened by rogue states such as North Korea and Iran, as well as terrorist organizations that may obtain nuclear weapons on the black market or from proliferators—and they may not be deterred by such threats.

Thus, U.S. strategic planning needs to adjust to new nuclear threat scenarios—including attacks on our critical infrastructure that could create havoc and major casualties. Terrorists willing to commit suicide to kill many Americans would not be deterred—nor might be others, especially Iranian leaders who have openly threatened to destroy the "Great Satan."

A high-altitude EMP (HEMP) attack is such a consequential threat. EMP Commissioners have stated that up to nine-out-of-ten American could die within a year from the societal collapse after such an attack shuts down the vulnerable electric power grid indefinitely.

Thanks to the EMP Commission, the technical nature of the EMP threat and especially how to harden against it was de-classified and made publically available in 2008. However, little

---

[14] This section is an edited and updated version of Appendix 2 of the June 28, 2015 letter from the Directors of the *Foundation for Resilient Societies* to President Barak Obama and the heads of all Departments and Agencies with responsibilities for countering the EMP threat. As of January 31, 2015 no response had been received. Our only evidence of government action beyond a White House receipt is that our letter is posted on the webpage of the Nuclear Regulatory Commission at http://pbadupws.nrc.gov/docs/ML1318/ML13183A027.pdf. See my June 24, 2014 discussion of this sad state of affairs a year later at http://highfrontier.org/june-24-2014-what-did-they-know-and-when-did-they-know-it/#sthash.QM91twLV.bOBUV4fl.dpbs. As of January 31, 2015, we still have received no response from any government office.

[15] Former Soviet planners confirmed their preemptive attack strategy in the early 1990s after the fall of the Berlin Wall and subsequent dissolution of the Soviet Union.

has been done to harden our critical infrastructure; and rogue nations, nuclear proliferators, and terrorist organizations are well aware of the devastating nature of an HEMP attack.

Because of increasing societal reliance on the current unhardened complex of electric power, sophisticated electronic devices and ubiquitous use of integrated circuits, an EMP attack by a single nuclear device today poses an existential threat to the United States and its population. We have not yet developed the conceptual framework or practical means to cope with this threat, even as rogue nations such as Iran threaten EMP attack in their rhetoric and military literature.

As former CIA Director R. James Woolsey testified on May 23, 2013 to the House Energy and Commerce Committee, our cyber and information warfare doctrines are dangerously blind to an all-out information warfare campaign—including EMP attack, designed to cripple U.S. critical infrastructures.[16] Because EMP would destroy both the electric power grid and integrated circuits essential to computers, EMP could be a key component of an information warfare attack.

Ambassador Woolsey noted that his assessment reflected the 2001-2008 work of the EMP Commission, the subsequent Congressional Strategic Posture Commission, and several other major U.S. Government studies—collectively representing a non-partisan scientific and strategic consensus that such an attack upon the United States is an existential threat. The foundation for identifying the existential nature of the information warfare and EMP threats was laid by the unanimous conclusions (based on all-source intelligence) of the 1998 Commission to Assess the Ballistic Missile Threat to the United States. In over 15 years since this Commission on which he served, subsequent Commissions and competent studies have reinforced this view, but little has been done to adjust U.S. strategic planning.

The EMP component of such an information warfare attack can now be executed by a long-range ballistic missile launched from the homeland of these states. However, the 1998 Commission identified a simpler—and perhaps less defensible—EMP attack strategy employing a short-range ballistic missile launched from a ship near the U.S. coast. Even unsophisticated and under-resourced terrorists could threaten EMP attack by mating a small nuclear device to a SCUD missile—or other missile of simple design—and mounting the missile and payload to a small freighter. We are most vulnerable to this threat from the Gulf of Mexico.

Perhaps the most troubling of these potential threats comes from North Korea and Iran, both of which employ nuclear and ballistic missile technology obtained from Russia and China.[17] Both have launched ballistic missiles in large numbers as part of military exercises; both have demonstrated intercontinental ballistic missile (ICBM) range capability; and both have placed satellites in orbit—notably launched over the South Polar region to approach the United States from the south in their maiden orbit at a few hundred miles altitude, just right for casting EMP effects over the entire continental United States. Our homeland missile defenses are currently arrayed against ICBMs that approach the United States from

---

[16] Former CIA Director Woolsey testified that Russia, China, North Korea, and Iran all include in their strategic doctrine and plans a wide spectrum of information warfare threats, including cyber-attack, sabotage and kinetic attacks on key system nodes, and wide-area EMP attack. See http://highfrontier.org/r-james-woolsey-testimony-before-the-house-committee-on-energy-and-commerce-may-21-2013/#sthash.wj3Fl4gP.dpbs.

[17] Russia and China have an excellent understanding of EMP effects, and their scientists, whether officially authorized or not, have proliferated this information to North Korea and Iran.

trajectories near to the North Pole, surely a well-known fact among North Korean and Iranian war planners.

North Korea has conducted three underground nuclear tests, including the most recent test in February 2013. Open source reports indicate that Iranian scientists have been present at North Korean nuclear tests—and it is not implausible to suggest that when North Korea is satisfied with a given nuclear design, Iran may be also.

Some reports have characterized North Korean tests as "failures" because of their low explosive yield. However, North Korea may be testing light-weight, low-yield advanced nuclear weapon designs obtained from Russia or China. These specialized devices may be designed to produce a low explosive yield, but a significantly higher output of gamma rays. In operational use, the gamma rays produced by such weapon designs would interact with the earth's magnetic field to produce enhanced EMP effects.

Low-yield entry-level weapons—even those without EMP enhancements—if detonated at an altitude of 60-70 kilometers will produce EMP fields sufficient to cause permanent damage to integrated circuits.

Because of technical interchanges between North Korea and Iran, there should be great concern that Iran will be following North Korea's lead in short order—perhaps even concurrently—to mate EMP-enhanced weapons to ballistic missiles or to include light-weight EMP weapons as satellite payloads.

On January 22, 2014, Caroline Glick in her *Jerusalem Post* article reported that Israeli Channel 2 showed satellite photos of an ICBM or satellite launcher being deployed near Tehran.[18] And Iran clearly understands how to leverage EMP effects created by nuclear weapons in its strategic and tactical planning. Former DCI Woolsey testified that Iranian doctrinal writings include assertions such as:

- "Nuclear weapons . . . can be used to determine the outcome of a war, without inflicting serious human damage [by neutralizing] strategic and information networks;"
- "Terrorist information warfare [includes] the technology of directed energy (DEW) or electromagnetic pulse (EMP);" and
- ". . . [W]hen you disable a country's military's high command through disruption of communications you will, in effect, disrupt all the affairs of that country. . . . If the world's industrial countries fail to devise effective ways to defend themselves against dangerous electronic assaults, then they will disintegrate within a few years."

Finally, Iran first launched a ballistic missile from a vessel in the Caspian Sea over a decade ago and, as former Director of Central Intelligence Woolsey testified, has several times demonstrated the capability to detonate a warhead at the high-altitudes necessary for an EMP attack on the entire United States. Thus, these tests are signatures of Iranian planning for an EMP attack that could be launched from a vessel off the U.S. coast.

In summary, rogue nations and terrorist organizations are aware of the destructive potential of EMP attack, have included EMP attack in their war plans, and could soon have an ability to execute such an attack. Time is short for the United States to develop EMP defenses.

---

[18] "Iran, Obama, Boehner and Netanyahu," The Jerusalem Post, January 22, 2015, http://www.jpost.com/Opinion/Column-one-Iran-Obama-Boehner-and-Netanyahu-388671

Gaps In Our Defenses Against EMP Attacks

Our strategic defenses should be designed to deter and defeat war-fighting doctrines of nations with substantial nuclear arsenals, rogue states with just a few nuclear weapons, and terrorist organizations that obtain nuclear weapons on the black market or from proliferators. Regrettably, our current defenses are focused on intercontinental missile attack via northern trajectories, and therefore leave the United States vulnerable to an EMP attack in at least three major ways:

- Nuclear-armed ballistic missiles launched from ships off our coasts and detonated a hundred miles or so over the United States;
- Nuclear-armed ballistic missiles launched from an aircraft and detonated over the United States; and
- Detonation of a nuclear weapon carried on a low earth orbit satellite as it passes over the United States.

None of these attack modes offer significant technological challenges to nation states with a modicum of nuclear weapon and ballistic missile technology. Indeed, in the 1960s, the United States launched Minutemen ICBMs both from a ship and a cargo aircraft. Iran launched a ballistic missile from a vessel in the Caspian Sea in the late 1990s. Israel regularly conducts its ballistic missile test involving missiles launched from off-shore vessels. Etc.

The Soviet Union deployed a Fractional Orbital Bombardment System (FOBS) designed to carry a nuclear weapon over the South Pole and to be de-orbited to attack anyplace on earth. Their dedicated FOBS site, operational between November 1968 and January 1983, was dismantled following June 1982 diplomatic commitments relating to the unratified SALT II Treaty.[19] No international agreement now prohibits a ready-to-launch FOBS that could detonate a nuclear weapon in outer space.[20]

The Outer Space Treaty of 1967 prohibits placing nuclear weapons in space orbit. This agreement can be circumvented simply by preparing a ready-to-launch vehicle with a nuclear weapon and placing the launch vehicle in reserve. Upon launch during international crisis, the satellite and nuclear weapon payload could be placed in a longitudinally progressive polar orbit that would eventually be above any point on earth. When above the location of choice, and upon command, the nuclear weapon could then be detonated to produce an EMP attack.

Not only Russia and China, but also North Korea and Iran have demonstrated an inherent capability to execute such an attack.

While satellite tracking systems could pinpoint the responsible nation for a satellite-based EMP attack, there is no similar assurance for an attack from a ship or aircraft. Without the

---

[19] See "The Soviet Fractional Orbital Bombardment System Program," Technical Report APA-TR-2010-0101 by Miroslav Gyűrösi, January 2010 (updated April 2012), available at http://www.ausairpower.net/APA-Sov-FOBS-Program.html, last accessed June 23, 2013.

[20] However, the *employment* of a space-based nuclear EMP weapon, whether launched by a FOBS system or otherwise, would constitute a "material breach" of the U.N. Convention on Environmental Modification, the ENMOD Treaty of 1977. This Convention entered into force on October 5, 1978; for the U.S. on January 17, 1980. It prohibits environmental modifications with "widespread, long-lasting or severe effects" as the means of "destruction, damage, or injury to any other State Party." North Korea ratified the ENMOD Convention on November 8, 1984. Iran became a treaty signatory on May 18, 1977, but did not ratify. Iran has a continuing duty not to act so as to defeat the "object and purpose" of the Convention.

National Command Authority knowing the origin of an EMP attack, the doctrine of deterrence based on massive nuclear retaliation fails. Retaliatory doctrines also fail for terrorists prepared to commit suicide to kill several hundred million Americans.

While terrorists might find it difficult to carry out an aircraft or satellite-based EMP attack, short range ballistic missiles and their mobile launchers can be easily purchased and carried covertly on any of the numerous vessels daily traversing near U.S. national waters.

In any case, defenses to counter the ship-based EMP attack scenario deserve top priority in rectifying our current vulnerability to EMP attack. Fortunately, there are operational capabilities that can be quickly adapted to provide such an EMP defense.

Near-Term Defenses Against EMP Attacks From Off-Shore And The South[21]
The nearest term defense against ship-based EMP attack can be provided by the U.S. Navy's Aegis Ballistic Missile Defense (BMD) system. In its impressive test record—29 successful intercepts out of 35 attempts, all executed by operational crews—the Aegis BMD system has already demonstrated it can shoot down short, medium and intermediate range ballistic missiles, in both their ascent (post-burnout) and midcourse phases of flight.

Today, there are at least 30 Aegis BMD Cruisers and Destroyers at sea around the world—currently funded plans will grow this number to 35 by 2018 and more of the approximately 80 Aegis ships could be given BMD capability for less than $50 million per ship. The marginal cost of the current SM-3 interceptor is less than $10 million per interceptor.

If Aegis BMD ships are to protect the United States from an EMP attack:

- Aegis crews must be operationally trained to intercept missiles in their ascent and midcourse phases of flight—as they are, and
- Aegis ships must be in the vicinity of the ship from which a potential attack is launched.

Normally, a few Aegis BMD ships are near our east and west coasts or in a coastal port—where they can maintain a BMD operational status if desired and so ordered. Furthermore, if these coastal ships were to be periodically tested against short and medium range ballistic missiles near our east and west coasts, such tests could contribute to deterring a terrorist EMP attack. On a random day in 2013, there were 4-6 Aegis BMD ships near the east coast or in an east coast port—all that is needed to provide an immediate defense is training and readiness operations.

However, defending against an EMP attack from the Gulf of Mexico is not so easily and quickly addressed, because our Aegis BMD ships do not normally traverse the Gulf—and these ships are needed overseas by our global combatant commanders. Except for an urgent requirement, perhaps on the basis of confirmed strategic warning, we will remain vulnerable to an EMP attack from the Gulf (or from the south, e.g., Venezuela) until we have a dedicated defense against this contingency is provided. But a "Quick Fix" solution (within a few years) exists as shown below.

---

[21] This and the next section elaborates "How to Protect America from the EMP Threat," by Henry F. Cooper and Robert L. Pfaltzgraff, *Investor's Business Daily*, October 2, 2014. http://news.investors.com/ibd-editorials-perspective/100314-720276-countering-an-emp-attack-on-america.htm

Important Quick Fix to Threats from the South: Aegis Ashore Sites Around the Gulf of Mexico

- *Aegis Ashore site in Hawaii is operational for testing purposes*
- *Have begun construction of Romanian Site*
  - *Operational by 2015 with a second site in Poland by 2018*
- *Site spacing around Gulf coasts depends on interceptor speeds*
  - *Have met with folks in Mississippi and Florida*
    - *Pascagoula , Miss. where Aegis ships are built*
    - *Panama City/Tyndall AFB, FL home of 1ˢᵗ AFNORTH*
      - *Command Links to 263ʳᵈ AAMDC in Anderson, SC*
- *Going to Texas this year—Corpus Christi possibilities?*

Aegis Ashore employs Aegis BMD shipboard components as "football size" ground-based interceptor system—no additional R&D cost

A near-term dedicated defense against short and medium range missiles launched from the south would be to deploy Aegis Ashore sites on several military bases proximate to the Gulf of Mexico. An Aegis Ashore site is operational in Hawaii for testing purposes, and the first overseas site will be operational this year in Romania. The second site is scheduled to begin operations in Poland in 2018.

No additional development costs are required to deploy the same system concept at key locations proximate to the Gulf of Mexico. Associated site selection and environmental impact studies would be required, of course. Four sites should be sufficient.

Of the above possible basing locations, I strongly recommend our first U.S. based Aegis Ashore sites be in Pascagoula, Mississippi, where our Aegis ships have been built for years, and Tyndall Air Force Base in Panama City, Florida, home of First Air Force which is responsible for air defense of the continental United States. Still needed are sites in Texas and Southern Florida.

The Defense Authorization Act for FY2014, reported favorably by the Senate Armed Services Committee (SASC) in June 2013[22] and not amended by the final Act, directed an expedited process to evaluate missile defense options against EMP threats to the homeland. But so far there has been no notable response from the administration.[23] The SASC called

---

[22] See S. Rpt. 113-044, accompanying S.1197, the Defense Authorization Act for FY2014 as reported to the Senate on June 20, 2013. Text of. Sec. 231 is available at http://www.gpo.gov/fdsys/pkg/BILLS-113s1197pcs/pdf/BILLS-113s1197pcs.pdf .

[23] The Secretary of Defense was supposed to submit to Congress within 180 days after enactment, a report on several potential future options for enhancing United States homeland ballistic missile defense.

for consideration of missile defense options to "defend the United States homeland against ballistic missiles that could be launched from vessels on the seas around the United States, including the Gulf of Mexico, or other ballistic missile threats that could approach the United States from the south, should such a threat arise in the future." This latter important threat is discussed below.

Near-Term Defenses Against EMP Attacks From Over The South Pole

Concepts for Aegis-based ballistic missile defense (i.e., both the currently deployed ships and future Aegis Ashore sites) should be integrated into the global missile defense architecture. Furthermore, the Aegis SPY-1 radar provides important tracking and warning information to this global system—and provides an important complement to the nation's BMD warning, attack assessment and tracking capability which historically has focused on detecting and countering ballistic missile attack via trajectories close to the North Pole.

In addition to the U.S. space sensors and other limited surface sensor capabilities, all the Aegis ships deployed worldwide—whether BMD capable or not—can help provide warning and tracking information to the BMD global command and control system. And this global system can provide critical information on attacks that come from either north or south.

In particular, a global tracking capability would help counter ballistic missile attacks that might come over the South Pole from North Korea or Iran—both nations have already launched satellites in such South Polar orbits that pass over the U.S. With such warning and track information on attacks over the South Pole, our ground-based interceptors, particularly those based in California, may be capable of intercepting an attacking satellite before it orbits over the United States.

If such a potential satellite-based attack is detected in time and tracked by our forward-based Aegis ships and other integrated sensors, other "downstream" Aegis BMD ships would also have a chance to shoot down the satellite before it overflies U.S. territory—even earlier than the longer range ground-based interceptors in California. (In 2008, the currently deployed Aegis BMD system shot down a dying satellite over the Pacific Ocean to protect cities from the toxic fuel it carried.)

Furthermore, existing Aegis air defense interceptors could be adapted to intercept a satellite launcher in its boost phase, while it is rising from its launch pad. Software changes and crew training are required to enable such a capability aboard an Aegis BMD ship appropriately stationed near the threat launch pad. This possible intercept configuration is illustrated below for a North Korean satellite launch, during its first and second stage burn phases.

TPY-2 radar at Aegis Ashore (or THAAD) site in the Philippines would help counter North Korean FOBS attack

- *TPY-2 X-Band Radar in the Philippines could cue Aegis BMD ships at sea and GBIs on Vandenberg AFB, CA*
- *First generation Aegis BMD shot down satellite in 2008; Aegis BMD ships at sea now and in the future will have improved capabilities*
- *Philippine cooperation is needed, as well as software modifications and crew training*

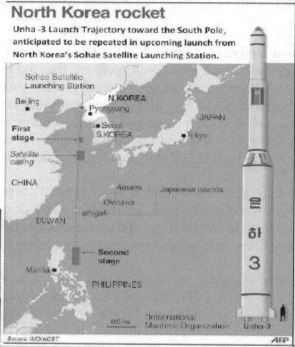

North Korea rocket

Unha -3 Launch Trajectory toward the South Pole, anticipated to be repeated in upcoming launch from North Korea's Sohae Satellite Launching Station.

Sohae Satellite Launching Station
Beijing
N KOREA
Pyongyang
First stage
Seoul
S.KOREA
JAPAN
Tokyo
Satellite casing
CHINA
Amami
Japanese islands
Okinawa
Ishigaki
TAIWAN
Second stage
Manila
PHILIPPINES
International Maritime Organization
Unha-3
Source: MOI/KCST
AFP

Interception Strategy:

- Boost phase intercept opportunities during first and second stage burn—possible with the Navy's SM-2 Block IV interceptor if an Aegis BMD ship is appropriately located, and its crew and system is prepared to do so.
- Subsequent SM-3 intercept opportunities after burnout if the Aegis BMD crew is prepared and needed sensor cuing is provided—recall that the first generation of the SM-3 was used in 2008 to shoot down a dying satellite with the help of such cuing information.
- The Vandenberg AFB ground based interceptors can be used to shoot down the satellite before it overflies the U.S.—again with needed sensor cuing information.
- An appropriate ground based radar—e.g., a TPY-2 radar—in the Philippines could help provide this needed cuing.

Americans need to wake up to FOBS threat & demand that their Representatives provide for the common defense!

Furthermore, as emphasized in this chart, cuing information provided from—say, a TPY-2 X-Band radar in the Philippines—would enable later intercept opportunities by other Aegis ships before the satellite overflies the United States.

Such a deployment could be implemented under the Enhanced Defense Cooperation Agreement (EDCA), signed by Presidents Obama and Aquino of the Philippines,[24] intended to meet 21st century challenges—a North Korean FOBS certainly qualifies. Such a deployment would "facilitate the enhanced rotational presence of U.S. forces; facilitate humanitarian assistance and disaster relief in the Philippines and the region; improve opportunities for bilateral training; and support the long-term modernization of the Armed Forces of the Philippines (AFP) as it works to establish a minimum credible defense."

Note that The TPY-2 radar is normally deployed along with the THAAD Theater Ballistic Missile Defense System—a site in the Philippines could help them protect their homeland from air and missile attack. And TPY-2 radars are being deployed in a number of other nations.

Also as indicated in the above figure, this cuing information also will help empower our operational ground based interceptors on Vandenberg Air Force Base, California.

---

[24] See "FACT SHEET: United States-Philippines Bilateral Relations," The White House, April 28, 2014
http://www.whitehouse.gov/the-press-office/2014/04/28/fact-sheet-united-states-philippines-bilateral-relations

In the case of satellites previously launched from sites near the southern coast of Iran, the same comments would apply for enabling a nearby Aegis BMD ship to shoot down a boosting launcher. However, if a satellite is launched to the south from the recently reported launch site near Tehran,[25] the Aegis BMD ships cannot get close enough for a boost-phase intercept. In that case, only more distant Aegis ships—and the Vandenberg AFB ground-based interceptors will have shots—and then only if they are provided needed cuing information.

In summary, a "South Pole" EMP attack via an orbiting satellite is within the near-term capabilities of rogue nations such as North Korea and Iran. A single-layer defense using ship-based or land-based AEGIS systems could provide substantial near-term deterrent effects. Deploying a multi-layered defense against such "Attacks from the South" should be feasible within three years and could provide both deterrent effect and high-certainty defense.

Associated Arms Control Challenge to Help Prevent Satellite-Based EMP Attack

Defending against a FOBS requires that, within seconds to a very few minutes after a satellite is launched to the south from North Korea or Iran (indeed from anywhere), the defense must be warned that it may carry a nuclear weapon—a serious challenge for arms control and diplomatic constraints. And the defense must be activated immediately. Cooperative measures are needed to accomplish such an objective.

Most helpful would be a multilateral agreement to inspect by appropriate means all space launch payloads once they are on the launch pad, shortly before launch, with the agreed understanding that all noncomplying launched payloads will be shot down. As previously explained, the Outer Space Treaty of 1967 already prohibits placing weapons of mass destruction in space orbit, but cooperative verification measures are lacking.[26] Effective verification of agreements banning potential satellite-based EMP attack would be very difficult, but not impossible.

Thus, developing acceptably-intrusive, mission effective sensors to assure compliance should be a high priority program to accompany negotiations to achieve such an international agreement. Given the practical difficulty of effectively shielding radiation emitted from a low-weight nuclear device to be placed on a satellite, cooperative verification of payload signatures may be useful. Nonetheless, it will be a significant challenge to assure detection of a nuclear weapon while at the same time not compromising national security secrets. Any verification procedure must apply to all parties and in particular must not compromise U.S. national security interests.

---

[25] "Column One: Iran, Obama, Boehner, and Netanyahu," Caroline Glick, *The Jerusalem Post*, January 22, 2015 keyed off a January 21st Chanel 2 Television report. http://www.jpost.com/Opinion/Column-one-Iran-Obama-Boehner-and-Netanyahu-388671

[26] Article IV of the Outer Space Treaty provides that "State Parties… undertake not to place in orbit around the Earth any objects carrying nuclear weapons or any other kinds of weapons of mass destruction." Both Iran and North Korea are signatory states, but without treaty ratification are not "state parties." With at least 102 State Parties, this treaty may constitute a peremptory norm of international law binding not only "state parties" but also "non-state parties."

    Complicating verification requirements for the Outer Space Treaty is the need to distinguish pre-launch nuclear power sources for space missions from pre-launch nuclear weapons payloads. United National General Assembly Resolution 47/68 of December 24, 1992 sets forth "Principles Relevant to the Use of Nuclear Power Sources in Outer Space." Highly enriched uranium 235 is a mandatory fuel source. When nuclear power sources are to be used for space missions, prior public reporting and prior notification to the United Nations are established U.N. procedures. See "Safety Framework for Nuclear Power Source Applications in Outer Space." [UN A/AC.105/934]

A possibly viable strategy follows:

- In addition to a declaratory policy threatening retaliation following a FOBS attack, the U.S. could demand that all satellite launch payloads be inspected by an appropriate body—e.g., the International Atomic Energy Agency (IAEA). If not, it should be our policy that we will shoot down such satellites launched without inspection. We should initiate programs to back up this strategy, particularly to deploy appropriately sited sensors to cue our currently operational defenses, as discussed in the following steps.

- Upon warning (e.g., of Iranian or North Korean satellite launch site preparations) and in the absence of such an independent payload inspection, Aegis BMD ships can be positioned to counter a satellite launch—either in boost phase or, with the aid of appropriate sensor cuing information, after its satellite is inserted into a southern directed orbit. The Aegis ship Captain should be pre-authorized by appropriate authorities, consistent with the warning provided by step one, to assure the intercept can be carried out without delay after the threat Iranian or North Korean satellite is launched. This requirement is no different than would be the case for any boost-phase, ascent-phase or early mid-course phase intercept defense. To assure high confidence, two interceptors might be fired.

- The ground based interceptors currently deployed at Vandenberg AFB in California probably have the range capability to intercept a FOBS from Iran or North Korea, if the Vandenberg command and control system is provided appropriate orbital parameters to cue its interceptors into the right battle space. The same sensors recommended in step 2 should be able to provide this needed cuing information. Since the Ground Based Interceptor system test record suggests only a 0.5 single shot kill probability, several interceptors—perhaps all four based at Vandenberg— should be launched to assure a high kill probability. (A shoot-look-shoot strategy could reduce the number required.)

- Finally, even a layered defense will not be perfect, so the electric power grid should be hardened as a top national priority. The appropriate strategy would be to harden first the critical nodes of the grid—e.g., their extra high voltage (EHV) transformers, which are not easily replaced and the survival of which would assure the grid can be quickly reconstituted after such an attack, provided other critically important components that could be destroyed by the EMP are stockpiled. Hardening the hundred or so U.S. nuclear power reactors, which produce about 20-percent of the nation's electricity, also should be a top priority. Implementing this strategy could take years, so we should enable a layered defense as quickly as possible. As noted above, we can and should **immediately** take inexpensive high-payoff steps to exploit our already existing BMD operational capability.

An adjunct to these steps should be to prepare to destroy the satellite launch vehicles on their launch pads—as former Defense Secretary William Perry and current Defense Secretary Ashton Carter originally recommended in their June 22, 2006 Washington Post article to deal with North Korean nuclear-armed ICBM threat.[27] The EMP from a southward launched nuclear armed satellite is currently much more dangerous than the ICBM threat, for which we have deployed at least a limited defense. We are completely vulnerable to the FOBS attacks from the south.

---

[27] "If Necessary, Strike and Deploy," Ashton B. Carter and William J. Perry, *The Washington Post*, Thursday, June 22, 2006. http://www.washingtonpost.com/wp-dyn/content/article/2006/06/21/AR2006062101518.html

Concluding Comments

EMP attack is an imminent threat and potential adversaries—including North Korea, Iran, and terrorists—well understand how to execute this kind of attack. Especially Iran, once it achieves a nuclear weapon that can be mated to essentially any of its many ballistic missile systems, poses an imminent existential threat to the United States. Iran might deliver such an attack directly (e.g., by launching a nuclear weapon on a satellite over the South Pole and detonating it in its first orbit over the United States); or it might engage surrogate terrorists to launch a high-altitude EMP attack from a vessel near our coasts.

Our current homeland missile defense systems are deployed primarily to defend against ICBMs that approach the United States from the north—over the North Pole. Urgently needed are defenses against EMP attacks that might be launched from vessels off our coasts—particularly off the coast of the Gulf of Mexico. Near term and relatively inexpensive defenses are feasible using existing Aegis ballistic missile defense systems, both ship-based and land-based.

We also need defenses and a companion diplomatic strategy to counter the possible threat posed by a nuclear weapon carried by a satellite in a south polar orbit, which might be detonated in its maiden orbit before currently deployed defenses can counter it. Confident warning and attack assessment information is needed to defend against this EMP attack scenario—which may be aided by an appropriate diplomatic strategy employing pre-launch payload inspections and related confidence building measures.

SELECT SOURCES

Congressional EMP Commission, *Report of the Commission to Assess the Threat to the United States from Electromagnetic Pulse (EMP) Attack*, Volume I: Executive Summary (Washington, D.C.: 2004).

Congressional EMP Commission, *Report of the Commission to Assess the Threat to the United States from Electromagnetic Pulse (EMP) Attack: Critical National Infrastructures* (Washington, D.C.: 2008).

National Academy of Sciences, *Severe Space Weather Events--Understanding Societal and Economic Impacts* (Washington, D.C.: National Academies Press, 2008).

Congressional Strategic Posture Commission, *America's Strategic Posture: The Final Report of the Congressional Commission on the Strategic Posture of the United States* (Washington, D.C.: United States Institute of Peace Press, 2009).

North American Electric Reliability Corporation and U.S. Department of Energy, *High-Impact, Low-Frequency Event Risk to the North American Bulk Power System* (June 2010).

U.S. Federal Energy Regulatory Commission (FERC) Interagency (White House, U.S. Department of Defense, and Oak Ridge National Laboratory) Reports:

--U.S. FERC, *Electromagnetic Pulse: Effects on the U.S. Power Grid*, Executive Summary (Washington, D.C.: 2010).
--John Kappenman, *Geomagnetic Storms and Their Impacts on the U.S. Power Grid* (Meta-R-319) Metatech Corporation (January 2010).
--Edward Savage, James Gilbert and William Radasky, *The Early-Time (E1) High-Altitude Electromagnetic Pulse (HEMP) and Its Impact on the U.S. Power Grid* (Meta-R-320) Metatech Corporation (January 2010).
--John Kappenman, *Low-Frequency Protection Concepts for the Electric Power Grid: Geomagnetically Induced Current (GIC) and E3 HEMP* (Meta-R-322) Metatech Corporation (January 2010).
--William Radasky and Edward Savage, *Intentional Electromagnetic Interference (IEMI) and Its Impact on the U.S. Power Grid* (Meta-R-324) Metatech Corporation (January 2010).

U.S. Department of Defense, *Pocket Guide for Security Procedures and Protocols for Mitigating Radio Frequency Threats*, Technical Support Working Group, Directed Energy Technical Office, Dahlgren Naval Surface Warfare Center.

President Barak Obama, Presidential Policy Directive-8, *National Preparedness* (Washington, D.C.: The White House, March 30, 2011).

U.S. Department of Homeland Security, *The Strategic National Risk Assessment in Support of PPD 8: A Comprehensive Risk-Based Approach toward a Secure and Resilient Nation* (Washington, D.C.: December 2011) http://www.dhs.gov/xlibrary/assets/rma-strategic-1.

North American Electric Reliability Corporation, *2012 Special Reliability Assessment: Effects of Geomagnetic Disturbances on the Bulk Power System* (February 2012).

House of Commons Defence Committee, *Developing Threats: Electro-Magnetic Pulses (EMP)*, Tenth Report of Session 2010-12, HC-1552 (London: Parliament, United Kingdom, February 8, 2012).

House of Commons Defence Committee, *Developing Threats: Electro-Magnetic Pulses (EMP): Government Response to the Committee's Tenth Report of the Session 2010-12*, HC-1925 (London: Parliament, United Kingdom, April 25, 2012).

Thomas S. Popik, C*omparative Analysis of "2012 Special Reliability Assessment: Effects of Geomagnetic Disturbances on the Bulk Power System" National Electric Reliability Corporation (NERC) and "Electromagnetic Pulse: Effects on the U.S. Power Grid" U.S. Federal Energy Regulatory Commission* (Foundation for Resilient Societies and Task Force on National and Homeland Security, March 2012).

Electric Infrastructure Security Council, *Detailed Review of the 2012 NERC Report* (Washington, D.C.: March 21, 2012).

U.S. Department of Energy, *Large Power Transformers and the U.S. Electric Grid*, Infrastructure Security and Energy Restoration Office of Electricity Delivery and Energy Reliability (Washington, D.C.: 2012).

Electric Power Research Institute, *Electromagnetic Pulses (EMPS) And The Power Grid* (September 2012).

U.S. Government Accountability Office, *Cybersecurity: Challenges in Securing the Electricity Grid* (Washington, D.C.: 2012).

National Research Council of the National Academies, *Terrorism and the Electric Power Delivery System*, Committee on Enhancing the Robustness and Resilience of Future Electrical Transmission and Transmission in the United States to terrorist Attack, Board on Energy and Environment Systems, Division on Engineering and Physical Sciences (Washington, D.C.: 2012).

U.S. National Intelligence Council, *Global Trends 2030: Alternative Worlds*, NIC 2012-001 (Washington, D.C.: 2012).

U.S. House of Representatives, Rep. Edward J. Markey and Rep. Henry A. Waxman, *Electric Grid Vulnerability: Industry Responses Reveal Security Gaps* (Washington, D.C.: May 21, 2013).

Dr. Peter Vincent Pry, *Electric Armageddon: Civil-Military Preparedness For An Electromagnetic Pulse Catastrophe* (Task Force on National and Homeland Security, 2013).

Dr. Peter Vincent Pry, *Apocalypse Unknown: The Struggle To Protect America From An Electromagnetic Pulse Catastrophe* (Task Force on National and Homeland Security, 2013).

Center for Security Policy, *Guilty Knowledge: What the U.S. Government Knows about the Vulnerability of the Electric Grid, But Refuses to Fix* (Washington, D.C.: 2014).

Electric Infrastructure Security Council, *EIS Council Comments on Benchmark GMD Event for NERC GMD Task Force Consideration* (Washington, D.C.: May 21, 2014).

John G. Kappenman and Dr. William A. Radasky, *Examination of NERC GMD Standards and Validation of Ground Models and Geo-Electric Fields Proposed in this NERC GMD Standard* (Storm Analysis Consultants and Metatch Corporation, July 30, 2014).

Thomas Popik and William Harris for The Foundation for Resilient Societies, *Reliability Standard for Geomagnetic Disturbance Operations*, Docket No. RM14-1-000, critiques submitted to U.S. FERC on March 24, July 21, and August 18, 2014.

General Pavel Andreevich Zhilin, *The History of Military Art* (Moscow: 1986) translated in JPRS-UMA-87-004-L (Washington, D.C.: Foreign Broadcast Information Service, March 27, 1987).

BIOGRAPHIES

Dr. Peter Vincent Pry is Executive Director of the EMP Task Force on National and Homeland Security, a Congressional Advisory Board that endeavors to continue the work of the EMP Commission. Dr. Pry is also Director of the United States Nuclear Strategy Forum, an advisory body to Congress on policies to counter weapons of mass destruction. Dr. Pry has served in the Congressional EMP Commission, the Congressional Strategic Posture Commission, the House Armed Services Committee, and the Central Intelligence Agency. Dr. Pry holds a certificate in nuclear weapons design. Dr. Pry has written numerous books on national security issues, including: *Apocalypse Unknown, Electric Armageddon: Civil-Military Preparedness For An Electromagnetic Pulse Catastrophe, War Scare: Russia and America on the Nuclear Brink, Nuclear Wars: Exchanges and Outcomes, The Strategic Nuclear Balance: And Why It Matters*, and *Israel's Nuclear Arsenal*. His books *War Scare* and *Electric Armageddon* have become the basis for documentaries by the BBC and National Geographic. Dr. Pry appears frequently on TV and radio as a national security commentator.

Dr. William R. Graham served as President Ronald Wilson Reagan's Science Advisor, Acting Administrator of the National Aeronautics and Space Administration (NASA), and Chairman of the Congressional EMP Commission. As a young defense scientist working for the U.S. Army, Dr. Graham was among the team that investigated and first discovered the EMP phenomenon in the aftermath of the 1962 STARFISH PRIME nuclear test. Dr. Graham is widely considered the Free World's foremost expert on EMP. Dr. Graham has served on several high-level study groups, including the Department of Defense Transformation Study Group, the Commission to Assess United States National Security Space Management and Organization (the Rumsfeld Commission on Space), and the Commission to Assess the Ballistic Missile Threat to the United States. From 1986-1989 Dr. Graham was director of the White House Office of Science and Technology Policy while he served concurrently as Science Advisor to President Reagan, Chairman of the Federal Joint Telecommunications Resources Board, and member of the Arms Control Experts Group. Dr. Graham was also Chairman of the Board and Chief Executive Officer of National Security Research Inc. (NSR), a Washington-based company that conducts technical, operational, and policy research and analysis related to U.S. national security. Dr. Graham is Chairman of the EMP Task Force on National and Homeland Security, a Congressional Advisory Board.

Ambassador R. James Woolsey previously served in the U.S. Government on five different occasions, where he held Presidential appointments in two Republican and two Democratic administrations, most recently (1993-95) as Director of Central Intelligence. During his 12 years of government service, in addition to heading the Central Intelligence Agency and the Intelligence Community, Mr. Woolsey was: Ambassador to the Negotiation on Conventional Armed Forces in Europe (CFE), Vienna, 1989-1991; Under Secretary of the Navy, 1977-1979; and General Counsel to the U.S. Senate Committee on Armed Services, 1970-1973. He was also appointed by the President to serve on a part-time basis in Geneva, Switzerland, 1983-1986, as Delegate at Large to the U.S.-Soviet Strategic Arms Reduction Talks (START) and Nuclear and Space Arms Talks (NST). As an officer in the U.S. Army, he was an adviser on the U.S. Delegation to the Strategic Arms Limitation Talks (SALT I), Helsinki and Vienna, 1969-1970. Mr. Woolsey serves on a range of government, corporate, and non-profit advisory boards and chairs several, including that of the Washington firm, Executive Action LLC. He serves on the National Commission on Energy Policy. He is currently Chancellor of the Institute of World Politics and Chairman of the Leadership Council of the Foundation for Defense of Democracies and Co-Chairman of the Committee on the Present Danger. He has also been a member of the Congressional Commission on the Strategic Posture of the United States; the National Commission on Terrorism; the Commission to Assess the Ballistic Missile Threat to the U.S.; and the President's Commission on Strategic Forces. He also presently serves as a Director the EMP Task Force on National and Homeland Security, a Congressional Advisory Board.

Ambassador Henry F. Cooper is Chairman of High Frontier, Chairman Emeritus of Applied Research Associates, and a Director of the EMP Task Force on National and Homeland Security (a Congressional Advisory Board), the Foundation for Resilient Societies, and the London Center for Policy Research. At High Frontier, he is working with local, state, and federal authorities to provide effective defenses against ballistic missiles, particularly those that pose an existential EMP threat to all Americans. Since 1979, he has been appointed by the President to serve as Deputy Assistant Secretary of the Air Force with oversight responsibility for Air Force strategic and space systems (1979-81); Assistant Director of the U.S. Arms Control and Disarmament Agency, backstopping all bilateral negotiations with the Soviet Union (1983-85); Ambassador and Chief U.S. Negotiator at the Geneva Defense and Space Talks with the USSR (1985-90); and Director of the Strategic Defense Initiative (SDI, 1990-93). He served on numerous technical working groups and high level advisory boards--including the Defense Science Board, the Air Force Scientific Advisory Board, U.S. Strategic Command's Strategic Advisory Group, the Defense Nuclear Agency's Scientific Advisory Group on Effects, and the Congressional Commission to Assess the U.S. Government's Organization and Programs to Combat the Proliferation of Weapons of Mass Destruction. He received the Defense Department's Distinguished Public Service Medal, the Defense Special Weapons Agency Lifetime Achievement Award, the U.S. Missile Defense Agency's Ronald Reagan Award, the U.S. Navy Aegis BMD Pathfinder Award, and Clemson University's Distinguished Service Medal. Ambassador Cooper taught at Clemson University and worked at Bell Telephone Labs, the Air Force Weapons Lab, R&D Associates, and JAYCOR. He holds BS and MS degrees from Clemson University and a Ph.D. from New York University, all in Mechanical Engineering.

Representative Andrea Boland served four terms in the Maine House of Representatives for District 142. Rep. Boland is a national leader in electric infrastructure security for geomagnetic storms and manmade electromagnetic pulse. She introduced the first State legislation in the nation to deal with EMP, which passed the Maine State Legislature in 2013 nearly unanimously. She served as a U.S. delegate to the international Electric Infrastructure Security Summit in 2012. Several States are now using her legislation as a model to protect their electric grids. Born and raised in the Boston area, Rep. Boland graduated from Elmira College in New York with a BA in International Relations and French. She studied at the University of Paris and earned her MBA from Northeastern University. She is self-employed as a real estate title examiner and has two children. She is a member of the Task Force on National and Homeland Security. Rep. Boland is a Democrat.

Senator David Farnsworth served as a Representative to the Arizona State House of Representatives 1995-1996 and was appointed to the Arizona State Senate on September 11, 2013. Born a U.S. citizen in Mexico City, Mexico in 1951, his family returned to Arizona in 1952 where he has been a resident ever since. An entrepreneur and small businessman, he owns a real estate investing and rental management company and is former owner of Farnsworth Auto Sales, Farnsworth Auto Recycling and Farnsworth Distributing.

Senator Farnsworth has worked as a licensed real estate and insurance agent, a supervisor for Home Depot, a crane and forklift operator for the Snowflake Paper Mill, and an underground diesel mechanic for Hecla Mining Company, a copper mine 30 miles south of Casa Grande, Arizona. Senator Farnsworth studied Business Administration at Mesa Community College. He is married to Robin Farnsworth. They have seven children and are active members of the LDS Church. Senator Farnsworth has a passion for good government, protecting the freedoms we enjoy, and is a Republican.

Senator Bryce Reeves in November 2011 defeated a 28-year incumbent to win the 17th District seat to the Virginia State Senate. As a freshman he was chosen to serve on four Senate standing committees, including the powerful Courts of Justice Committee, the Privileges and Elections Committee, the Social Services and Rehabilitation Committee, and the General Laws and Technology Committee. He is Co-Chair of the Military Caucus and is the Senate representative to the Virginia Military Advisory Council to the Governor. Senator Reeves was appointed to the Commission on Military Installations and Defense Activities. He is a standing member of the National Conference of State Legislatures Task Force on Military and Veterans Affairs. Senator Reeves holds a BS degree from Texas A&M University, recognized as a Distinguished Military Graduate. He earned a Master of Public Administration on Public Policy from George Mason University and has completed advanced leadership courses at Harvard University's JFK School of Government. Senator Reeves began his public service with a commission as a 2nd Lieutenant in the U.S. Army as an Airborne Ranger in the Infantry. He lives in Spotsylvania County, Virginia, with his wife Anne and their two children, Nicole and Jack. Senator Reeves is a Republican.

Senator Ralph Shortey was elected in 2010 and continues to serve in the Oklahoma State Senate. He is a member of the Rosebud Sioux Indian Tribe. Senator Ralph Shortey was born in Casper, Wyoming. He spent part of his childhood on the Rosebud Sioux Indian Reservation in Grass Mountain, South Dakota before moving to Oklahoma City where he attended Moore Public Schools. Shortey graduated from West Moore High School in 2000, and following graduation he attended Heartland Baptist Bible College in Oklahoma City in preparation for mission work in Uganda. In 2002, Ralph married his high school sweetheart, Jennifer and continues to make his home in south Oklahoma City with their two children, Kaitlyn and Elena. With a growing family, Shortey decided against pursuing mission work and instead entered the oil and gas industry, working as a production consultant. In 2010 Shortey, a long-time political volunteer, decided to run for the Senate District 44 seat. In addition to serving in the Oklahoma State Senate, he is currently pursuing a degree in finance and economics. Senator Shortey' s priorities in the Legislature include personal liberty, fighting illegal immigration and strengthening public safety in Oklahoma.

Representative Michelle Rehwinkel Vasilinda was elected in 2008 and is serving her third term in the Florida House of Representatives. She has been appointed to numerous committees of the Florida State Legislature, including Agriculture and Natural Resources Appropriations, Education Choice and Innovation, Economic Development Policy, Health and Family Services, Rule Making and Regulation, and the Select Committee on Government Reorganization. Stating in the Florida House: "Common sense has no lobbyist! It's up to us to use common sense for the common good," Rep. Rehwinkel Vasilinda is a champion for the common good and common sense policies for business and consumers, the energy and construction industries, healthcare, the environment, education, the arts, our nation's veterans, and national security. She has worked hard to make the world a better place, as a volunteer, attorney, college professor, and now a legislator. Rep.

Rehwinkel Vasilinda attended New College, the honor college of the State University system of Florida, and graduated from the University of South Florida in 1982. She graduated from the Florida Levin College on Law in 1985. She is a member of the Task Force on National and Homeland Security. She has two daughters and three stepsons. Rep. Rehwinkel Vasilinda is a Democrat.

Dr. William A. Radasky holds the Lord Kelvin Medal for Electromagnetic Protection Standards and is one of the few people on planet Earth who has actually designed national electric grids to be protected from EMP. Dr. Radasky served on the Congressional EMP Commission and has worked on high power electromagnetic applications for more than 44 years, beginning his career at the Air Force Weapons Laboratory in 1968 where he evaluated the threat of the high-altitude EMP to military systems. He has published over 400 reports, papers, and articles dealing with electromagnetic environments, effects and protection during his career. In recent years he has worked extensively in performing assessments for critical infrastructures to the threats of HEMP, IEMI and severe geomagnetic storms. He is Chairman of IEC SC 77C (EMC: High Power Transient Phenomenon), Chairman of IEEE EMC Society TC-5 (High-Power EM), and a working group convener for Cigre C4. Dr. Radasky founded Metatech Corporation in 1984 in California and is the President and Managing Engineer. He received his B.S. in Electrical Engineering and Engineering Science from the Air Force Academy in 1968; his M.S. in Electrical Engineering from the University of New Mexico in 1971; and his Ph.D. in Electrical Engineering from the University of California at Santa Barbara in 1981.

John G. Kappenman is widely considered the world's foremost expert on the threat posed by severe space weather to national electric power grids. Mr. Kappenman served on the Congressional EMP Commission, where he innovated the scientific case for severe space weather posing a potentially catastrophic threat to national electric grids. Mr. Kappenman was one of the chief contributors to the 2008 National Academy of Sciences Report *Severe Space Weather Events--Understanding Societal and Economic Impacts*. He has testified before Congress on numerous occasions on the potential threat of a geomagnetic super-storm and on the necessity of protecting the U.S. power grid. He has served as a principal investigator for the Federal Emergency Management Agency on the vulnerability of the electric power grid to severe geomagnetic storms under U.S. Presidential Executive Order 13407. Mr. Kappenman served as a Keynote presenter and member of the U.S. delegation for the first and second World Summits on Electric Infrastructure Security in 2010 and 2011, convening respectively in Parliament's West Minster Palace, London, and in the U.S. Capitol, Washington, D.C.. He holds several patents and numerous awards for his inventions including the Westinghouse Nikola Tesla Award. Mr. Kappenman is the owner of Storm Analysis Consultants, located in Duluth, MN. He is a 1976 graduate of Electrical Engineering from South Dakota State University, and has held numerous senior management and technical positions, including at Metatech as manager of their Applied Power Solutions Division, which focused primarily on space weather and EMP effects on power grids. Mr. Kappenman has published over 50 papers, including several major studies on space weather and EMP threats to power grids for the U.S. Federal Energy Regulatory Commission.

Dr. George H. Baker III. Dr. Baker's professional background spans academia, industry, and government. Baker is Professor Emeritus, James Madison University where he taught applied science from 1999-2012 and organized/directed JMU's Institute for Infrastructure and Information Assurance (IIIA). He is CEO of BAYCOR, LLC – a consulting company primarily devoted to preparedness for and protection against major electromagnetic threats to critical infrastructures including nuclear EMP, solar storms, and RF weapons. He is a member of the Board of Directors of the nonprofit Foundation for Resilient Societies and the Board of Advisors for the Congressional Task Force on National and Homeland Security. He is consultant with Integrity Consulting Engineering and Security Solutions on vulnerability assessments of critical national security installations and systems. From 2002-2008 he served as principal staff on the Congressional EMP Commission. From 1996-1999 he directed the Defense Nuclear Agency's Springfield Research Facility, directing research and assessments related to hardened facilities, including organizing the first JCS Force Protection assessment teams. He is a charter member of Virginia Secure Computing and Networking, a consortium of Virginia university cyber security principals. In addition, he has provided consulting services to the Defense Threat Reduction Agency, the Department of Homeland Security, the National Research Council, Northrop Grumman, the Institute for Defense Analyses, the National Science Foundation, George Mason University, the Federal Emergency Management Agency, the Assistant to the Governor for Commonwealth Preparedness, the National Park Service, SAIC, Defense Group Inc., National Security Research Inc., CACI, ORSA, the Maritime Emergency Preparedness Project, ENSCO Inc., EMPRIMUS, Instant Access Networks, and the Infrastructure Security Partnership.

Michael G. Hoehn is an attorney licensed in Washington, D.C. and Missouri with an office in the District of Columbia. Mr. Hoehn graduated cum laude from Westminster College in Fulton, Missouri in 1979 and received his J.D. from Washington University in St. Louis, Missouri in 1983. He also attended Concordia Seminary in St. Louis. In addition to his law practice, Mr. Hoehn has served as the Executive Director of a non-profit organization, The Alliance for Vigilance since 2007. Mr. Hoehn has worked as a political consultant for a number of political campaigns and has spoken at various places around the country on the threat posed by Sharia and militant Islam as well as the threat posed by EMP. Mr. Hoehn has also worked as a grass roots organizer and serves as legal consultant to the Counterterrorism Caucus in the Oklahoma State Legislature.

William R. Harris is the Corporate Secretary and a Director of the Foundation for Resilient Societies, a research and education non-profit. Resilient Societies supports federal and state regulatory agency initiatives to strengthen resilience of critical infrastructures. Mr. Harris is an international lawyer specializing in arms control, nuclear non-proliferation, energy policy, and continuity of government. He worked on Hot Line upgrades, creation of linked Nuclear Risk Reduction Centers (1982-84), and was a co-drafter of arms limitation treaties in 1986-87, 1991, and 1993. Mr. Harris supervised research projects at RAND in 1972-2002. He served as Special Counsel to the Senate Committee on Foreign Relations on ballistic missile defense issues, and organized a Task Force on Competitive Position of the U.S. in High Technology Industries in the Reagan Administration. He holds a B.A. from Harvard College and a J.D. from Harvard Law School.

Thomas S. Popik is a co-founder of the Foundation for Resilient Societies, a public advocacy group concentrating on protecting the U.S. electric grid from natural and manmade disasters and currently serves as its Chairman. Mr. Popik is the principal author of Petition for Rulemaking PRM-50-96, first submitted to the Nuclear Regulatory Commission in draft in February 2011, before the Fukushima nuclear accidents proved his warnings prescient. PRM-50-96, if approved, would require nuclear plant licensees to install backup power to protect against loss of commercial grid power due to solar storms. Mr. Popik has been an Observer and active participant in the Geomagnetic Disturbance Task Force for the North American Electric Reliability Corporation. Mr. Popik started his professional career as a U.S. Air Force officer assigned to Electronic Systems Division at

Hanscomb AFB, serving first as an engineer for the Distant Early Warning (DEW) Line Upgrade and then serving as Project Manager and Acting Program Director for the Berlin Radar Program. In his later career, Mr. Popik became a noted expert on the U.S. housing and mortgage markets, appearing on CNN, CBS, and Fox Business News and quoted in the New York Times, Washington Post, and Wall Street Journal. Mr. Popik holds a Master of Business Administration from Harvard Business School and a B.S. in Mechanical Engineering from MIT. He is a co-founder of the Academy for Science and Design, New Hampshire's charter High School for scientific education. Mr. Popik is a member of the Task Force on National and Homeland Security, a congressional advisory board.

Lori Frantzve and Larry Guinta own and operate AZ-Techinc International, a high-tech firm that does research and development on innovative technologies to protect the electric grid and other critical infrastructures from various threats, including natural and nuclear EMP. Lori is Director of AZ-Techinc, located in Scottsdale, Arizona. Larry is Vice President of Operations and Engineering. He is a technical automation problem solver, highly knowledgeable in multiple diverse technologies to create solutions to difficult problems. He has developed systems and control software for seven software patents and one critical infrastructure protection mechanism patent for GMD and EMP. Larry graduated from Illinois State University with a BS in Mechatronics, Robotics, and Automation Engineering.

WITHDRAWN
BY
WILLIAMSBURG REGIONAL LIBRARY

CPSIA information can be obtained
at www.ICGtesting.com
Printed in the USA
LVHW05s1425130618
580604LV00009B/447/P

9 781517 621391

Goodnight

by Charlotte Zolotow • pictures by Pamela Paparone

goodnight goodnight goodnight

the sun is down
it's time to sleep

the trees whisper
the birds are still

goodnight   goodnight   goodnight
sweet dreams are waiting

close your eyes
close your eyes
sleep
sleep deeply   sleep softly   sleep sweetly

goodnight

now you have finished "Goodnight." turn the book around to read "Wake Up"

now you have finished "Wake Up." turn the book around to read "Goodnight"

WAKE UP

trees are singing

birds are winging

things are thinging

wake up wake up wake up

the sun is out
the night is over

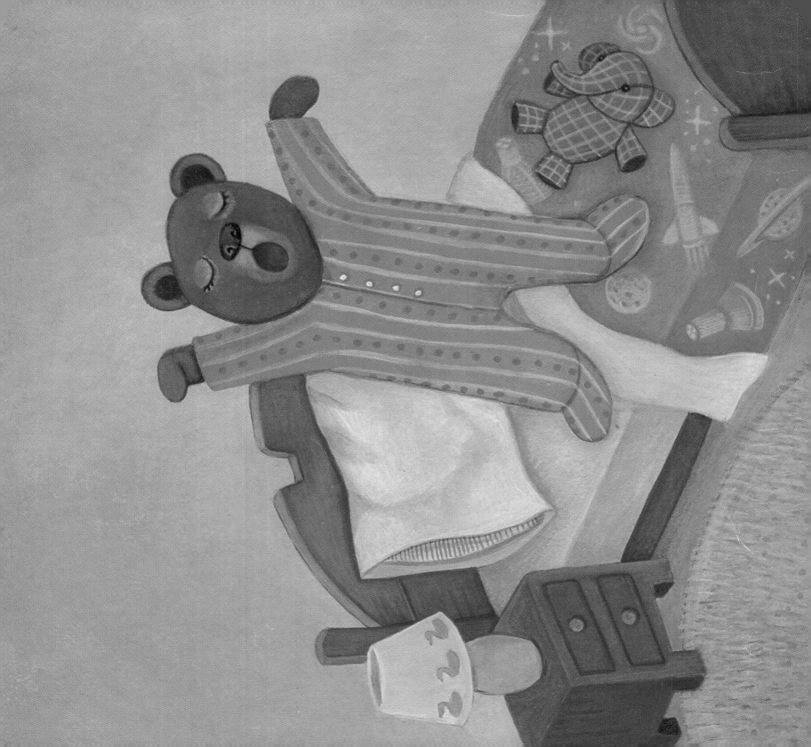

WAKE UP WAKE UP WAKE UP

the night is over

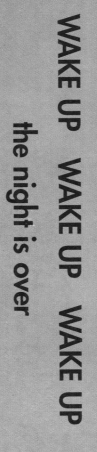

wake up wake up

wake up wake up

the day's begun

Wake Up

by Charlotte Zolotow • pictures by ... ne

HarperFestival®
A Division of HarperCollinsPublishers